"Ana Homayoun has written the very book I've yearned for, a must-read for teachers and parents. I have been recommending Ana's work for years, but *Social Media Wellness* is her best yet—a thorough, well-researched, and eloquent resource for parents and teachers seeking guidance about how to help children navigate the treacherous, ever-changing waters of social media and the digital world."

—Jessica Lahey, Author
The Gift of Failure: How the Best Parents Learn to Let Go So Their Children Can Succeed
Lyme, NH

"This is the book I've been waiting for. Ana Homayoun gives concrete strategies for parents to talk with their teens without using judgment and fear as tools. This is a guidebook you can pick up at anytime, and which your teen can read, too. I'll be recommending it to everyone I know."

—Rachel Simmons, Author
The Curse of the Good Girl: Raising Authentic Girls with Courage and Confidence
New York, NY

"This is the essential guide to navigating the ephemeral and transactional communications woven into the language of social media online and IRL. I relished every page of this book. It is jam-packed with sound and seasoned self-management and executive-functioning tips and systems. The research and artfully reconstructed narratives, tools, ideas, and reflective questions feed the systematic and practical approaches the author shares to empower students, parents, and educators alike. I can't wait to add this to my professional library and share it with all of my teachers!!!"

—Lisa Johnson, M.Ed, Author of *Cultivating Communication and the Classroom* and High School Educational Technologist
K-12 1:1 iPad School District
Austin, TX

"I wish every parent, teacher, teen, and tween knew Ana Homayoun as I do. As a journalist, she's long been my go-to source for advice on social media dilemmas affecting families because she is smart, wise, and—above all—empathetic. I'm so glad to see *Social Media Wellness* is now available to everyone. Buy it. Like it. Share it."

—Steven Petrow, "Digital Life" Columnist
USA Today
Chapel Hill, NC

"Ana Homayoun demonstrates how social media and our digital lives have reoriented relationships and how we think. In her book she offers vital tools and strategies for this revolution—whether you're a teacher, parent, or student. I found myself challenged from each of these viewpoints!"

—Homa Tavangar, Author and Global Education Adviser
Growingupglobal.net
Villanova, PA

"Keeping up with tweens and teens on social media often seems like a dizzying task that leaves us, the adults, lost and confused—too often giving up. *Social Media Wellness* brings great clarity to the matter, offering actionable advice for parents and schools. In her typical style, Homayoun is realistic, pragmatic, and refreshingly straightforward. She gets our attention without using scare tactics and then gives us, parents and educators, the tools to most effectively help children find wellness in the social media age."

—Andrew Davis, Head of School
Mt. Tamalpais School
Marin, CA

"In our selfie society, teens and tweens encounter constant temptations and threats to their social, emotional, physical, and academic health. Ana Homayoun's new book provides strategies to 'unselfie' our teens and develop a healthy, balanced relationship with social media."

—Michele Borba, Ed.D.
Author of *UnSelfie: Why Empathetic Kids
Succeed in Our All-About-Me World*
Palm Springs, CA

"Rich with stories and thoughtful interpretations of tweens' and teens' online habits, curiosities, and consequences, Ana Homayoun provides parents and educators an especially powerful resource to confidently guide our students and children with tools, counsel, and reassurance as they navigate social media. Bravo!"

—Stephanie Balmer, Head of School
Harpeth Hall School
Nashville, TN

*To my younger sister, Allia, whose in-real-life commentary
and observations are some of the most brilliant, witty,
and wise I have ever been privileged to experience.*

Social Media
WELLNESS

Helping Tweens and Teens
Thrive in an Unbalanced
Digital World

Ana Homayoun

A JOINT PUBLICATION

A SAGE Publishing Company

A SAGE Publishing Company

FOR INFORMATION:

Corwin

A SAGE Company

2455 Teller Road

Thousand Oaks, California 91320

(800) 233-9936

www.corwin.com

SAGE Publications Ltd.

1 Oliver's Yard

55 City Road

London EC1Y 1SP

United Kingdom

SAGE Publications India Pvt. Ltd.

B 1/I 1 Mohan Cooperative Industrial Area

Mathura Road, New Delhi 110 044

India

SAGE Publications Asia-Pacific Pte. Ltd.

3 Church Street

#10-04 Samsung Hub

Singapore 049483

Acquisitions Editor: Ariel Bartlett

Senior Associate Editor: Desirée A. Bartlett

Editorial Assistant: Kaitlyn Irwin

Production Editor: David C. Felts

Copy Editor: Amy Marks

Typesetter: C&M Digitals (P) Ltd.

Proofreader: Sally Jaskold

Indexer: Marilyn Augst

Cover Designer: Gail Buschman

Marketing Manager: Anna Mesick

Printed in the United States of America

ISBN 978-1-4833-5818-5

SUSTAINABLE FORESTRY INITIATIVE

Certified Chain of Custody

Promoting Sustainable Forestry

www.sfiprogram.org

SFI-01268

SFI label applies to text stock

17 18 19 20 21 10 9 8 7 6 5 4 3 2 1

About the Author

Ana Homayoun is a noted teen and millennial expert, author, speaker, and educator. Her work focuses on promoting organization, time-management, personal purpose, and overall wellness for young people. Her first book, *That Crumpled Paper Was Due Last Week: Helping Disorganized and Distracted Boys Succeed in School and Life*, quickly became a classic among parents and educators for the pragmatic approach to executive functioning issues. Her next book, *The Myth of the Perfect Girl: Helping Our Daughters Find Authentic Success and Happiness in School and Life*, explores the real-life dilemmas of young women today and provides strategies for finding authentic success and happiness. Her latest book, *Social Media Wellness: Helping Teens and Tweens Thrive in an Unbalanced Digital World*, decodes the new language of social media socialization, and provides practical strategies to encourage better choices online and in-real-life.

In addition to her individualized consulting services, Ms. Homayoun travels around the world working with schools, and frequently provides parent education, student presentations, and professional development presentations. Her work has been quoted or featured in the *New York Times, San Francisco Chronicle, USA Today, San Jose Mercury News, Chicago Tribune, Washington Post,* and ABC News, among others, and is a frequent guest on NPR.

She is the founder of Green Ivy Educational Consulting, a Silicon Valley-based educational consulting firm. For more information, please visit www.anahomayoun.com and www.greenivyed.com.

Contents

Prologue

If you've picked up this book, it's likely that you've experienced some of the ways social media has utterly changed all of our lives, and especially changed the lives of today's tweens and teens. For many parents and educators, teens' and tweens' social media socialization can quickly become irritating, fascinating, bewildering, scary, and overwhelming all at once, and it can be easy to fall into the trap of wanting to ignore it all and hope it goes away.

The reality is that social media and related technology are unlikely to go away but instead will continue to evolve. Over the past fifteen years, I've come to realize that we are having the wrong conversations with our kids when it comes to social media and related technology. We can't ignore our tweens' and teens' social media use, and we need to resist talking about social media and online use from a place of fear and misunderstanding. Our efforts will be more effective if we can focus on helping the next generation to develop better ways to manage and organize their time online and in real life. To do so, it is important to recognize and appreciate how rapidly social media and related technology have evolved and how much we all struggle to keep up with the changes.

To give you a better sense of how quickly things have changed, I encourage you to think about it in terms of presidential elections. In February 2007, then-senator Barack Obama announced his candidacy for president. At the time, there was no iPhone (the first iPhone was released in June 2007).[1] Snapchat and Instagram, two social media apps later used by the White House during President Obama's time in office, had yet to be invented. By the 2016 presidential election, virtual reality became an emerging topic in education, as did personalized learning programs focused on online learning experiences.[2]

Some observers say that the mass sharing of "fake news" could have played a role in the 2016 presidential election, and studies showing that students are often unable to recognize fake news sources are concerning.[3] Part of the transfer of power from the 44th to the 45th president involved transferring the @POTUS Twitter account, and archiving President Obama's tweets as @POTUS44 for historical legacy. When we step back and think about it, so much has evolved in such a short period of time that it can be difficult to fully appreciate the impact.

By the time you read this book, there will likely be new social media apps and technology innovations in use—which makes everything seem temporary. After all, when I began writing this book a few years ago, some of the most popular social media apps, like Snapchat, were in their infancy, whereas others, like Musical.ly and live.ly, didn't exist. Even so, many of the issues surrounding teen wellness existed long before social media. In many ways, social media amplifies what already exists, and the dopamine release and corresponding feelings of pleasure that can result from social media interactions may encourage addiction among tweens and teens who struggle to self-regulate. Research suggests that heavy media multitasking, or switching between tasks and juggling multiple forms of media, which many students do daily, can have an effect on information processing and memory use, thereby affecting learning and retention.[4] One of the most important things we can do is to help today's tweens and teens understand that their online and in-real-life experiences are more intertwined than they have been led to believe. In doing so, we can help them to develop a new perspective and framework for understanding how we can work together to promote social media wellness.

This book is organized so that Chapters 1–3 provide a foundational understanding, and the remaining chapters (4–8) offer practical, implementable, prescriptive exercises and strategies that can be adapted to different scenarios, situations, and social media innovations. What works for one family, school, or community might not be appropriate for another. This book doesn't attempt to provide all the answers for every situation, but it does offer a student-focused, wellness-driven perspective. In the end, I hope that working through the exercises and implementing the suggested strategies will help you, your family, your school, and your greater community to find solutions that work well for your circumstances.

An important note: I've always said that no one walks into my office hoping to be featured in a book someday. This book is a result of nearly fifteen years of working with tweens and teens in the heart of the Silicon Valley, and visiting some of the first schools to implement one-to-one programs. To protect the anonymity of students, parents, and educators, I've changed some names and identifying details, as appropriate, and in several cases used composites to simplify the examples.

Finally, even though the title of this book is *Social Media Wellness*, it addresses more broadly the various technologies that affect today's tweens and teens. In the end, I hope this book inspires you to find effective solutions.

With all that said, let's dive in.

CHAPTER 1

Landscape

What Today's Social Media World Looks Like for Tweens and Teens

A few years ago, I was walking through the hallway of a middle school when Danielle stopped me. "You're the lady who gave that presentation last week, aren't you?" she asked me. Sitting on the floor of the school hallway, Danielle looked at me with knowing brown eyes. Her school uniform had an end-of-the day rumple to it, and her ash-blonde hair was pulled back loosely in a ponytail. It was a couple of weeks into the school year. I had given a presentation on back-to-school wellness to her and her middle school classmates the week before and had returned to give a corresponding talk to parents that evening.

"Your presentation was super helpful. A lot more than I thought it would be," she volunteered. She quickly shared that she was in the seventh grade and was waiting for her mom to pick her up after school. Enjoying our conversation and curious to get her feedback, I asked what part of the presentation she found most useful.

"Well," she started slowly, "all last year I had a profile on Ask.fm.[1] Lots of kids at my school are on it. Most nights, I would go into my room to do my homework, but I was really spending hours on Ask.fm. Have you used Ask.fm?"

I nodded.

She went on to reveal that she never told her parents about her profile on the site, because Ask.fm, like many social media sites, including Facebook, Instagram, and Snapchat, has a minimum age requirement of thirteen years.[2] (Some apps ask users to be eighteen.)

As a sixth grader, she was twelve years old when she first created her Ask.fm account and wasn't even supposed to be on the site.

"People posted mean things on my profile page," she continued, her voice softening, "and I didn't know who was saying what, and it stressed me out so much. Pretty soon, I couldn't focus. It got hard to concentrate, and sometimes I would stay up late thinking about what people were saying. A lot of nights I had a hard time sleeping. But after your presentation, I realized I had choices on how I spent my time, and I wanted this year to be different—so I went home and deleted my Ask.fm account."

"Wow," I replied, both surprised and impressed by her decisiveness and courage to take action. "How do you feel?"

"I feel amazing," she gushed, her face beaming with a huge smile. "It's as though a big weight has been lifted off of my shoulders. In the last week, I've gotten my homework done a lot more quickly and have time to do whatever I want. I feel like this is going to be a great year."

A few moments later, I ran into the principal and asked if she knew of Ask.fm or had ever used it. The principal gazed at me with a look of slight obliviousness and shook her head. A few hours later, I asked the three hundred parents in the audience how many were familiar with Ask.fm. Only two raised their hands. This discrepancy, I soon realized, was part of our new challenge for social media wellness.

I became a social media "expert" somewhat by accident. Like many adults in my mid-thirties, I came of age in a time of nascent social media opportunities. Even though I grew up in the Silicon Valley, I wasn't that interested in the Internet as a high school student, and I only vaguely remember using my high school email address to trade five-line emails with a pen pal from the Midwest in a corresponding chemistry class. In 2001, I started an educational consulting firm with the goal of helping students with organization, time management, personal purpose, and overall wellness. Our main office is located in the heart of the Silicon Valley, but back then, there was no Facebook, Instagram, Snapchat, Musical.ly, Tumblr, YouTube, or WhatsApp.

About a decade ago, I noticed a shift in the way students managed their distractions and completed their work. At the time, they did most of their homework on worksheets or loose-leaf paper and then stored it all in hardback binders. Schools typically gave students written day planners to track assignments (whether or not those were used is another story altogether). My work was focused on helping students develop and manage their time so that they had more time for fun and rest, and the organizational system I developed became encapsulated in my first book, *That Crumpled Paper Was Due Last Week*. As a result of the success of that book, I began traveling to schools around the world, helping administrators, teachers, parents, and students promote academic success and personal wellness in the school and greater community.

Through my work, I've regularly seen students' grade point averages (GPAs) improve from a 2.5 to a 3.6 within six months, and I've helped college students on academic probation improve to a B+ average simply by transforming when and how they do their work. In addition to the improvements in test scores and overall grades, I believe the most important indicators of success are our students' increased confidence and engagement in their school and greater community. Once students design a system that works for them, they feel more in control of their lives and are excited to take healthy risks, try new activities, and get involved in a way they might not have before. They become purposeful, thoughtful, and resilient young leaders who are more likely to set audacious goals *and* improve their overall wellness with better sleep and nutrition habits. My work has always been about helping students dream big and make daily choices and develop habits around their own personal values. It is amazing to watch students go through this process, and positively influencing young people to make intelligent choices at such a pivotal time in their lives is extremely gratifying.

Over the past decade, I've witnessed first-hand the effects of technology and social media in the classroom and on young adults' lives more generally. As more and more schools brought personal technology like computers and tablets into the classroom, I soon realized that all the traditional strategies we were employing were not enough. In the beginning, I noticed how the technological creep that was the online social world created another layer of distractions that needed to be addressed in my daily work with students. What began as a trickle of diversion—Facebook was first focused on college students, after all—quickly became a watershed of distraction (and disturbance) with the prolific abundance of iPhone and Android use and an explosion of instantly accessible free mobile apps.

I developed expertise around social media because I knew that doing so was a professional imperative. It created a crucial lifeline to help me reach students who were increasingly disconnected from adults who could—and should—provide guidance at a critical time in their social and emotional development. I began giving presentations to school faculty and parents on the new "language" of social media, because I realized that they were in need of a translator to thread the connection between the older generation's pre–social media experiences and today's younger generations' way of living a life online.

Though students have long managed to find distractions anywhere and at any time, new social media innovations, especially anonymous and ephemeral social media apps and live-feed video, present new challenges for students and adults. Students who once identified food, daydreaming, pets, and siblings as major distractions are now far more likely to name certain social media apps or online websites. One of my high school seniors proclaimed that he spent the majority of his waking day on "the entire Internet," and many of my other students admit doing the same. Another one of my students, a high school sophomore, recently listed her main distractions as the following:

1. Snapchat (x 100)
2. Instagram
3. Facebook
4. YouTube
5. Thinking about my life
6. Sleeping

Like many teens today, this young woman looks to online sites and mobile apps as a way to connect, communicate, and acquire new information. I will be the first to admit that technological innovation has improved all of our lives in many ways, and we all know that the story is nuanced and more complicated than technology being simply good or bad. Over the past decade, we—and by *we* I mean parents, educators, and students—have experienced a seismic shift in communication and interaction that we are only now beginning to understand and address. Much of the current work around students and technology addresses and highlights the challenges but doesn't always provide crucially needed practical solutions.

According to 2015 Pew Research data, 92 percent of teens go online every day, which comes as no surprise to people who work with teens (see Table 1.1).[3] What's disconcerting, however, is that 24 percent report being online constantly—their phones are mere inches away from their heads when they hit the pillow, and they think nothing of waking up in the middle of the night to check notifications and respond to messages.[4] Girls are much more likely than boys to send and receive texts, and girls between the ages of thirteen and seventeen send by far the most text messages, nearly 4,000 text messages on average per month, which works out to well over 100 text messages per day.[5] (Those texting statistics are dwarfed quickly by the number of messages sent through messaging services like Facebook Messenger and WhatsApp, which, combined, have 60 billion messages sent through their systems *each day*.[6]) Twenty-five percent of American teenagers admit to being connected to a device

TABLE 1.1   Teens and Social Interaction: Texting Is Only Part of the Story

COMMUNICATION PLATFORM	PERCENTAGE OF TEENS WHO USE PLATFORM	PERCENTAGE OF TEENS WHO USE PLATFORM DAILY
Texting	88	55
Instant messaging	79	23
Email	64	6
Video chat	59	7
Video games	52	13

Note: For many teens, texting is the dominant way that they communicate on a daily basis with their friends. Along with texting, teens are incorporating a number of other devices, communication platforms, and online venues into their interactions with friends.

Source: Pew Research Center. (2015). More than half of teens text with friends daily. Retrieved April 7, 2016, from http://www.pewinternet.org/2015/08/06/teens-technology-and-friendships/2015-08-06_teens-and-friendships_0-02/

within five minutes of waking up.[7] The latest research suggests that teens between the ages of thirteen and eighteen spend about nine hours per day using some form of entertainment media, and tweens between the ages of eight and twelve use nearly six hours per day of entertainment media.[8] This time does *not* include time spent online during school or while doing homework.[9] And because so much of that time is spent on media multitasking, or using multiple forms of media at once (texting while listening to music, for instance), students can actually pack far more hours of actual use into that daily time.

> What gets lost or overlooked in this shift toward technology is the importance of carving out and creating time for some of the most crucial elements for child and adolescent identity development—solitude for self-reflection, opportunity for greater self-awareness, and, quite simply, sleep.

In many communities today, it is commonplace for students to have a mobile phone at their disposal, ostensibly "for emergencies" and "just in case." Given some of the horrific events of the past two decades—9/11; Hurricane Katrina; the school shooting in Newtown, CT; and other tragedies—it is understandable that many parents feel more comfortable if their children have a phone. At the same time, today's tweens and teens are spending more time online and are shifting their personal efforts to maintaining and building an online presence. What gets lost or overlooked in this shift toward technology is the importance of carving out and creating time for some of the most crucial elements for child and adolescent identity development—solitude for self-reflection, opportunity for greater self-awareness, and, quite simply, sleep.

THE NEW LANGUAGE OF TECHNOLOGY AND SOCIAL MEDIA

In the summer of 2014, I gave a presentation to a group of women on the impact of social media in our everyday lives. The women in the audience were between eighteen and forty-five years old, and most were active on some form of social media. At that time, Snapchat was still gaining momentum and popularity, and most of Snapchat's primary user base was under twenty-five years old. When I mentioned Snapchat to the audience, the majority of women under twenty-five were readily familiar with the app and in many cases had downloaded it onto their mobile devices. Most of the older audience members, however, were unfamiliar and somewhat uninterested.

This same sort of generational divide is currently happening with many students, educators, and parents. Over the past fifteen years, we have seen a remarkable shift in language and communication, and this shift has directly affected tween and teen wellness inside and outside of the classroom. Since I gave that talk in 2014, Snapchat has exploded in popularity, and new apps and messaging tools continue to change the way students interact, communicate, and consume content. In many ways, social media has created a new language of communication, and different generations are using and understanding the options differently. Students download and use new apps on a regular basis, and teachers, with all their other responsibilities, may not have the time or inclination to stay informed on all the latest social media trends. Recently, a teacher at a school I worked with was dumbfounded to learn that nearly all of her students were using a mobile app *during class* that she barely even knew existed. A head of school at a prestigious independent day school told me that he didn't need to keep up with all the different social media trends because "everything will change in six months anyway." Even when teens need their parents' support and guidance, they are less likely to seek it if they think their parents won't understand the problems they face, in particular with regard to their online activities. A 2015 study by Common Sense Media found that 25 percent of teens who are online think their parents are in the dark (knowing only "a little" or "nothing") about their online activities. A slightly larger percentage (30 percent) think their parents are similarly uninformed about their use of social media.[10] Even adults who want to stay involved and informed face a constant struggle to understand the new language of social media, which has new dialects and nuances evolving on a seemingly daily basis. Plus, in many ways, keeping up with all the changes is exhausting. Nancy Jo Sales, author of *American Girls: Social Media and the Secret Lives of Teenagers*, traveled around the country documenting the social media habits of tween and teen girls, and revealed that after some days of researching, she would "have to sort of just sit for a while and take it all in."[11]

Over the past five to ten years, technology has utterly transformed the way students think, learn, communicate, and process information. In her recent TED talk, "We Are All Cyborgs Now" anthropologist Amber Case explores the long-lasting impact of being dependent on devices for our everyday functioning.[12] Students in today's learning environments face the ultimate paradox: The same devices and tools they are required to use to complete much of their schoolwork also serve as their main sources of distraction from getting any of that work done. More and more schools encourage students to use laptops and tablets in the classroom. According to data from the U.S. Department of Education, teachers at public schools reported that 69 percent of their students use computers during class most or some of the time. Internet connections were available for 93 percent of computers located in classrooms and for 96 percent of the computers brought into classrooms.[13] Many independent schools and private schools throughout the United States and abroad have implemented one-to-one tablet or computer programs, or have similar programs in the works. More and more public and charter schools are doing the same—and with the price of a new Chromebook hovering around a few hundred dollars, it can be far cheaper to buy a Chromebook than to separately purchase all the textbooks it could potentially store. Regardless of whether or not a school has a one-to-one (or one-to-many) program in place, it is important to recognize that many schools are moving toward increasing the amount of educational technology in the classroom. Students spend at least some of their time online completing homework, and online socialization and distraction sneaks in and becomes a deterrent from completing work. How easy is it for students to block the Internet, when they need to use the Internet to complete their homework? Not so easy, as many of my students readily attest.

Early on, I realized that knowing the abbreviated language of texting and how to post Instagram photos or send Snaps gave me crucial credibility with students, and made them more open to listening to my recommendations and working with me to find pragmatic solutions. Students relax when they realize I am not against social media, and that I simply want to help them devise healthy ways of managing their work and life that are in accordance with their own vision of personal and academic success. In the end, my work is all about empowering students to align their daily behavioral choices with their goals and values. Through my work, I've personally developed greater empathy for our youngest generation's struggles with technology and social media, because it didn't take long for me to recognize how much time *I* could spend perusing my Instagram feed or doing "research" on the latest popular apps when I wanted to procrastinate. In the midst of my research, I found that my iPhone was filled with so many social media apps that it could have been mistaken for a teenager's phone. I added flattering filters to photos, shared interesting articles, liked others' check-ins at worldwide hotspots, and messaged friends and family internationally without affecting my data plan. All of those little moments of connection and communication quickly added up to a whole lot of time.

Regardless of their level of awareness around current social media trends, parents, teachers, and administrators are typically at a loss for how to support students because they do not fully appreciate the problem. And this is a significant issue, because 58 percent of teens say their parents are the biggest influence on what they believe is appropriate (and inappropriate) online.[14] Although most adults over the age of forty can remember a time in their school days when they felt slighted or were stressed by sex, drugs, alcohol and/or social and romantic relationships, virtually none has a memory of being broken up with via text message two days before prom and having the whole school discover and discuss the breakup via multiple social media networks.

Social media shouldn't be seen as strictly positive or negative. Instead, it should be addressed as a new language and cultural shift that provides different opportunities to connect and communicate. In some ways, it provides another layer for potential interaction and socialization. This new language and cultural shift creates a whole host of challenges that this book attempts to address and navigate. When parents and educators aren't comfortable speaking the "language" of social media, they are less able to provide relevant guidance and reassurance for the multitude of new issues students juggle online and in real life. They are also less able to be a proactive, preventive resource, because their inability to connect may keep young people from reaching out to them as a support or resource. In many ways, parents and educators now have the added responsibility to learn and become comfortable with this new way of communicating and interacting so they can provide young people with the tools and structure needed for self-control and safety.

Social media shouldn't be seen as strictly positive or negative. Instead, it should be addressed as a new language and cultural shift that provides different opportunities to connect and communicate.

It's true that every generation, in some ways, has its own new language, and it's easy to underestimate this sense of generational divide or drift. But there are many reasons why the stakes are higher now and prescriptive solutions are needed more desperately than ever before. We'll look at some of the reasons as they relate to social and emotional development in Chapter 6, but for now, one of the key issues is how more and more young people seek advice and guidance from peers or an anonymous online media community instead of seeking support from the adults in their lives.

Some of this movement away from parental influence is, of course, a normal part of development. As kids grow up, they rush to create their own community away from the influence of their parents as a way of separating from them. But the key difference is that today's parents and educators, on the whole, remain dangerously unaware of the new language and culture that social media and related technology create for our youngest generation. Other books delve into the issue in greater detail, and I provide a resource list at the back of this book. My focus is on how we all need to build better awareness and close this language gap so we can promote overall wellness for today's tweens and teens. The goal for my work has always been to help young people develop the skills they need for future success and happiness, and social media has simply created an added layer that must be addressed.

Think back to Danielle's story at the beginning of the chapter. Danielle's after-school devotion to Ask.fm is an example of risky online social behavior. Her parents thought she was in her room doing homework, and her quiet and diligent nature made it impossible for them to think anything else was going on. Her social standing and popularity was important to her, and being on Ask.fm had somehow been deemed cool by her peer group. Danielle's online experience clearly had an adverse effect on her well-being, and she didn't have support strategies in place if something didn't go as planned. My presentation resonated because I used the language of social media she was comfortable with, and conveyed my message without being judgmental or creating fear. As a result, she was able to reframe her thinking and realize she had choices around how she spent her time. When she ultimately decided that this school year would be different, she proactively made the choice to spend her afternoons without the daily drain of negative online interactions. She was able to get the guidance she needed in order to make choices to promote her overall social and emotional wellness—in part because I spoke her language.

SO MUCH HAS CHANGED, YET SO MUCH REMAINS THE SAME

I was recently speaking to a group of summer camp directors and senior administrators at a large conference in the Northeast, and many were frustrated and confused about the paradoxical role that social media plays in their work. Many camps, like schools, use social media to highlight how a positive camp experience provides the opportunity to take healthy risks, make lifelong friendships, and promote an inclusive community. However, camp directors of both sleepaway and day camps are sometimes at a loss for how to deal with certain issues, like campers posting photos of counselors online without permission, or overzealous camp parents who take helicopter parenting to a new level by trying to "friend" or "follow" counselors online as an another way to check up on their children (for example, sent via Facebook Messenger: *Is Johnny doing okay in your cabin?*").

In the past few years, camp directors have dealt with more issues around day campers going home at the end of the day and posting certain photos or comments on social media. In the same way that social media has created a world where the school day no longer ends at 3 p.m., the camp world no longer ends when the camp day or session is over. Sleepaway campers might wait until the end of summer when they are back home to re-create a secondary camp experience online, but the exclusionary nature of certain postings and photo tagging creates the same heightened challenges that schools experience around online socialization—which in many ways goes against the very tenets of a camp's mission. For example, a camper could post a photo of the campfire on Instagram and tag all the other campers in his or her designated group of friends, silently and subtly signaling who is part of the group (#squad) and who is not. More and more, camp directors and senior staff spend hours fielding calls and emails from concerned parents whose children feel slighted and excluded as a result of after-camp postings. On some level, it is important for kids to understand that not everyone is included in everything all the time, but at the same time, it is also crucial for camps to use social media as a learning tool for the greater life lessons that are an essential part of personal development—namely, developing empathy and compassion for others, and working collaboratively to foster a sense of community and belonging.

My consulting with camp administrators made me realize how very few, if any, of these camps had a written social media policy for parents, staff, and campers, and many didn't really know where to start. Like school administrators, many of them felt overwhelmed and under-informed.

I wasn't too far along into my presentation before one of the camp directors put me on the spot. "How are we supposed to monitor and enforce social media when so much of it happens off camp grounds?" I could hear the frustration in her voice, and I recognized an argument that is often used by school administrators: We can't (or won't) deal with a social media issue if it happens off school grounds.

"Well," I replied, "you have certain rules at camp, right? Rules and policies that people have to follow to be part of the camp community, don't you?" She nodded.

"Most of those rules focus on issues around socialization, self-regulation, and safety," I continued, "and you've hopefully created a camp culture and sense of tradition that people want to return to again and again? I mean, many of you have camps that have the same campers return year after year." She nodded again, and by then most of the rest of the room was in agreement.

"Here's the thing: There are always rules and policies that we are expected to follow in order to remain a part of a community, whether that is a school community, camp community, municipal community, or our greater world as a whole. Ultimately, we always have a choice, but in order to remain part of a community, we generally have to follow a certain set of rules and guidelines. This isn't that different. I encourage you to reframe your thinking and approach social media as an opportunity to teach the things we always to seek to instill in young people—integrity, resilience, determination, kindness, leadership, and personal values. If people don't follow the rules, there are consequences—and one of the consequences might be that they are no longer able to be part of the community. If you've spent time creating a unique and inclusive camp culture, that is not a risk your campers will want to take." I likened it to the many schools I have dealt with that have suspended or expelled students because of social media issues, or to communities where children and young adults have been prosecuted based on evidence found on social media.

Suddenly, something clicked. I wasn't asking them to use social media policy to threaten campers or to create a sense of fear. Instead, I encouraged these summer camp leaders to reframe their thinking and use social media as a tool to teach the same important life skills they had been instilling in campers for decades. I wanted the camp directors to use social media to create and implement policies as a way to help campers understand they had choices around how they spent their time online and in real life, and how those choices had potential benefits and consequences.

Many of the underlying issues teens and young adults encounter as a result of online experiences existed long before the dawn of the Internet. It's not as though feelings of insecurity or inferiority began when people started using Facebook or Instagram, or that children started making questionable decisions with the advent of Snapchat. In reality, insecurity and poor decision-making are rather typical experiences for many tweens and teens. Most adults can recall a time when they somehow felt excluded in their younger years—perhaps by not making a sports team or winning a leadership role, or not being included in party or prom plans, or feeling as though everyone else was better/smarter/stronger/better-liked than them. Many can also recall how they did something that was ill-advised or, for lack of a better word, dumb. Social media use didn't cause these feelings or decisions, but it's easy to see how social media expands and amplifies such feelings to near-overwhelming levels while creating a long "paper" trail that can radically alter the long-term consequences of bad choices.

Our role as parents and educators is to help young people identify and process their feelings, to provide them with opportunities to reflect and build self-awareness and their own set of personal values, and to encourage them to create coping strategies and find resources when things don't go as planned. This role has certainly become more challenging with the increased opportunities for ephemeral and anonymous online interactions, which I discuss in greater detail in Chapter 2. And, there are things we now need to think about and address earlier and more thoroughly than ever before. Regardless, it remains our responsibility to help students understand that their online and real-life experiences and interactions are more intertwined than they've been led to believe. We also need to collectively reframe our thinking about the importance of speaking the language of social media, and recognize that building a greater awareness provides us with the opportunity to enhance our conversations with tweens and teens around real-world personal and academic development issues. In doing so, we can encourage the next generation to be values and purpose-driven, engaged, and enthusiastic members of their school and greater communities.

> It remains our responsibility to help students understand that their online and real-life experiences and interactions are more intertwined than they've been led to believe.

HOW SOCIAL MEDIA AND TECHNOLOGY AFFECT THE OVERALL EDUCATIONAL EXPERIENCE

In 2010, I began visiting schools and learning more about their classroom technology and, in many cases, helped them understand how to more effectively implement their tablet and computer programs. I realized quickly that schools regularly spent a great deal of time and resources updating their classroom technology to state-of-the-art levels and thinking through the logistics of giving every student a computer or tablet. These same schools had not thought through their social media use policy, especially as it dealt with faculty-student-parent interaction and off-campus postings and occurrences. Many schools assumed that whatever happened off campus would stay off campus (they were wrong). The few who did develop technology and social media use policies rarely extended their policies to include the actions of both faculty and parents. Many school administrators felt stuck because they didn't fully understand all the different options or potential issues and became overwhelmed over the new apps and updated devices becoming available every day. As one issue is addressed, another issue pops up.

Today, many schools have a terms-of-use policy for technology and social media, in many cases reacting to past incidents by putting preventive measures in place. Still, many administrators, educators, and parents struggle with how they can use social media as an opportunity for a greater teachable moment. It's hard to know how and when to create programming that encourages students to better manage themselves in a world of so many options. I encourage parents and educators to think about family and school policies through the lens of three Ss—*socialization, self-regulation,* and *safety.* Later chapters suggest specific tools and ways to present the conversation, but let's take a moment now to think about how social media has affected the overall educational experience through each of these contexts.

Socialization

A few days before the recent school year was set to start, I was running a small-group workshop for incoming ninth-grade boys at a high school near our office. The workshop focused on organization, time management, distractions, healthy risks, and overall wellness and goals. It was developed as a way to help students ease into the transition to high school. At one point, I asked the teens, "If you were going to need to have an important conversation with someone, how would you go about doing so?" I was trying to encourage them to seek out healthy communication styles.

Without missing a beat, one of the young men enthusiastically raised his hand to respond, "Facebook Messenger!" I was bemused, thinking more along the lines of a face-to-face conversation as the ideal way to avoid potential misunderstanding and miscommunication. He genuinely believed that using the online intermediary would allow him to be clearer in thought and expression for a tough conversation, and he's certainly not alone. In her book *Reclaiming Conversation,* author Sherry Turkle describes how more and more families choose to "fight over text" instead of having a face-to-face dispute.[15] Parents and students sometimes believe fighting over text allows them to maintain composure in the face of a difficult discussion. In reality, it can actually prevent kids (and adults) from building crucial skills that come from having tough conversations face-to-face, where facial reactions provide powerful nonverbal communication tools typically unavailable through a screen.

> Handling disputes via social media can actually prevent kids (and adults) from building crucial skills that come from having tough conversations face-to-face.

Social media adds a layer of complexity by altering how and when students socialize with one another, and changes how young people communicate and interact with their teachers and parents. For most students, the social part of the school experience no longer ends at 3 p.m., with conversations and content shared long after the final school bell rings. With social media, the secondary social experience begins at 3 p.m., and home, more specifically a child's bedroom, no longer offers a sanctuary from the challenges of navigating tween and teen friendships. As a result, there's less time for social and emotional processing, and less of an opportunity to slow down and regroup from a negative social interaction, that, given a little time and space, might seem more manageable. For students struggling socially in the hallways and cafeterias, going online after school can become yet another reminder of the world in which they may or may not feel as though they belong. (Conversely, it can also provide an opportunity for them to feel connected to others outside of their immediate school community, which I'll discuss more in Chapter 6.) Even those who feel a sense of connectedness may also experience low-grade anxiety about what they might be missing out on if they are not online and available. You might have heard students refer to this situation as "fomo" or the *fear of missing out*. This underlying anxiety quickly affects how they are or are not able to self-regulate during and after school hours.

Part of this anxiety also stems from the complicated way social media interactions blur the lines of friendship. After all, the notion of what constitutes a friend has shifted. When I was writing my second book,

The Myth of the Perfect Girl, I ran several focus groups of middle school and high school girls. One middle school girl explained how there were several classmates who would chat with her online every afternoon for extended periods of time, but wouldn't greet her in the hallway the next day. Their conversations online were warm and friendly, but the next day, it would seem as though they had never met. She felt confused as to what constituted a genuine friendship, and the juxtaposition between friendly online chatter and real-life silence became anxiety provoking for her. With Facebook, our "friends" can include our closest friends from childhood, our accountant we see once a year, and the college classmates we haven't spoken to in fifteen years. When adults talk about their friends, there are various degrees of friendship that sometimes need to be classified (but are often over-looked). *Is she a close friend, or an acquaintance I met once who likes and comments on my online postings?* Another of my students, a high school sophomore, had long drifted away from friendship with one of her classmates, but neither could bring themselves to end their Snapchat streak, a novelty that develops when users send photos or messages to one another every day. The Snapchat streak was now over 270 days long, and even though neither girl would reach out to the other for any other reason, the prospect of ending the streak seemed overwhelming.

Middle school and high school have always been, in some greater sense, about developing important interpersonal social skills and critical thinking. If you ask an adult what they most remember about school, it might be a teacher or a class, but more likely it would be related to a social experience or interaction. Navigating relationships with peers, teachers, and parents can be complicated and exhausting, especially when there are so many lessons learned and moments of self-discovery. Friendships shift, alliances fade, and who-likes-who and does-he/she-like me takes hours of thinking and processing time, time that no longer seems to exist in today's always-on, always-available social world of online and real-life relationships.

In later chapters, we'll delve deeper into the social and emotional effects of social media on teens, especially as they relate to identity development and empathy, but for now understand that social media has changed socialization for tweens and teens such that the school day never seems to end.

Self-Regulation

When students come into my office for the first time, I usually spend part of that session asking where and when they complete their work, where their phone is while they complete work, what other websites or media are open when they are trying to complete work, and what they believe to be their biggest distractions. Most of my students say they complete their work in their room, with their phone nearby. Students quickly admit that they might have several different tabs open for websites they might need to complete their work or sites they might want to peruse to take a break (online shopping, YouTube, Tumblr, ESPN). It never takes long for them to begin media multitasking while doing their homework. Even though they initially believe otherwise, students begin to realize that the small trickles of distraction combine to create an environment in which little is completed with any sort of efficiency.

Part of the challenge around self-regulation is related to perception—many students don't fully recognize how much answering a few texts here or there, watching a few YouTube videos, sending a Snap, or scrolling through their Instagram feed affects their ability to do work. Research shows that nearly half of teens admit to watching television or using social media while completing their homework, and most believe that media multitasking has no effect on the quality of their work.[16] Two-thirds of those who media multitask while completing work don't believe watching television or texting has any impact on the quality of their work, and over half say using social media has a negligible impact on the quality of their work.[17] As someone who has worked with thousands of sleep-deprived, stressed-out, anxious tweens and teens, I beg to differ. There's long been a myth surrounding the potential of multitasking to improve productivity, which I explored in *The Myth of the Perfect Girl*. The reality is that multitasking results in nothing being completed well.

During my presentations to students, I typically give an example of the incremental creep of text message conversations. It goes something like this: In the middle of completing math homework, you notice a phone notification because you have a text message from someone—*who could it be?* Maybe a friend, or perhaps a romantic interest. It could be a relative asking a quick question, or a teammate wanting to know when practice starts. Receiving a text message creates a sense of urgency, and the natural inclination is to answer the message. But then what happens? It's not as if you then fully return to completing math problem #3 once the message is sent. (Students usually nod in agreement.) More likely, you sit and wait for a response, to which you might need to think up a funny, witty, and spontaneous reply. Thirteen messages later, you are still on math problem #3—and you've convinced yourself the past half-hour has been dutifully spent on math homework. If you are in your room, your parents likely think you are hard at work as well.

> The reality is that multitasking results in nothing being completed well.

Whenever I give this "math problem #3" example, nervous laughter erupts from the audience, because nearly all tweens and teens who message their friends experience a similar scenario on an ongoing basis. It's no secret that students struggle with self-regulation, especially when it comes to understanding how to compartmentalize work so they can remain productive and focused. Some of this struggle is developmental and is affected by where tweens and teens are in terms of brain development. Boys' brains are still developing until they are about twenty-four years old, and girls' brains aren't fully developed until they are around twenty-one years old.[18] The prefrontal cortex, the area of the brain that regulates impulse control and sound decision-making, still has a good ways to go for many tweens and teens, and the pleasure principle often reigns supreme. Various forms of media often provide an instant gratification and distraction that can be hard to overcome in the face of longer-term goals related to academic performance and overall wellness.

When it comes to helping students with self-regulation, adults often make the mistake of coming from a place of punitive anger and frustration about distraction and off-task behaviors. In reality, adults have their own struggles regulating technology and social media use. Research suggests that adults check their smartphones an average of once every six minutes—or over 150 times *per day*.[19] Some 93 percent of 18–29 year olds admit to using their smartphones to avoid being bored, and 57 percent of phone users report that their phone use leaves them feeling distracted.[20] Today's employers go to great lengths to try to manage employee productivity during the workday, blocking access to personal email or websites that might be distracting, hiring consultants to provide professional development around increasing mindfulness, and managing technological distractions so that work can be completed more efficiently.

Given the issues adults in the workplace experience related to online distractions and productivity, we need to shift our perspective and understanding of self-regulation and create opportunities for students to develop their own intrinsic motivation to make behavioral changes. At the same time, we also need to provide students with concrete tools to make those changes. Later chapters will suggest strategies for promoting a shift away from multitasking toward compartmentalization and single-task focusing, and finding ways to encourage time and energy management on a daily basis.

Safety

I encourage parents, educators, and students to think about safety in terms of offering protection rather than creating a sense of punitive fear. Safety issues have become far more complicated over the past five to ten years, and from an online perspective it's important to recognize issues related to privacy, data mining, and how and where tweens and teens are sharing information in cyberspace. When we think in terms of physical and emotional safety, parents and educators have to work with students to create emergency and contingency plans for when something doesn't go as planned and to help students feel as though they can reach out to multiple people and places if they make a decision that puts them in harm's way.

One of the first schools I consulted with on technology policies decided, for financial and logistical reasons, to have students' families purchase iPads instead of giving students school-issued devices. Since the tablets were owned by the families, students kept their devices year round, and the school had little say on what apps and games students used or added to the devices. In one case, a middle school girl began using her iPad to communicate with someone she thought was a fifteen-year-old boy through Minecraft, an open-world game that allows players to build designs from textured blocks. Though Minecraft is most known as a game focused on creative building, it has a social component that allows players to communicate and interact with one another. When law enforcement officers showed up at the family home to inform the young girl and her parents that she was actually spending her time communicating with a man in his mid-forties in another state, the parents rushed to blame the school. The parents reasoned that it was the school's fault for making students use iPads and thus exposing her to potential harm.

There were several issues in this case, namely, that schools should generally issue devices and create policies and guidelines for parents and students around smarter choices and appropriate use. This school had no policies in place and provided no real guidelines for parents (this has since changed). At the same time, many parents blame schools and are frustrated with tablet and computer programs that encourage students to be online for many hours in the day. Parents often fail to realize that the mobile devices they readily purchase for their children (smartphones with cameras and videos, for example) can be bigger triggers for the onslaught of school social-networking disasters. When Andrew Davis was the head of the middle school at Crystal Springs School in Hillsborough, California, he noted that nearly all of the disciplinary actions regarding social media and device misuse involved students who were using devices brought from home and purchased by their parents.[21] The school had a one-to-one tablet program, and in some cases, parents remained unaware of their children's use of personal devices. As with most other schools, students could bypass school filter systems by using their mobile phones on school grounds. Yet, when the mobile phones were used on school grounds in a way that resulted in disciplinary action, parents were quick to assume the school-issued tablet was to blame.

When we think of social media, technology use, and safety for tweens and teens, one of the first things that come to mind is the need to protect young people from chatting and meeting with potential predators online. This increased vulnerability is especially true for students who might feel socially isolated at school or within their community. At the same time, issues related to online and in-real-life safety go beyond protecting young people from interacting with strangers and potential predators to also include serious topics such as data mining, privacy, and security. For instance, when a school has students sign up for a free file-sharing service to store and turn in assignments, the students are exposed to potential data mining and are regularly exposed to targeted advertisements. Imagine my surprise when

I asked a group of two hundred students what their biggest distractions were when they were completing homework and one blurted out, "The ads that pop up when I use [a popular file-sharing service]!" I glanced over at the school principal, who looked chagrined as she realized the school's requirement to set up free accounts on the file-sharing service had caused this problem.

Even though ad-free educational accounts were an option, the school was unsuccessfully attempting to save tens of thousands of dollars by having students create free accounts (though nothing is really free, and the ads clearly came with a cost). A later conversation with school administrators revealed that in requiring those fifth- and sixth-grade students to sign up for free accounts on the file-sharing service, the school was also making the students indicate falsely that they were thirteen years old, which was the minimum age according to the service's terms of use. Shortly after my presentation, the school principal told me the school decided to pay for the educational accounts.

In addition, many classrooms use educational sites and apps that may have dubious data-security practices or questionable data-mining practices, making students' personal information and records vulnerable to being unknowingly stored or exposed. Hundreds of companies, including Facebook and Google, use data to target ads, and how and what is being targeted at students based on their search practices can lead to a host of questions that don't necessarily have clear answers.[22] A February 2015 *New York Times* article entitled "Uncovering Security Flaws in Digital Education Products for Schoolchildren" reveals how software engineer Tony Porterfield discovered the website his children were assigned to use to complete a reading assessment had a number of security flaws that made it easy for unauthorized users to potentially gain access to students' names, voice recordings, and skill levels.[23] Similar vulnerabilities expose students using educational tools as part of their classroom learning experience to hacking, identity theft, and unsolicited contact from strangers. Reporter Natasha Singer notes that "some privacy scholars, educators and technologists contend that federal protections for student data have not kept pace with the scope and sophistication of classroom data mining." Even though the Family Educational Rights and Privacy Act (FERPA) places limits on how student information is handled, those limits often don't extend to the free apps and sites teachers use in the classroom to supplement their daily instruction.[24]

There are so many unique layers to address when we think about maintaining and supporting the safety of tweens and teens, but foundationally, parents, educators, and students need to work together to offer support and find solutions. During a recent Q&A after a presentation to parents, one mother cornered me and begged me to tell her exactly what she needed to do to keep her daughter safe. As much as I want to be able to provide a simple solution, I told her what I tell all parents and educators: There is no one-size-fits-all answer. Designing successful solutions requires a nuanced and flexible approach, and building awareness is the first step.

SUMMARY

Social media creates a new language of communication and connection and, in many cases, widens the generational divide between children and the adults they may look to for guidance. Tweens and teens today often look to their peers and an entire online media culture for advice and input, and adults need to become more aware and understanding of how this new language is key to helping young people grow up into thoughtful, resilient, active members of the school and greater communities. Even though social media and related technology introduce new layers of complexity to learning and relationships, we still hold many of the same values for our children, and we need to find better ways to reach kids and give them the tools and resources they need to make better decisions. In terms of how social media and technology affect students' educational experiences, it is helpful to think of the ways in which socialization, self-regulation, and safety play a role. Today's tweens and teens socialize differently with one another and have a difficult time self-regulating when experiencing the ultimate paradox: The device they need to use to complete their work is their biggest distraction from getting work done. When we think about maintaining and preserving the safety of students, it is important to remember the growing complexity around maintaining students' safety. It is not simply a question of having them avoid meeting unsavory strangers online. They also must find ways to protect their privacy, identity, and personal data as they use more and more educational apps and online tools.

CHAPTER 2

Background

Where We've Been, Where We're Going, and Why It Matters

In the fall of 2001, I worked briefly as an investment banking analyst in the Silicon Valley office of a big bank. Analysts typically work long hours with an inordinate amount of downtime in between projects or tasks, and many spend time attempting to appear busy during the lulls, toggling deftly between computer screens to avoid the potential glare from a manager or superior walking by. In those days, there were not many websites to help us waste hours of time, but one that gained quick notoriety was HOTorNOT.com. Developed by Berkeley grads James Hong and Jim Young in 2000, Hot or Not became popular with the initial premise that users could submit photographs of themselves (or others) to be judged by the general public through a 1-to-10 rating system.[1] Photos of two people were also put side by side so that users could determine the "hotter" of the two.

In many ways, Hot or Not influenced today's top social media sites, because it was one of the first websites to successfully capitalize on and monetize the comparison culture integral in today's social media. As a college student, Facebook CEO Mark Zuckerberg was brought before the Administrative Board at Harvard in 2003 for creating Facemash, a version of Hot or Not specifically using photos of Harvard undergrads.[2] A decade later, in 2013, Instagram "beauty pageants" consisted of groups of girls' photos being posted in a grid-like fashion and users being asked to determine the most attractive by leaving their choice in the comments section.[3] These girls, some as young as nine or ten years old, were harshly evaluated on their appearance by anyone who could access the photos, and it's unlikely they were socially and emotionally able to process the potential onslaught of public commentary.[4] In many ways, though, these Instagram beauty pageants were simply Hot or Not 2.0.

I mention Hot or Not because the site's instant popularity stemmed from some of the very same qualities that make so many social media sites popular today. Hot or Not's original website was easy to use, and new photos were uploaded regularly to provide a constant flow of new content. The website offered a seemingly quick and gratifying way to interact with the content—that is, judging people based on their physical attractiveness, and seeing how those ratings matched up with the opinions of other users. Many of today's most popular social media apps—including Facebook, Twitter, Snapchat, Instagram, YouTube, and Musical.ly—share some of those same qualities. For instance, Instagram is relatively easy to use, has new user-generated content uploaded constantly, and provides a quick and easy way of interacting with content by offering feedback through a "heart" or comments on a photo.[5] On YouTube, users can quickly upload or watch videos, there is a consistent stream of new content, and there are easy ways to share and comment on photos. Tween and teen girls post "Am I Pretty or Ugly?" videos on YouTube asking for public feedback on their attractiveness, but as with the Instagram beauty pageants, they are usually not emotionally or mentally prepared for the anonymous feedback in the comments section.[6] In essence, the inherent popularity of some of today's most widely used social media sites can be traced to a site developed by two young men after a dispute over a passing woman's attractiveness ("Is she hot or not?") and the algorithm that was built as a result.

HOW WE GOT HERE

It's helpful to step back and take a brief look at how much has changed in so little time. To say that social networking applications haven't been around for long is an understatement. One of the main reasons the new language of social media is so difficult for parents and educators to fully understand and address is that there always seems to be some new development upending what was previously on trend. Many of the earliest forms of social networking, like Friendster, focused on open socialization and free creative expression. In 2002, Friendster exploded in popularity (relatively speaking) to become one of the first social networking sites to have more than

1 million users. The site grew to have over 3 million users before its rapid decline. Despite its collapse, Friendster identified people's need to and interest in interacting and socializing with one another online. (Today, Friendster has been relaunched as a social gaming site in Asia.) In 2004, Myspace became popular by allowing people to personalize their pages with colors, graphics, photos, music, and background images.[7] For those interested in music, MySpace's customizability gave them a powerful, inexpensive way to showcase their talent, and for a short while, it was one of the more important music marketing sites. Though the site has gone through ownership changes and has experienced a significant decline in users, it remains in existence.

Nothing has utterly changed the social media landscape quite like Facebook. Facebook was first designed as a virtual picture book for Harvard students, after founder Mark Zuckerberg took down its predecessor site Facemash amid rampant criticism.[8] Its popularity quickly led to its becoming available to students on other college campuses, and I first heard about Facebook in the fall of 2005, when one of my students who was a sophomore at Boston College told me about the profile she had just created on what was then known as "the" Facebook. She explained that she put all her information online so that her friends could quickly find her dorm room location, instant messaging handle, class schedule, and phone number. At the time, her online naïveté, combined with Facebook's initial focus on college student populations, gave her (and many of her peers) a false sense of privacy and security. In those early days, it was common for students to openly share photos not likely meant for public consumption. Some students were dismayed to find that future employers gained access to their postings, evaluating them as a way of gauging prospective employees' decision-making skills and judgment.[9]

It didn't take long for Facebook to expand to a much wider audience. Now, virtually anyone with an email address and Internet access can create a Facebook profile. In May 2009, Facebook surpassed Myspace in number of users, and by the end of 2016, the site had grown from 1 million monthly users to over 1.79 *billion* active monthly users worldwide.[10] In August 2015, Facebook announced that it had over *a billion* daily users—or approximately one out of every seven people on Earth.[11] It is clearly no longer just for college students. In all likelihood, your neighbor's pet sitter and grandmother are both active users, sharing their vacation photos, status updates, and daily frustrations with their Facebook "friends."

Over the past twelve years, Facebook's digital fences have gone through significant changes. Though Facebook initially insisted that people use their real names, it clarified its "real name" policy to allow for greater flexibility in response to continued protests from the lesbian, gay, bisexual, and transgender (LGBTQ) community and now allows people to post using their "authentic" names, or names by which they are known.[12] In compliance with federal laws, Facebook's minimum age of use in its terms of service is thirteen years old, though it is ostensibly difficult for any social media site to verify users' self-reported age. For years, the profiles of users under eighteen years old could be viewed only by those within the young person's friend group. In 2013, Facebook made a somewhat controversial decision to alter the company's privacy rules and allow teen users to make their posts public. Even though Facebook defends its decision, the potential for increased exposure has led to criticism.[13] Today, all Facebook users have access to "public" posts, and privacy groups have raised concern over how data shared on the site are stored and used.[14] The company is currently focused on finding ways to unite the world online—and now has a growing suite of popular social media apps, including Facebook Messenger, Instagram, and WhatsApp.

I highlight Facebook because historically it provided many middle school and high school students with one of their first experiences with social connection—and confusion. Even though many of today's tweens and teens are likely to be on Snapchat, Musical.ly, and Instagram long before they create a Facebook account, many still use Facebook and Facebook Messenger as a base camp of sorts. There are so many different apps—including the music-, podcast-, and video-streaming service Spotify or the high-school-focused app After School—that allow or require users to sign in via a Facebook account.[15] Those who are active on social media likely regularly use another product in its suite of apps. As of September 2015, Facebook Messenger—the messaging app Facebook spun off as a separate app to download in 2014[16]—is the second most popular app in the United States (behind the Facebook app).[17] Many middle school and high school students spend the bulk of their time on Snapchat or Instagram, which was acquired by Facebook in April 2012 and quickly became a favorite for its ease of use and focus on photo filters and editing tools.[18] When I once asked a high school freshman how she was doing, she replied brightly, "I am GREAT! The photo I posted on Instagram got 192 likes today!"

Some teens I work with equate Facebook to more of a professional and personal networking site—it keeps them connected, and they might check in weekly, daily, or even hourly, but it is not where they typically go when they want to share their deepest secrets, poignant thoughts, or silliest photos online, in part because their grandparents, neighbors, and family friends might all be their Facebook friends. Teens who might want to disconnect from Facebook can find it difficult because some social planning (sharing invitations, setting times and places for events) is done through the site. At some schools, teachers use Facebook groups to maintain school or class communication, or students might create their own Facebook groups to manage collaborative projects. So, even as they may use Facebook regularly, many students actively shift some of their online time and efforts to mobile apps and sites that provide an illusion of more intimate daily interactions.

For many tweens and teens, their time spent on social media comes at a time of crucial identity formation and growth development. It gives some young people the opportunity to connect and share in a way they may not be comfortable doing in person, and to keep up with friends and family regardless of geographic distance. At the same time, spending time perusing other people's posts and photos creates a false sense of intimacy and inclusion, as the concept of online friends and followers has blurred the lines related to what constitutes friendship. For example, frustration and hurt feelings can crop up regularly when tweens and teens (and adults, too) realize they weren't invited to a party or event after postings show up in their "newsfeed," the ever-changing cultivation of others' postings.

THE NEW SOCIAL MEDIA

The past decade has radically transformed the tween and teen experience. There are so many different ways to think about what *new* really means—does it refer to sites that began within the last ten to twelve years that are still in use today, including Tumblr or Twitter?

Or does *new* refer to how iPhone and Android apps have moved so much of our daily life to mobile? Is the focus mainly on mobile apps whose popularity has exploded since 2009, like Musical.ly, Snapchat, and Instagram? Or do we want to focus on the global explosion in popularity of messaging apps like WhatsApp, Line, and WeChat, all of which are used to send and receive messages, photos, and voicemails? Indeed, there are so many ways to look at the idea of new social media trends among young people that, for the sake of brevity, I want to highlight some general trends and how they affect tween and teen culture and experience. Although much may happen outside of the classroom, smartphones have made it more likely that the majority of social media use takes place during the school day. In a 2013 *New York Times* profile of Snapchat, the app's founders reported finding "unusual spikes in activity, peaking between 8 a.m. and 3 p.m.," which led to the realization that some use was centered around high school students.[19] Tween and teen users were (and are) likely sending Snaps (and creating posts, updating profiles, shopping online, and checking ESPN) in the middle of math class.

> Videos and photos are now the most popular ways tweens and teens express their taste and distinguish themselves.

Today's tweens and teens are hyperfocused on sharing, curating, and communicating through customizable text messages, photos, and videos that can be created quickly and disseminated instantly. We've seen shifts to and from many trends, and it's impossible to say when and if one trend has completely gone away before another starts—trends often vary based on a student's age, geographic location, peer influence, and social habits. Videos and photos are now the most popular ways tweens and teens express their taste and distinguish themselves. In the upcoming sections, I focus on the overarching trends of public profiles, private messaging, anonymous and ephemeral interactions, and video and live feed. For purposes of discussion, I've separated out these topics, even though they all overlap in many ways (for example, a teen can receive private messages through a public profile). At the same time, it's fascinating to think about how all these trends have evolved, intertwined, and changed in less than three presidential terms.

Public Profiles

Tweens and teens create online profiles for many reasons. One of the most common is to project their own identity within a unique personal space. In the way teenagers' bedrooms might have once been the main reflections of their individuality, so now are their digital spaces. Myspace originally allowed for highly personalized spaces, and then Facebook profiles exploded with popularity after allowing individuals to personalize a highly formatted template with their own content. Twitter users are able to have both a banner photo (an option added in 2012) as well as a profile photo, and Tumblr accounts can be individualized in many ways with or without the help of templates. The individuality once limited to decorating the private space of one's room (or wall, in the case of shared bedrooms) has expanded to profiles filled with postings, photos, and commentary now open for public consumption. The once-private time and space for individual identity development has shifted to have the potential for worldwide liking, sharing, and feedback.

The term *public* can be rather confusing—is it "public" simply if everyone else can see it? Does a person's identity also have to be known? For instance, teens create Instagram or Snapchat accounts with an anonymous handle or username that is publicly viewable, even though their identity remains shielded. Some social media accounts might be open to the anonymous feedback and questions of others. An Instagram account may be deemed private, though followers who have been accepted are freely able to view the content. I define a "public profile" as one that is meant to be viewed by others, whether "others" comprises only a user's ten closest friends or, in the case of Internet sensation Kim Kardashian, the 86.6 million followers of her Instagram account as of November 2016.[20] A real name or identifying information does not need to be used, and even though nearly all social media apps and sites allow content to be made private or have limited access, I use the term *public* if the content is accessible or meant to be viewed by others.

Here's an important point: We've created a false sense of security with private accounts. Tweens and teens are often advised to make their accounts "private," to limit others' access. Teen girls tell me that they have public "rinsta" or real Instagram accounts for all followers and then private "finsta" Instagram accounts for their "closest" friends.

But, usernames remain searchable, and those who do have access to posts and photos can easily take a screenshot and repost images to make them accessible to a wider audience. In many cases, some information thought to be private is still available to the wider public. For instance, Dara was a sixth grader I worked with whose parents allowed her to have an Instagram account as long as she kept her account "private," or visible to followers she approved. When I looked up Dara's profile, I saw that her username was her real name, and that her "tag line" that was publicly visible included particular identifying information that could be used to locate her easily. Her last name was unique, and her parents were high-profile, well-known figures who didn't realize Dara had inadvertently provided a great deal of information to the wider public audience with her "private" account.

Many young people now use Instagram as their main public profile. With over 500 million active monthly users uploading approximately 95 million photos/videos per day,[21] Instagram's popularity is rooted in its remarkable simplicity. Accounts can be personalized quickly

Amanda Jones

SOCIAL MEDIA WELLNESS

with photos, memes, and reposts of others—with little to no written content needed. Since so many students have smartphones with camera and video capabilities, photos can now be filtered and enhanced within seconds and can easily be uploaded for others to view, like, and comment upon. Looking at others' photos and receiving likes and comments on one's own photos can be time consuming, and Instagram users spend an average of over ten hours a month perusing photos.[22] Nearly 42 percent of teens who use Instagram access it on their mobile devices, and 23 percent of teens consider it their favorite social networking app.[23]

Even if an account is "public," keeping a teen's identity less visible has advantages. (I use the term *less visible* because very little is truly anonymous on the Internet.) Several years ago, Alexa felt disconnected from her peers at school and was simply trying to "ride out" her senior year in high school. She confided that she found a sense of community online through her Tumblr account, where people from around the world would follow her posts and comment on how her writings had helped them deal with their own issues. Alexa felt her Tumblr page gave her an outlet to express her creativity, and the feedback she received improved her self-esteem and self-confidence at a time when she didn't feel as though she was finding the same level of support in school. For some people, posting to a Tumblr account is a way of keeping an online digital journal. Alexa remained anonymous online, and none of her followers knew she was a high school student from the San Francisco Bay Area. Even so, she felt a sense of community from the online world she helped create with her daily musings.

> Public profiles give tweens and teens the opportunity to create their own unique space and identity.

There are several reasons why public profiles are so popular with teens and tweens. Most obviously, public profiles give tweens and teens the opportunity to create their own unique space and identity. One component of adolescent development is wanting to be liked or feeling included in something. The ability to interact with others, whether friends or followers, gives an appearance of belonging and being liked in a world in which likes and followers have become the new barometers for popularity.

Public profiles have the potential to transform the lives of ordinary teens who boast hundreds of thousands or even millions of followers (on Facebook, Instagram, Musical.ly, or Twitter) or subscribers (to a YouTube channel), to a level of fame that can be financially lucrative if not emotionally fraught. A 2015 survey found that teens are more influenced by digital stars than Hollywood celebrities; teens stated they had a greater emotional attachment to YouTube stars and found them more engaging and extraordinary.[24] In her book *American Girls: Social Media and the Secret Lives of Teenagers*, Nancy Jo Sales interviews Amanda, the teen behind the handle MakeupbyMandy24.[25] With 2.8 million YouTube subscribers, 2.6 million followers on Instagram, and 800,000 followers on Twitter in 2016, Amanda is a recognizable star in the world of YouTube celebrities. At the same time, her world has quickly narrowed, as she explains to Sales: "YouTube has taken over my whole life . . . everything about my life now is from the Internet . . . . All my friends are from the Internet, it's really awesome . . . 'cause we all relate to each other."[26]

When so much of a tween's or teen's life revolves around sharing photos and messages online, there is inevitably an amplified opportunity for confusion, self-doubt, and harm. Stan Kutcher, an adolescent psychiatry expert, explains that many young teens hoping to gain notoriety within a larger community might create postings using tags like "self-harm," "depression," and "sadness" as a way to garner attention.[27] Social media gives tweens and teens the ability to be validated and acknowledged nonstop, which can quickly nourish their developmental need to feel liked and wanted. At the same time, it can also encourage them to interact in ways that are more focused on garnering positive reactions and praise—provocative photos, for instance—and in doing so, can be another deterrent to allowing them to reflect upon their own personal values and intrinsic motivation. Over time, the reactionary feedback loop creates an environment in which tweens and teens make more and more decisions based on the affirming and derogatory reactions of a greater online community.

Private Commentary (i.e., Messaging)

Messaging remains a popular way for tweens and teens to stay connected to classmates, friends, and family members. The 2015 Pew Research study "Teens, Technology and Friendships" notes that text messaging is a consistent part of teens' daily lives and interactions: Over half of teens (55 percent) text their friends on a daily basis, and 88 percent of teens text their friends on at least an occasional basis.[28] For many teens and young adults, text messaging via phone and other messaging apps has replaced email for regular communication. In my own daily work, I realized the heightened importance of messaging when my office manager told me she no longer emailed our millennial staff members when she needed an immediate response because she realized sending them a text message was far more likely to garner a quick reply.

Tweens and teens use so many different forms of messaging that it can be difficult for parents and educators to keep track (see Table 2.1). There's basic SMS text messaging, of course, and private messaging

TABLE 2.1   Most Popular Messaging and Social Media Apps Among Teens[1]

COMMUNICATION PLATFORM	PERCENTAGE OF TEENS WHO USE THE PLATFORM
Snapchat	72
Facebook	68
Instagram	66
Twitter	36
Kik Messenger	29
Pinterest	27
Tumblr	24
Google Plus	21
WhatsApp	10
LinkedIn	9
Tinder	4

Note: [1]As of February 2016.

Source: U.S. teens: Most popular social media apps 2016. Statista. Retrieved November 7, 2016, from www.statista.com/statistics/199242/social-media-and-networking-sites-used-by-us-teenagers/

through social media apps like Instagram or Twitter. In addition, most adults don't realize that online games like Minecraft also have messaging tools that tweens and teens use to interact with one another on a regular basis. And then there are the many different messaging apps, including Facebook Messenger, WhatsApp, Line, WeChat, and GroupMe, all with slight nuances and different features that appeal to different audiences. It's easy for large groups to communicate—and potentially miscommunicate—with one another using group messaging apps like GroupMe, which reported in June 2012 that over 4.6 million users were sending an average of 550 million messages through its app each month.[29] An active conversation between several individuals on a group message app can feel like sitting around a table where everyone is talking at the same time—making it impossible to fully read and digest. And the potential for misunderstanding and miscommunication is naturally amplified when there are so many ideas, tangents, and tidbits flying around at once.

Ultimately, there are so many ways to message that if one way is unavailable, another is likely found within seconds, and many students actively shift between texting, direct messaging on social media, video games, video chat, and messaging apps like WhatsApp and Facebook Messenger to directly communicate with others. At one school I worked with, when school administrators decided to block the messaging feature on the school-issued iPads, students quickly shifted to using their email accounts as a way to message one another within the school system.

Private messaging—whether through texting, group messaging, or other means—creates the opportunity for a more intimate level of communication than posting a comment or question on a public profile. Messaging allows for conversation, and in a world in which 57 percent of teens between the ages of thirteen and seventeen have made a new friend online, it is seen as a way to create connections.[30] It also creates a whole new language of communication between tweens, teens, and adults that is not always fully understood and can quickly lead to misunderstandings. What if someone doesn't respond right away? How is sarcasm conveyed? And don't forget the underappreciated importance of emoticons and exclamation points in communication—an issue often lost on adults. A 2015 study suggested that text messages sent with a period were perceived as being less sincere. The principal researcher, Celia Klin, noted that "[t]exting is lacking many of the social cues used in actual face-to-face conversations. When speaking, people easily convey social and emotional information with eye gaze, facial expressions, tone of voice, pauses, and so on."[31] In other words, there's a big difference between responding "OK" and "Okay!!!! SO EXCITED!!!!" A little emoticon and exclamation point use can go a long way—a person could be responding quickly with a "K" to note understanding and acceptance and come to find out later that the intended recipient spent hours wondering if the person was angry or irritated. (This has happened to me more than once.)

In terms of educators and students, schools need to address the heightened sense of intimacy in messaging when they are developing policy. I've visited schools where teachers are allowed, and in some cases encouraged, to give students their personal cell phone number as a way of maintaining communication after hours for help with an assignment or a school issue. I've long argued that most inappropriate teacher–student relationships begin with text message communication and that schools need to have more proactive policies around teacher–student communication. As Terry Abbott, former chief of staff at the U.S. Department of Education, argues in the *Washington Post,* "two things have become popular and had a massive effect on the prevalence of sexual misconduct in schools: social media and text messaging. . . . Classroom sexual predators have been exploiting these new, unsupervised modes of communication to develop improper relationships with students out of sight of parents and principals."[32] A first step in policy is to require educators to communicate with students over a third-party platform that can save and store messages and communication. This requirement obviously won't deter those who choose to actively disregard the rules, but it does provide parameters and structure that can help avoid the potential for inappropriate behavior to develop. For example, Remind is an app that allows teachers to communicate with parents and students without revealing phone numbers, and it stores all messages within the app. As of September 2016, Remind had over 20 million monthly active users (educators, parents, and students), and the app is used in approximately half of the 100,000 public schools in the United States.[33] Remind gives educators a way to communicate with parents and students without providing an illusion of intimacy that can develop through seemingly surreptitious interactions.

Ephemeral and Anonymous Interactions

Tweens and teens want to socialize online without worrying that conversations or images from the seventh grade will pop up in a future search by a college admissions officer or potential employer. Some of them have been online since birth, as some parents set up online accounts for their children at birth. On average, parents post nearly 1,000 images of their child before the child reaches two years old. (The term *sharenting* refers to the way in which many parents look for validation of parenting experiences through social media.)[34] The notion of ephemerality in apps initially became popular with teens who realized that public online interactions had a long shelf life and wanted to share posts and images quickly and continuously without creating a long trail of content. As public profiles grew to have such a wide potential audience, many tweens and teens were simply trying to find a way to socialize online without added fear and consternation. Today, many apps provide features that combine to make ephemerality a commonplace feature, and what started as a way to go underground has now become much more mainstream.

Snapchat, the most popular app promising ephemerality, became popular in part because of its incredible success in creating an addictive element of fun and suspense—*the message will self-destruct in ten seconds, better look fast!* There's an illusion—and I use the term *illusion* because nothing is really as anonymous or ephemeral as hoped—that the funny photo or witty commentary will disappear within seconds of viewing. It can be fun to receive a Snap from a friend making a silly face, thinking that the photo will seemingly disappear a few seconds later. Snapchat streaks, described in Chapter 1, have an addictive quality because no one wants to be the one to break the streak. Snapchat Stories, launched in October 2013, allows users to combine content (messages, images, and videos) viewable within a twenty-four-hour period. In August 2016, Instagram launched Instagram Stories, which also allows users to share photo and video slideshows that disappear after twenty-four hours.[35] After that time, the content disappears, which encourages users to share new content often. Universities and colleges have created their own Snapchat Stories as a way to remain relevant and reach students. In many ways, the explosive popularity of Stories with universities and corporations has come from an ability to successfully "gamify" the dispersal of content by transforming content sharing into a fun game to be played.

The short shelf life also gives users the confidence to share content without worrying about perfection. In many ways, tweens and teens (and users in general) feel as though the barriers to produce and share content are much lower when it is ephemeral—making users more likely to share raw, "real" content without second-guessing themselves. This opportunity for quick sharing without excessive agonizing can have potential benefits and consequences, of course, especially for those who might be impulsive.

Apps that encourage the potential for anonymity feed adolescents' developmental desire to explore their own identity and idea creation. As is sometimes the case, middle schoolers might believe others will share their true feelings and are more likely to be open without the pressures of being "on" and constantly evaluated. Ultimately, it sometimes boils down to a version of *does he or she really like me?* Ask.fm allows users to anonymously ask questions or post comments on another person's profile. Whisper allows people to post their secret thoughts online, for others to comment and reflect upon. At the same time, many public profiles can be made anonymous when users create a username or handle that is not explicitly identifiable—that is, without using their real name, location, or other identifying information. According to the Pew Research Center, one in four teens (26 percent) on social media say they post fake information online to protect their privacy.[36] "Finstagram" and "Finsta" are terms used to highlight "fake," friends-only or private Instagram accounts—and some tweens and teens create two accounts, one that is accessible by their parents and another that their parents might not be aware of.[37]

The "fake accounts" can also be used to bully and harass classmates while dodging parental supervision and school discipline. Guidance counselors and college advisors have shared stories of "fake accounts" posting photos of girls and calling them ugly, and the school was never able to figure out who was behind the postings. One teenage girl at a school I work with learned that a fake Instagram account had been created in her name with inappropriate photos and comments posted, and people initially followed the account thinking it was her. She felt mortified and humiliated, and the school was unable to find out who created the account.

Why does all this matter? Protecting privacy is obviously important, and young people putting more care into what they choose to share online is a definite win. At the same time, the underlying fear we've created around social media use motivates many tweens and teens to go "underground" and use apps anonymously beyond the reach of parental guidance and adult supervision. The unfortunate side effect is that potential safety nets may not be in place when something doesn't go as planned. There also might be a missed teachable moment. I liken it to when I was younger and might have done something mildly inappropriate in public and one of my parents would have shot me "the look"—the one that said, "that's probably not a good idea, and we will discuss that later." It's perfectly normal for tweens and teens to make mistakes as part of the developmental process. It becomes infinitely more problematic when they make those mistakes anonymously on apps and are exposed to things they might be unprepared for socially, emotionally, or otherwise. Without guidance and support, issues can snowball and have increasingly dire consequences if not addressed immediately. Think back to my opening story in Chapter 1 about Danielle, who used Ask.fm without the knowledge of her parents and teachers. When things began happening online that she considered mean and nasty, she wasn't comfortable seeking guidance from those adults and felt she had nowhere to turn. At what point would she have felt comfortable asking for help? It is hard to know.

Issues arise when tweens and teens underestimate the potential for something they share online to gain a much wider audience than intended. Photos and videos can quickly go viral, and young people who send images and notes sent under the assumption of private, anonymous, and/or ephemeral messaging can become mortified in the face of a more public audience. The most common challenge comes from the seemingly private interactions between young adults in the context of a potential or existing romantic relationship. Sexting—or sending explicit photos or messages via private messaging—is used by teens (and adults) as a form of flirting within the context of a romantic relationship. A 2014 study from Drexel University found that over half (54 percent) of college students said they had sent or received sexually explicit messages or photos when they were under age eighteen.[38] Laws vary among the states, and, in some cases, teens have been prosecuted for sending explicit photos of themselves and others.

The legal, social, and psychological consequences of sexting are often addressed inadequately, yet they are a major aspect of social media wellness for tweens and teens. The bigger issue with private messaging remains clear: What happens when the private turns public, and there are no safety nets in place?

Most adults recognize that nothing is truly ephemeral or anonymous, and it's important to build that awareness in tweens and teens in a way that is not fear inducing or anxiety provoking. Snapchat, for instance, admits on its company blog that it has and will turn over photos and messages to law enforcement officials if it is given a warrant. In other words, nothing really disappears.[39] In 2014, Snapchat settled charges with the Federal Trade Commission (FTC) after allegedly misleading consumers into thinking Snaps and videos disappeared when those photos, messages, and videos actually remained accessible, as well as for not being forthcoming with users about how data were collected and stored.[40] Snaps can easily be captured if the recipient manages to save a screenshot, and there have been cases of Snaps being saved and distributed using third-party apps, including the now-defunct Snapsaved.[41] The false sense of security from ephemeral apps often masks a harsh reality. In early 2015, Snapchat added a Safety Center to its website with guidelines discouraging users from sending pornography, explicit photos or messages to minors, intimidating notes or threats, or content that could be seen as an invasion of privacy.[42]

For many teens, having a safe space where they are free of their digital footprint can help them to better navigate the rough waters of adolescence. In my second book, *The Myth of the Perfect Girl*, I discuss the importance of having multiple clusters of connection—or communities where a teen feels supported and validated. Social relationships can be fluid during adolescence, and close friends one day might not be as supportive the next, so having several places to turn for support can be critical for overall health and wellness. For Alexa, one of her clusters was the online Tumblr community. Proponents of anonymous apps and sites say it is crucial to allow teens the opportunity to explore their personal identity and perspectives without fear of retribution or worrying that something will be attributed to them. Teens wanting to explore their sexuality might find a community online that might feel easier and safer to navigate, especially if they live in a small community or a place where they feel their beliefs may be questioned. Teens who might not feel comfortable openly asking about sexual or mental health resources might feel more comfortable seeking that information in an anonymous setting. Teens or young adults who have different political or social values from their family or friends might find a community of like-minded people online, where they feel safer sharing and discussing issues of interest.

In my own work with teens, I've recognized the complexities of anonymous and ephemeral apps. Several years ago, I created an account on Yik Yak, a mobile app launched by two former college fraternity brothers that was first available for download in November 2013 (on April 28, 2017, Yik Yak announced it was shutting down its once popular app—another example of the ever-changing nature of social media).[43] Yik Yak initially allowed users to anonymously post brief, 200-character comments. Originally, those posts could be viewed only by users within a 1.5-mile radius of the poster's location, though posters could later view Yaks from anywhere and designate their "base camp," or main geographic location, where they were able to post and respond even if they were out of the vicinity.[44] College students going home for the summer, for instance, could still plug in to their campus community by designating that location as their base camp.

According to the founders, Yik Yak was intended to give users access to relevant, hyper-local content (for example, the line at the local coffee place is so long that it extends out the door, or there is an accident on a nearby side street). When teens began anonymously using Yik Yak to post hyper-local content on their middle school or high school campuses, it became an utter disaster. Unsubstantiated rumors and mean comments regarding students' (and faculty members') appearances and personal lives quickly endangered campus safety and community.[45] On some campuses, Yik Yak use resulted in cyberbullying, potential legal action, and bomb threats, while other schools remained virtually unscathed.[46] One of the reasons for the wide discrepancy in effects is that much of the app's potential was based on the number of Yakkers posting within a given location. Yik Yak worked most effectively when many users posted within a small geographic area with a free flow of information and commentary. If one of two people occasionally posted at a given location, with no feedback or interaction from others, there was far less potential for negative repercussions.

In the app's short time invading high school campuses, Yik Yak's creators realized the potential negative impact of their app. The founders chose to change the app's age requirement to 17 and older, and blocked use of the app on the grounds of elementary schools, middle schools, and high schools across the United States.[47] The age requirement change was somewhat cosmetic, since 39 percent of online teens admit to lying about their age in order to access a website or account.[48] After the change, anyone trying to access or post on or near school grounds that have been blocked, they received a message saying something along the lines of this: "It looks like you are using this at a high school or middle school, which is not allowed. Sending and reading messages is disabled."

Even though Yik Yak's creators have tried to remove the app from middle school and high school campuses (and I have found instances where it *does* work on campuses, particularly private and independent school campuses), it is still easily accessible in areas just past school grounds. I created a Yik Yak account because I wanted to see what teens around my office were discussing. Once I tapped into the local network, I surmised that most Yik Yak posters in my immediate vicinity seemed to be in junior high or high school, and most posts dealt with issues typical of teen angst—love, homework, friends, and family drama. A few weeks after creating my account, I saw one user ask for a referral to a therapist for help with teen depression. I wondered about potential responses and considered posting a few good local resources. Before doing so, I was pleasantly surprised to see that others had anonymously provided the OP (original poster) with great resources. A few were places I would have recommended. Responders also chimed in with genuine encouragement and empathy. It was heartening to read and, at the time, made me reexamine my own perceptions of anonymous apps.

One of the main challenges of monitoring activity on anonymous apps is understanding when the subtext is inappropriate, crude, and vulgar. In 2015, the app After School quickly became a sensation among high school students who wished to share their ideas in an anonymous format. The app claims to be on over 22,300 high school campuses and allows users to post messages anonymously.[49] Unlike Yik Yak, After School is designed to be accessed only by high school students, where students from each school are able to openly share observations, reflections, and issues in a designated message board. Even though the app's founders say they want to encourage an open dissemination of positive musings, After School has struggled with the issues common to most apps that promise anonymity.

Mean comments and threats of violence have prompted schoolwide response, and some public school administrators struggle to find ways to discipline students for untraceable comments and postings. As of April 2015, After School keeps track of cell phone data to identify the origins of postings and also offers text crisis counselors to users who post messages that are deemed potentially problematic.[50]

Like so many things, the world of ephemeral and anonymous app use is complicated. There is no easy answer, but the first step is building awareness and allowing tweens and teens to express why they are spending time using certain sites, and what they feel the benefits and drawbacks are to their time, energy, and personal motivation. For a summary of the ephemeral and anonymous apps that are currently available, see Table 2.2.

Video and Live Feed

Much of today's video-sharing and live-feed streams are intertwined with public profiles, private messaging, and anonymous and ephemeral interactions. Marketers focus on making videos as part of their content marketing strategy, and nearly every popular social media site—including Facebook, Instagram, Snapchat, Tumblr, and Twitter—makes it easy for videos to be uploaded and shared so that others can watch and interact.[51] The rise of iPhone and Android use allows students to create and consume content with little effort, and today's tweens and teens can create and disperse a video several different ways via multiple platforms within a matter of minutes. A video created using an iPhone could be edited using Snapchat tools, uploaded to YouTube, and shared on Facebook and Instagram. It could be sent via messaging to a small group of intimate friends, or posted publicly to a wider audience. With all these interconnected ways to create and disperse content, it is easy to underestimate the remarkable power of video production and consumption in the world of tweens and teens.

One of the most popular social video-sharing apps is Musical.ly, a music-sharing app that allows "Musers" (as users are aptly named) to post videos of themselves lip synching to songs. Musical.ly has exploded in popularity since launching in August 2014, and as of October 2016, the app boasts over 133.5 million Musers worldwide (60 million in the United States). Musical.ly claims that half of all

TABLE 2.2 Anonymous and Ephemeral Apps Informational Chart

APP	DATE FOUNDED	SIGN-UP PROCESS	MINIMUM AGE TO USE	FEATURES	POPULARITY	PERCENTAGE OF USERS UNDER AGE 18
After School	2014[1]	Each school creates the account, which is a closed community; students log in via Facebook with their school name and age verification.[1]	13[2]	Can be used anonymously or with names attached; all users are held to After School's community guidelines and are not permitted to post harmful or inappropriate content to their school's feed.[1]	Over 80% of high schools use this app, making it the largest social network for teens[1]; between 2 and 10 million users.[3]	N/A
Ask.fm	2010; bought by Ask.com in 2014[4]	Download free app; name and birthdate required.[4]	13[4]	Anonymous Q&A website; syncs to Twitter and Facebook.[4]	Largest Q&A website in world, with 150 million users in 150 countries.[5]	42% (under 17)[6]
Instagram	2010[7]	Download app; create profile with name and email address.[8]	13[9]	Can edit and use special "filters" on posted photos and can tag other users in photos and use your location[7]; many teens create Finstagram or fake Instagram accounts (fake = more candid, private profiles shared only with select friends, a "real" version of their lives)[10]; Instagram Stories (est. 2016) are collections of photos or videos posted to show your friends what you've been up to in the last day. They exist for 24 hours and can be replayed as many times as the user wants.[11]	300 million active monthly users; considered most important social network by 32% of American teens.[8]	52% of Internet users age 13–17[12]

(Continued)

TABLE 2.2 (Continued)

APP	DATE FOUNDED	SIGN-UP PROCESS	MINIMUM AGE TO USE	FEATURES	POPULARITY	PERCENTAGE OF USERS UNDER AGE 18
Kik Messenger	2009[13]	Download free app and create profile; email and birthdate required (data use charges may apply).[13]	13[13]	Free messenger app, simple alterative to email or SMS messaging; password-protected, username-based setup; can be used anonymously.[14]	200 million users; over 40% of U.S. teens and young adults use Kik; biggest cross-app messenger in the U.S. market.[15]	27% (age 13–18)[14]
Periscope	2014; bought by Twitter in 2015[16]	Download app and create profile with phone number; can use existing Twitter profile to create account.[17]	13[18]	Live video-streaming app that allows users to broadcast themselves to users who join the broadcast; can be replayed many times; taken down after 24 hours.[19]	10 million total users; 1.85 million daily users.[20]	N/A
Snapchat	2011[21]	Download app; create profile with name, email address, and birthday.[22]	13[23]	Place to post images with commentary; posts "disappear" within seconds, but they can still be retrieved[23]; 9,000 photos are shared per second[21]; Snapchat Stories (est. 2013) are collections of photos or videos posted to show your friends what you've been up to in the last day. They exist for 24 hours and can be replayed as many times as the user wants.[22]	More than 60% of U.S. 13- to 34 year-old smartphone users are Snapchatters[24]; 100 million active daily users[21]; on average, at 500 million Snapchat Stories per day (calculated at 10 seconds each), it would take over 158 years to watch an entire day of Snapchat Stories.[25]	45% of Snapchat's users are 18–24 years old (under 18 N/A)[26]

APP	DATE FOUNDED	SIGN-UP PROCESS	MINIMUM AGE TO USE	FEATURES	POPULARITY	PERCENTAGE OF USERS UNDER AGE 18
Spotafriend	2015[27]	Download app, register, and use.[28]	17; but marketed to 13–19 demographic.[29]	Functions as a "Teen Tinder" designed for teens ages 13–19, although advertised as a way to meet friends in your local area and build community; integrated chat feature.[30]	#1 free teen swiping app in the United States, Australia, United Kingdom, and Canada; has more than 1 million members.[28]	Not reported, but nearly all, based on its marketing campaign.[28]
Tumblr	2007[31]	Register with email and username.[32]	13[33]	Microblogging platform that allows users to post text, photos, quotes, links, music, and videos from browsers, phone, desktop, or email; users can customize everything, from colors to theme's HTML.[31]	288 million blogs; 132 billion posts.[31]	15%[33]
Twitter	2006[34]	Download free app; sign up with full name and phone number or email.[35]	13[36]	Users send short 140-character messages to their followers; can "retweet" others' messages and direct message other users.[37]	305 million active daily users; consistently named one of the most popular social media apps for teenagers.[37]	50% of teens who go online use Twitter[38]
Whisper	2012[39]	Download app and create profile; requires no personal information, not linked to other social networks, and requires 4-digit pin every time you log on.[40]	13–18 with parental permission[41]; must be 17 to download app.[42]	Lets users anonymously share their secrets with millions of others in acts of contrition, catharsis, and some degree of nameless performance.[43]	45% of users post something every day[43]; 10 million users per day.[44]	4%[45]

Note: N/A = not available.

Sources: See table notes on p. 198.

teens are on the app, and the company launched live.ly, which allows users to easily livestream themselves.[52] Musical.ly's premise is simple, given that lip synching and music videos were popular with teens long before the advent of the Internet and mobile apps. The app allows tweens and teens to quickly create, share, and comment on videos. In his *Billboard* article "Musical.ly's Teenage Revolution: How the Trend-Setting Lip-Sync App Is Changing the Music Industry," Chris Martins reveals how this relatively young app has rapidly powered through to create its own generation of star-power.[53] For instance, 14-year old Maria Shabalin quickly gained a following after she began using Musical.ly and sharing her videos. By the fall of 2016, Maria had over 2 million followers online and was profiled in the *New York Times* on how she spends her Sundays (some of her time was spent making Musical.ly videos, obviously).[54]

Parents have voiced concerns over the use of explicit lyrics in Musical.ly music videos, as well as the sexually explicit and suggestive nature of videos posted online. Nonetheless, Musical.ly does encourage a certain amount of creativity, and it encourages the use of privacy settings. Like everything else in the social media world, parental awareness and understanding is key.

The ease with which video clips are created and shared makes it difficult to separate out what is actually being watched online. For example, it can be impossible to distinguish the difference between watching television shows or online videos, because some short video clips have been created from longer television episodes. Still, according to Common Sense Media's *Common Sense Census*, 61 percent of tweens like watching television a lot and 46 percent like watching online videos a lot, with 62 percent and 24 percent saying they watch TV and online videos every day. Among teens, 45 percent like watching TV and online videos a lot; 58 percent watch TV and 34 percent watch online videos every day.[55]

The rise in video translates into an increased focus on and fascination with live-feed video, which promotes this idea of newer and ever-changing content that highlights the ability to be raw and authentic. Periscope, a live-streaming video app owned by Twitter, allows users to "explore the world through the eyes of somebody else" and boasted 200 million live broadcasts as of March 2016.[56] Facebook Live, officially announced in April 2016, allows any

Facebook user with a smartphone to share live videos on the site and see how many people have tuned in to view the video feed.[57] There are filters to alter video quality, and in many ways, it makes sense the new social media would gravitate toward live-feed video, because so much of social media is about current and ever-changing content. Live-feed videos are similar to ephemeral content in that users often perceive that there is a lower barrier for creating and sharing content, which makes them more open to sharing and posting without worrying about long-term perception. For instance, a teen user creating a permanent post on Instagram might spend time making sure everything looks "just right" (anyone who has watched someone spend forty-five minutes trying to take a photo with a selfie stick knows what I mean), whereas a real-time, live-feed video has a lower barrier for sharing because the content feels raw, real, and right now.

Even though live-feed video provides a never-ending stream of new content, it also challenges notions around privacy and personal protections from being video-recorded. It is almost as if live-feed video is the new *new* social media, and with that brings a whole host of new opportunities and challenges. When individuals post live-feed videos showing exactly where they are located at any given time, there can be natural safety concerns. In the spring of 2017, Facebook Live worked to address issues that arose from crimes (including violent crimes and murders) being streamed live.[58] From a social media wellness perspective, many individuals have been disturbed by these videos, and tweens and teens may likely be traumatized after watching them. Given the newness of it all, it is difficult for proper guidelines and policies to address every potential pitfall, and parents don't always realize that if their children are on social media, they could potentially be accessing real-time violent content involving friends, classmates, or others in a way that is quickly socially and emotionally overwhelming.

There are certainly more than a few social and emotional drawbacks to the ease with which videos can be viewed and shared. In addition to concerns around viewing violent content, parents and safety advocates express concern that the ease of video viewing also gives rise to increased access to pornography. Most of the sexually explicit images and videos available online are free, and videos are often pirated and reposted on multiple websites as a method of potentially luring customers in to pay for different pornographic content.[59] In an interview with *The Atlantic* magazine, Shira Tarrant, a professor of women's, gender, and sexuality studies at California State University, Long Beach and author of the book *The Pornography Industry*, reveals that porn figures are hard to discern because the industry "is mostly online, as opposed to DVD sales or magazine sales, which you can track more easily."[60] Few research studies have looked at the effect of porn use on teen relationships, but a research study found that, among twelve-to-fifteen-year-olds in the southeastern United States, 53 percent of boys and 28 percent of girls had watched sexually explicit media, most often using the Internet.[61]

When I talk to parents about tween and teen social media use, I sometimes find it surprising that many parents don't fully realize how easily accessible sexually explicit content is on their children's smartphone. The mother of a sixth-grade boy once came up to me after a presentation with the most horrified look on her face because she had realized, midway through my talk, that she hadn't set any controls on her son's phone, and it was statistically likely that he had seen (a fair amount of) pornographic content. Part of the issue is how we, as Americans, view sexual health and education, and how many tweens and teens feel as though they are driven to look at sexually explicit content as a sort of sex education reference material to supplement the conversations they may or may not be having with adult figures in their lives. I'll discuss this topic more in Chapter 6, but in general, the rise of video and ease of accessibility of sexually explicit content is another part of the new language of social media that needs to be addressed. More often than not, teens' attempts at procuring sexual education materials leave them with images that completely distort reality and distill emotionally healthy relationships to quick and often violent physical interaction between dominant males and submissive females.

VIRTUAL REALITY

On August 24, 2016, White House chief photographer Pete Souza captured an image of President Barack Obama that was highlighted in the 2016 Year in Review. In the photograph, President Obama watches a virtual reality (or VR) film that was captured during an earlier trip to Yosemite National Park, and the president seems fully engaged and enthralled by his experience.[62] In a short time, the development of virtual reality has allowed for computer-generated simulation and interaction in a way never before thought possible. Users can have a seemingly real experience using equipment like the headset President Obama wears or a helmet and gloves with special sensors.

Virtual reality, unlike other forms of social media, can be a completely immersive experience—with potential benefits and drawbacks. Users who wear a headset and gloves or suit with sensors can have movements tracked—and feel as though they can track the movements of others. Virtual reality gaming allows players to experience a fully three-dimensional experience (as opposed to the two-dimensional experience of playing on a keyboard while watching a screen) and has the potential to provide a more intimate interactive experience. Users are able to create an identity using an avatar and interact and communicate in a world that can seem all too real. Jordan Belamire was playing a virtual reality game and felt sexually assaulted by another player within the confines of the game when the other player began "virtually rubbing her character's chest" and then assaulted her character by groping and grabbing at the character's breasts and crotch area.[63] For Belamire, the experience felt all too real, but no clear rules and regulations are in place regarding behavior toward an avatar or character in a virtual game. Many of the same issues around inappropriate behavior, social and emotional impacts, and addiction can exist when people interact in a world that feels as though it is an escape from their own reality.

In many ways, we are only beginning to see the potential benefits of virtual reality in terms of tween and teen learning and development. The emerging opportunities for learning and engagement include ways to close the gap in opportunity and access to resources. For instance, Google's Expeditions, which was announced in 2015, enables teachers to bring synchronized virtual reality field trips to their classrooms. Google provides schools with kits that include curriculum resources and viewers, and students are able to virtually take students "to places a school bus can't."[64] Virtual reality education has provided ways to augment classroom learning with three-dimensional interactive experiences that increase the potential impact of lessons.

One of the most promising areas for virtual reality and education is in helping students to develop empathy by figuratively enabling them to walk a mile in someone else's shoes. The health industry has used virtual reality to train professionals on what it might feel like for patients experiencing a certain disease or disability. In the school setting, virtual reality games could potentially be used to help combat bullying and the bystander effect by allowing students to see what it feels like to be a victim or to role-play different scenarios of how students could react when they see something inappropriate taking place.

WHY ALL OF THIS IS A BIG DEAL IN TERMS OF TWEENS, TEENS, AND THE SCHOOL EXPERIENCE

With the new social media world in a constant state of flux, the overall issue remains prevalent and somewhat overwhelming to all involved: How can we work together to promote wellness in an ever-changing time of heightened social media socialization? How can we use the framework of socialization, self-regulation, and safety as guiding principles for the basis of our work? What is the appropriate role for school administrators and educators in promoting wellness and better decision-making among students? What is the responsibility of parents while schools are so focused on increasing technology use in the classroom?

I was recently flying home from a "writing vacation" to finish this book and was seated next to the mother of an eighth-grade boy. We began discussing some of the issues in this book, and she was vehement that it was parents' responsibility to teach values and good decision-making around social media use. I calmly asked her what she knew about a few notable apps that kids in her community were actively using, and she looked perplexed. She assumed that since her son was what she termed "a talker"—meaning he told her everything—she was covered. I pointed out that was not exactly true—especially since his peers' social media choices likely affect classroom interactions and behavior. We all want to help students to navigate and adjust when things don't go as planned, and to understand how their choices online and in real life are more intertwined than they've been led to believe. Even though social media happenings can occur off campus and after hours, and frequently involve non-school issued mobile devices, many tweens and teens are making potentially life-altering decisions online and are in need of guidance and support. Sleep deprivation, sexting, and cyberbullying all affect the energy and attitude of students inside and outside the school community, and our goal should be to create an environment in which students have multiple avenues to seek out resources.[65] The aftermath of negative social media and online interactions overwhelmingly affects students' overall school experience and can irrevocably alter our classroom and school communities.

Regardless of where social media interactions occur, the entire social networking experience seeps into school culture, and it can put even greater pressure on students' mental health and overall wellness. The statistics are overwhelmingly not in girls' favor: Girls are twice as likely as boys to be bullied electronically, and perceptions of school climate and culture can directly impact their overall wellness. Those who have been cyberbullied are three times more likely to consider suicide.[66] Researchers at the University of South Florida surveyed 415 high school students to look at the correlation between students' perceptions of school climate and their own mental health wellness. They found that girls who had a negative perception of school climate were far more likely to also have greater self-reported mental health issues. For boys, the correlation was not nearly as strong.[67] Even so, all students benefit from a safe, welcoming, inclusive learning environment, and that potential community is easily disrupted when social media interactions are ignored or overlooked. In the coming chapters, we'll look more closely at the five side effects of increased social media and technology use, and what we can all do to make a difference.

SUMMARY

In terms of technology and social media, it can be hard for adults (and nearly impossible for tweens and teens) to fully comprehend how so much of our world has changed in so little time. Tweens and teens today spend time enhancing their own public profiles on social media sites like Facebook, Instagram, Twitter, and Tumblr, and a profile can be considered public if it is meant to be viewed by others. Nearly all teens with a phone use some sort of private messaging, communicating with family, friends, and acquaintances via text messaging and/or apps like Facebook Messenger, WhatsApp, and WeChat. Many of the initial fears regarding consequences of social media use have led to increased popularity of apps promoting anonymous and ephemeral interactions, even though nothing is truly anonymous or ephemeral on the Internet. Nearly all social media sites enable users to upload, view, and share videos, which provides easily consumable content for tween and teen users, and the latest developments, such as Facebook Live, live.ly, and Periscope, give users the opportunity to participate in live-feed video.

Today's social media provides ample opportunity for connection and interaction, but it can also be challenging for students to make good choices every day with so many potential distractions. Sleep deprivation, cyberbullying, and sexting can affect the social and emotional well-being of students, and these issues make it imperative that we create a new conversation around social media wellness.

CHAPTER 3

Side Effects

Five Ways Social Media Affects Today's Tweens and Teens

As soon as Ellie posted her latest selfie on Instagram, their phones started buzzing.

"I just posted a photo on Insta—can you like it?"

"PLZ like my Insta photo!! THX."

The two girls knew that if they didn't like Ellie's photo, she would be annoyed with them. Ellie had likely texted at least twenty of her friends, if not more, and if her photo didn't get what she considered to be "enough" likes within the crucial first five minutes it was posted, she would most likely delete the Instagram post. A photo receiving fewer than 100 likes was unlikely to be kept as part of her curated collection of selfies, fun location shots, memes, and pictures of her dachshund (#weinerdog), Dolly. Ellie's self-imposed rules around brand management were highly regulated and well-thought-out—every photo contributed to her highly controlled image, and she shamelessly sought out likes and comments with the determination of a seasoned public relations professional. She used hashtags like #squad and #squadgoals to refer to her friends and identify or solidify her status within a self-defined clique or social group. It didn't matter that she was only twelve years old—technically not even old enough to legally have an Instagram account. It was the likes and comments that counted most.

In my work with students, I've long noticed how the bulk of students' energy on social media isn't spent on posting, sending texts, and scrolling through social media feeds. Instead, most of their time is spent navigating relationships, waiting for responses, and analyzing the meaning of responses and response time. *Who liked my photo? If someone I like romantically likes my profile photo or selfie, does that mean they like me back? Will my comment be liked by the original poster (OP)? Why did he take four hours to respond to my message (I know he saw it hours ago)?! Why isn't he/she responding to my text message? Did I say something wrong?* All the data on tween and teen social media use can't really account for the number of minutes, hours, and days spent analyzing the meaning of how, when, and if people respond.

For tweens and teens today, social media isn't simply a matter of posting photos and seeing who likes and comments on them. In reality, the social machinations and political maneuverings going on behind the scenes—for example, liking certain photos to send a message or tagging people to solidify #squadgoals status—would make even the most seasoned politician squirm. Many people—especially older women, now the moms of tweens and teens—rightfully argue that these social manipulations have always existed, and I agree to an extent (who hasn't been on the receiving end of an eye-roll or a look of judgment?). At the same time, social media and technology use has changed the overall day-to-day experiences of Generation Z, the cohort born between the mid- to late 1990s and 2010, and ultimately has had long-term effects on their social and emotional development. Generation Zers are characterized by, among other things, their extreme fluency in Internet and social media use. Although the overarching impact of using technology and social media so early in their lives and so often during the day (and night) has yet to be determined, through my work I've seen five main effects: altered expectations, mixed messages, information overload, an on-all-the-time mentality, and an "all about the likes" development of personal values.

ALTERED EXPECTATIONS

A few years ago, Nick walked into my office looking rather glum. He was a typically upbeat young man with a good sense of humor and an easygoing demeanor, but on this day he seemed unusually distraught and agitated. I immediately sensed something was up and casually asked what was going on.

When we met the week before, he had just received his SAT scores electronically and seemed pleased with his marked improvement from several months of intense studying and preparation. He generally struggled on standardized tests, and he was initially happy and proud of the results of his hard work and effort. But now, after many of his friends posted their (notably higher) scores online, Nick felt stressed out, anxious, and sad—as if nothing he did would ever be able to compete with his friends' numeric achievements. In rapid succession, he started down what I like to call the rabbit hole of never feeling "enough"—never feeling good enough, smart enough, strong enough, well-liked enough, or successful enough. This feeling of *never good enough* is not new. But, in today's social media age, it has become amplified.

In the academic world, altered expectations aren't simply a result of more rigorous college admissions standards and lower college admissions rates; they are also a result of the amplified expectations brought on by the online comparison culture. It is not as though sharing grades or scores is in any way a new phenomenon. In the time before social media sharing, Nick could have found out his friends' scores in any number of ways: They could have freely discussed scores over lunch, passed notes in class, or shared them in late-night phone conversations. The tendency for comparison is certainly not new—but when Nick's online newsfeed became filled with scores from people he barely spoke to or interacted with, he felt as though his internal newsfeed (his mind) became cluttered, hindering his ability to process and think clearly. He went from being proud of his personal improvements to becoming disappointed, frustrated, and annoyed. So even though the culture of comparison has always existed in some way, the ease of sharing through social media and the online world now amplifies that culture to overwhelming levels. There are too many choices, too many opinions, too many scores to hold as comparison. Today, it only takes a few clicks to see what everyone else seems to be up to at any given moment. No matter what, someone could be doing it better/faster/more beautifully. And now, those results are at our fingertips, ready to be consumed and internalized.

There are definitely situations in which an increased amount of information can be beneficial (think about a student researching college options and seeing schools beyond his or her rural community). At the same time, all that oversharing has the potential to paralyze young people who constantly feel less than or not good enough. This comes, of course, at a crucial time in their emotional and social development, when young people already feel an intense desire to compare themselves to others and seek commonalities—which is in some ways an appropriate part of their developmental process. But the online oversharing of grades, scores, and accomplishments can also lead to altered expectations and amplified feelings of inadequacy.

These altered expectations are not limited to academics, nor are they felt only by students. Socially, the qualitative metrics created by our social media culture gives numeric values to being liked and receiving approval and acknowledgment. Students begin to equate their social success and self-worth with the number of likes or followers who respond to their daily musings and public postings, as Ellie does when she deletes Instagram posts that fail to receive what she deems an appropriate response. Students evaluate their personal likeability or social success on the parties they may or may not be invited to on their feed, or the photos posted by others that they may or may not be tagged in—which all combines to contribute to increased anxiety and worry around how they are perceived online and in real life. A 2011 study released by the American Academy of Pediatrics cited "Facebook depression" as a very real effect of adolescent overexposure to social media, adding more complexity to the adolescent experience.[1]

It doesn't take long for the increased level of anxiety and feelings of inadequacy to be felt by parents, who can easily become stressed out by their child's academic performance or perceived social success. I recently spoke to a group of mothers of middle school students, and one by one they openly expressed how stressed they became if they went on social media and found out they weren't invited to a gathering of moms or asked to join a certain school committee. A 2015 University of Michigan study found adults became more lonely and depressed the more time they spent on Facebook.[2] A 2014 research study by a team at the University of Pittsburgh concluded that young adults who spend more time on social media are more likely to be depressed.[3] This finding is significant, since public officials believe depression could be the leading cause of disability in industrialized countries by the year 2030.[4] Research suggests that middle school moms are the most stressed out, and I can't help but wonder what role their children's intertwining school and social media experiences play.[5]

In my office, I've seen heightened social expectations fully highlighted during high school prom season, beginning with how a teen is asked, to what dress a girl chooses, to transportation decisions, and what pre- and post-prom plans entail. Even if teens aren't prom-goers, the associated tumult and social media postings likely show up in their school hallways and social media feeds. *Promposals*, the term given to high school prom invitations involving a level of fanfare and creativity that make them look and feel more like elaborate wedding proposals, have elements of fun, surprise and stress.

At first glance, promposals seem sweet and romantic—Instagram, Snapchat, Twitter, and Pinterest are filled with a bevy of photos and captivating descriptions from promposals. Marketers have even gotten involved with the promposal phenomenon, as Snapchat partnered with clothing retailer Men's Wearhouse in March 2016 to create a special promposal filter to encourage increased sharing of related images.[6] But, the planning and effort required for a successful promposal make a genuine phone call or bouquet of flowers seem painfully inadequate. And they create another layer of expectations that wouldn't exist if not for the online sharing and commentary. Teens' efforts are quickly lauded or criticized by online commenters, giving a traditional teenage rite of passage the added elements of judgment and evaluation. High school administrators and principals at schools overtaken by the promposals say they regularly see teens (mostly boys) coming into their office concerned and anxious that their efforts will be woefully inadequate in comparison to the cookie cakes, cardboard cutouts, and choreographed dance routines of others.

It's not just the online postings from peers, classmates, and parents that contribute to these altered academic and social expectations. Celebrities who cultivate their online presence and develop their personal brand by documenting their daily happenings and excursions create aspirational lifestyles for others to admire and want to emulate. *She's on a private jet! Wearing those jeans! With that lipstick color!* Hip-hop musicians, professional athletes, and actors all have ways of using their social media accounts to promote their own idea of aspirational living. I once sat next to an up-and-coming hip-hop artist on a plane who asked me to take no less than five posed photos of him sitting on the plane, eating breakfast, drinking champagne—all to store for later to make sure he had a constant stream of Instagram excellence. His real life, I learned, was much quieter than his online presence. He was making ends meet by doing graphic design work and lived with his girlfriend and one-year-old son in the Seattle suburbs. Some people might find it fun to be voyeuristic in the complicated world of celebrity living, but others may mistake the curated reality for real life.

It could be argued that, in terms of voyeuristic accessibility, celebrity Instagram accounts aren't that much different from reading *People* or *Us Weekly*, or watching the once-beloved *Lifestyles of the Rich and Famous* (or MTV's more hip *Cribs,* or any of Bravo's *Real Housewives* series). At the same time, magazines and television shows that follow the lives of celebrities provide a natural distance and limited content, whereas social media makes the experience seem much more intimate in access. Liking a celebrity photo provides the illusion of interaction with that celebrity—and that access seems much more within reach. More often than not, it does little more than provide more content for distraction.

Most of us inherently know that social media gives us a mistaken sense of access and insight into others' lives, and we recognize that individuals curate their postings to give an incomplete and usually aspirational version of their lives. But, for many teens (and their parents), this constant stream of content combines to heighten expectations and create a low-grade anxiety and underlying feeling of inadequacy.

These altered expectations can also unintentionally contribute to what famed Stanford researcher Carol Dweck terms a "fixed mindset," which is the underlying belief that our intelligence and ability is fixed and immutable. Under a fixed mindset, we either have the ability to do something—or we don't. A "growth mindset," by contrast, allows us to believe we always have the ability to improve and cultivate new knowledge, and that effort and determination are the keys to improving and developing new skills over time.[7] Individuals with a growth mindset are usually quite accurate in evaluating their abilities and believe in their own personal development—in many cases, they are more open, perseverant, and resilient.[8] Much of a growth mindset comes from an innate belief in potential and possibility—which in many ways can be challenged when spending hours online scrolling through the amazing curated accomplishments of others.

When tweens and teens spend time looking at accomplishments online, or compare their real lives to the online aspirational lives of others, they can judge themselves and fall into the trap of the fixed mindset. Students with a "fixed mindset prefer effortless success" and are less tolerant of anything that hampers their ability to seem successful.[9] Much of the permanent postings and images on social media culture promote this idea of effortless success, though backlash to Beyonce's "I woke up like this" philosophy certainly exists. For the most part, students with a fixed mindset believe imperfections are cause for shame and have been found to be more likely to lie about their scores on exams.[10] Think back to Nick and his SAT scores. When Nick saw his peers' SAT scores online, he quickly switched from the growth mindset to the fixed mindset. He no longer recognized that his effort led to improvement and instead became fixated on the mistaken belief that his ability to do well on standardized tests was fixed and unable to be developed or changed.

> When tweens and teens spend time looking at accomplishments online, or compare their real lives to the online aspirational lives of others, they can judge themselves and fall into the trap of the fixed mindset.

The fixed mindset can also affect students' focus on personal appearance, for example, when they focus on looking a certain way in response to what others deem beautiful. In 2015, teen girls began emulating Kardashian family member Kylie Jenner's voluptuous lips by sucking on a bottle cap before taking photos. Known as "bottle lips," the viral challenge had tween and teen girls posting photos of themselves on social media with the hashtag #kyliejennerchallenge.[11] These girls were fixated on the idea that certain features, in this case, plump lips, were the most desirable feature and worthy of spending time and effort on documenting and sharing. (This obsession faded away when Kylie's lips, admittedly temporarily enhanced using lip fillers, became noticeably less enhanced.)[12] When the fixed mindset becomes planted into tween and teen minds through altered expectations, it can quickly and detrimentally pervade every part of their lives.

To be sure, the altered expectations resulting from social media interactions can be motivating, inspiring, and healthy—think of online accounts encouraging us to worry less, practice self-care, meditate, and rest. I'll talk about more options in Chapter 6, but apps like

Headspace, which encourages mediation, and Color Therapy, which promotes mindful relaxation through online coloring books, can certainly have a positive and influential daily impact. At the same time, tweens and teens can gravitate toward perceiving themselves as less than, and the resulting altered expectations can be socially and emotionally stressful.

MIXED MESSAGES

Whenever I think of the mixed messages we send kids around technology and social media use, I imagine the parent who bans cell phone use at the dinner table and is tapping away at his or her own cell phone underneath the table. It's no secret that adults have a difficult time putting away their devices or avoiding the temptation to check what is going on. That, in essence, is the epitome of the mixed messages we send children. We are generally so worried they will overuse technology and social media that we often don't stop to evaluate our own habits and what messages we silently send our children through our actions.

I am the first to acknowledge that I use social media and technology on a regular basis to communicate and complete my own work, but I am concerned that, both at school and home, we overlook how so much of our social media and technology rules with kids boils down to some version of "do as I say, not as I do." Many parents and educators admit, sometimes grudgingly, that they are tethered to their phone, tablet, and/or computer. Some try to pass it off as necessary for their work, but in reality, many adults are likely unable to follow the basic technology boundaries—no phone use after 10 p.m., keep phones out of the bedroom at night, refrain from texting or making a phone call while driving—that we want to encourage children to follow to promote their socialization, develop healthy self-regulation skills, and protect them from external harm (*socialization, self-regulation, safety*).

The idea of modeling healthy social media use is important, and it is tough because as adults we often haven't created our own standards. Even when we develop standards and boundaries, they quickly seem to be rendered useless or somewhat impractical. An easy example is calendars and appointment books, which used to be kept in paper-and-pen form in some type of day planner. Though written planners are still used regularly (and I encourage my students to use them), many people keep an online version of their calendar so that it can be readily shared with coworkers and family members. Children who spend time in two households might have parents who use Google Calendar to keep track of activities, or parents might manage multiple sports calendars with a color-coded online system. Even with the best of intentions to stay off our phones, it might not always be possible if that is where we keep our notes, compile to-do lists, and plan for the next day's agenda. Even if we wanted to put away our phones, we might have our music stored there and want to listen to tunes while relaxing. In so many ways, much of our lives are compartmentalized into small devices that are harder and harder to let go of.

Peer pressure and parental pressure are two reasons why tweens and teens receive mixed messages. Kids want to be using the same social media apps their friends are on, particularly in middle school, when they are all trying to work out friendship dynamics. For parents, it can be easy to get caught up in the latest parenting trends without fully understanding what will and will not work for your children and family. Parents sometimes look at me as though I am archaic when I ask what they think about following the Children's Online Privacy Protection Act (COPPA), which requires social media account holders to be thirteen years of age.[13] Parents and tweens (often together) counter that Instagram is harmless and that their entire fifth- or sixth-grade class is on the site, thereby deeming it an appropriate way to socialize. By that extended logic, any time a group of students decides to do something, it becomes appropriate and safe, which we know is not the case. When parents allow younger children to set up social media accounts, they may inadvertently send the message that some rules are okay to break—and the notion of bendable rules can become a slippery slope when it comes to teaching teens about following rules (and laws) online and in real life. Of course, there was the parent who bluntly announced in front of me, "I don't want my child thinking they have to follow the rules! They should be able to question authority, especially when the rules are stupid!" before stomping off after a school presentation.

Even with the influx of celebrities and media role models, tweens and teens still look to parents to send clear messages through modeling appropriate behavior. Distracted driving—more specifically, texting or talking on the phone while driving—is one of the most common ways parents underestimate the mixed messages being sent to kids. No parent wants to encourage his or her child to do something that dramatically increases the chance of being in a fatal crash, but they might not think twice about looking down at their own phone and sending a quick affirmation or an "on my way!" when running late. Some parents train their kids to respond to text messages right away, and then teens say the reason they text while driving is to answer their parents' text messages.[14] Both texting and cell phone use have been linked to an increased number of deaths from distracted driving, so much so that all drivers are banned from texting while driving in forty-six states and Washington, D.C. Similarly, fourteen states and Washington, D.C., do not allow drivers to use hand-held cell phones while driving.[15] In 2012, the National Highway Traffic Safety Administration found that 18 percent of all fatal accidents were caused by distracted driving, with 3,328 people killed and 421,000 people injured.[16] According to Pew Research's 2010 report "Adults and Cell Phone Distractions," 44 percent of adults and 40 percent of teens report that they "have been in a car when the driver used the cell phone in a way that put themselves or others in danger."[17] At the same time, one in four teens (26 percent) of driving age report that they have texted while driving, and half of all teens report being a passenger in a car when the driver has texted while driving.[18]

When it comes to students using tablets and computers in schools, I've seen all sorts of mixed messages. Much of it comes down to the central paradox that the same devices students use to complete their work can also serve as their main distraction from getting work done. YouTube, for example, has millions of videos for users to choose from—some that may help students understand and solidify concepts they are learning in class, and others that can lead them to watch hours of irrelevant content. One charter high school tried to block YouTube from the school website and then add back specific videos that administrators deemed useful for content instruction (videos from Khan Academy, for instance). That approach became too complicated and cumbersome for the school to manage (especially as students simply bypassed the school restrictions and watched videos on their phones), and they soon lifted the block.

Still, the school's attempts to regulate YouTube use highlights the complication of mixed messages in the classroom, as students today are increasingly forced to navigate their online world while they study. In 2000, Congress passed the Children's Internet Protection

Act (CIPA) with the hopes of protecting children from "obscene or harmful content."[19] Schools and libraries receiving discounted E-Rate services are required to follow certain rules, including blocking or filtering Internet access to photos that are deemed "(a) obscene, (b) child pornography, or (c) otherwise harmful to children."[20] (E-Rate services are discounted Internet and telecommunications services provided by the Federal Communications Commission [FCC] that are available to certain schools and libraries).[21] The hope was that minors would be protected from exposure to inappropriate content while doing research at schools or in local public libraries and that CIPA would offer a protective layer of regulation.

In wanting to protect students from the potential onslaught of social networking, schools are often caught in a bind, and attempts to protect students can sometimes thwart actual learning, and efforts to police backfire. For example, a student doing research in the school library for a class assignment can find that a keyword has been blocked because of multiple potential meanings or that a website has been blocked because the content is deemed inappropriate even though it is relevant to a topic being discussed in class.

A recent report from the American Library Association suggests "many schools are going beyond the requirements set forth by the Federal Communications Commission (FCC)" in CIPA.[22] Nearly all schools (98 percent) filter their content, according to the 2012 national longitudinal survey of the American Association of School Librarians (AASL), with the top four filtered content areas being social networking (88 percent), IM/chatting (74 percent), gaming (69 percent), and video services (66 percent).[23] Only 51 percent of respondents said their school had a filter mechanism in place that would address when students bring their own devices to school—as is often the case these days, either because they use their own devices for class work or because they bring their cell phones and other devices for social use. Others said their school's acceptable use policy helps reassure them that students will make good choices.[24] It's not clear whether schools with filtering policies tell students why the filters are in place and what those filters are meant to protect against or promote in relation to the school's mission and acceptable use policy. At the same time, schools send mixed messages when their filtering system blocks the social media sites (namely, Facebook, Instagram, YouTube, and Twitter) that they use to post athletic highlights or event announcements for students to access.

When students find that topics are filtered through their school-issued device or library computer, they turn to their personal devices, which typically do not need to access to the school's Wi-Fi network. In essence, the filter system required to protect students so they can learn more effectively sometimes prevents them from obtaining the knowledge and information needed to help with their own learning process.

Ultimately, there are mixed messages everywhere. Still, tweens and teens are always listening and watching us (whether they admit it or not), and the mixed messages we inadvertently send encroach upon their own healthy development of personal values and good decision-making skills at a most critical time in their identity formation. To mitigate against these mixed messages, adults need first to come up with their own clear terms of use (and CIPA, which was last updated in 2011, may need to be revisited).[25]

INFORMATION OVERLOAD

Posters at Facebook's Menlo Park campus scream the words "RUTHLESS PRIORITIZATION" in bright orange letters, and it's fitting that a company that aggregates and curates so much content works to keep its employees focusing and filtering at all times. Students and educators should take a signal from the social media giant and use the concept of ruthless prioritization to manage the intense volume of information—both personal and academic—coming their way every minute.

During an average minute, Snapchat users share 284,722 Snaps; YouTube users upload 300 hours of new video; and Instagram users like 1,736,111 photos.[26] Part of the never-ending allure of social media is that, at any given second, there could be something bigger/better/faster/snappier right around the corner. When I give presentations to students, I joke about how it seems scientifically impossible to watch only three minutes of YouTube videos because *just one more* three-minute video quickly morphs into thirty-five minutes of nonstop watching. All successful social media apps and sites—and by "successful" I mean sites and apps that have a large base of users who frequently come back and are "sticky," meaning that those users stick around for a while—design their sites to provide an enticing, never-ending stream of new and relevant (and irrelevant) information.

Those apps and sites targeting the "dream demographic" of tweens and teens have a level of simplicity that makes them quickly addicting: It doesn't take long to figure out how to use Instagram (Snapchat, in my personal opinion, takes a bit more time), but once you do, there are so many ways to process, post, and interact. Students can (and do) scroll through Instagram feeds and Snapchat Stories and, once they arrive at the end of the new photos and messages, will refresh their feed or find other ways to look at new and fresh content. The idea of constantly being exposed to new and different information is appealing to many tweens and teens, which is why they gravitate to ephemeral apps or online games that are constantly changing and adding new features.

For students trying to manage their work and life online, this constant stream of content easily becomes crushing, as there always seems to be something to keep up with, and new data to store and process. In terms of schoolwork and learning, today's research databases and search tools have made an overabundance of information readily available with a few simple clicks. When I was a research assistant for a college professor in the late 1990s, my job mainly consisted of going to the library, walking through the stacks on the different floors, pulling bound copies of research journals, and copying studies that she wanted to read for her own work. I loved the work because it was straightforward (except when the journals weren't where they were supposed to be) and somewhat relaxing, and because in a few hours I would have all these neatly copied articles for her to review, and my job was done. Now, that same task that once took me several hours is finished in less than ten minutes and usually doesn't even involve my walking to the library.

At the same time, the amount of readily available information now means a simple search can return a back-breaking amount of content. Jessica Lee, who is currently the head of an independent school outside Washington, D.C., was the head of a middle school in Northern California when I interviewed her for this book.[27] She noticed that when middle school teachers asked students to research a broad topic, like the Roman Empire, for example, students quickly became so overwhelmed by the amount of raw data they would find in a Google search, or even a scholarly literature search, that teachers would preselect the documents needed for the research project and have students focus on reading and analyzing those documents. These teachers wanted students to ultimately develop their own solid filtering and decoding skills, but they also recognized the amount of content available online made it somewhat counterproductive for students to use their limited time trying to figure out what information was reliable and what was not worthy of being cited in a research project.

I agree with the spirit of the teachers' efforts in giving preselected documents, but I also realize one of our main (and often overlooked) roles as educators in this new learning environment is to help tweens and teens build skills and develop methods for actively filtering, managing, and processing the overwhelming amount of data and information coming their way on a daily basis. Students who receive a high volume of information without finding ways to determine what to pay attention to and what to ignore can easily become over-whelmed and anxious. There's just so much out there, and so little time to deal with it at all.

The problem of staggering amounts of content also applies to social and personal information. Tweens and teens share and follow people who share glamorous and mundane posts with equal intensity. In a student's mind, what someone ate for breakfast is a Tumblr post, how they did their makeup becomes a YouTube video, how they rocked out to a song becomes a video using Musical.ly, and how they found something totally irreverent becomes a Snap. These minute choices can be weighted with equal or greater importance as information for next week's history project or English essay. Much of this new content is cap-tured in real-time, quickly becoming addicting and all-encompassing, especially for tweens and teens trying to figure out their own values and identify what is important to them in a world where so much is coming at them without explanation, reflection, or analysis.

If we want to promote social media wellness, we have to find ways to promote ruthless prioritization and filtering techniques as second nature; otherwise, a small trickle of distraction quickly becomes a watershed of content and information that, without a purpose or a plan, can leave students drowning. When I was a kid, my parents let me watch two television programs—*Sesame Street* and *Mr. Roger's Neighborhood*—and only with their permission. The only real computer game I had access to was *Where in the World Is Carmen San Diego?* because my parents refused to purchase Super Mario Brothers. My exposure to media was limited, so there was no real need for filtering and boundaries. Today, kids are regularly exposed to millions of different options, without any real way of learning to determine what is important. Students using the Internet for school can become exhausted, because they are constantly trying to filter and process without any real skills or conscious thoughts on how to ruthlessly prioritize. In later chapters, I look at how to encourage students to develop their own appropriate boundaries and filters so that they can focus their efforts on what they deem worthy of their limited time, given their own hopes and expectations, and how to encourage students to take a proactive stand to determine what is superfluous and to be avoided (*hint:* it all has to do with time and *energy* management).

In my work, I've found that nearly all students want to do well, and many struggle with underdeveloped habits related to organization, time and energy management, and overall wellness. To do well, students have to *feel* well, and being buried beneath a crushing amount of content translates into less time and space for the quiet reflection, personal regrouping, and digital detox that are crucial for sustainable success and happiness.

ON-ALL-THE-TIME MENTALITY

We know that the school day no longer ends, academically or socially, at 3 p.m. It's not just that students socialize with one another through texts, messaging, and other online and in-real-life interactions. Many teachers no longer announce homework in class and instead encourage students to "look online" for assignments posted through the school homework portal, sometimes after school has ended. Some teachers do what I call "stealth posting," announcing an assignment or test furtively online with no classroom announcement. Many of these teachers say they want to encourage students to proactively check the online portal, but I wonder why they enjoy leaving students scrambling and raising anxiety levels late on a Sunday night. Other teachers, wanting to be a helpful resource, encourage students to send emails or text messages late into the evening and on weekends asking for clarification about an assignment or about material on an upcoming exam. Although the intention to promote learning is certainly laudable, it also promotes burnout—for teachers and students.

Not too long ago, I visited a large independent school to present and speak with parents, faculty, and students. Upon my arrival, I had an informal lunch with several school administrators, and the high school principal off-handedly mentioned the school's recent Power Down Day. Students had been told to leave their iPads (usually used for classwork) at home and their phones in their backpacks on the previous Friday. The goal, developed out of a recent visit and talk from a meditation coach, was to encourage students to spend the entire day with as little technology as possible. This simple act is far from revolutionary, and, indeed, some readers may wonder why a Power Down Day was really needed. But it was—and it was remarkably successful. During lunch that day, the school put out board games and other activities throughout campus, and encouraged students to mingle and converse with one another. Some students sat by themselves and read (physical books!), while others just seemed to relax on the campus. Students were given the permission to be "off" by the requirement to Power Down—and in my later conversations with students, they repeatedly told me how much they enjoyed that day. "It was the best day," one told me. "I didn't feel as rushed, and I could just hang out with my friends," said another. Administrators noted that nearly all students actively participated, some playing board games and others just sitting and talking without a phone in front of their faces. Given the intensely positive feedback, I openly wondered why they couldn't create a Power Down afternoon or set amount of time on a weekly basis, and it seemed to me the school was still figuring out how to bring that element into a school day already packed with activities and opportunities.

The result of today's increased technology and interconnectedness is that many tweens and teens feel as though they are always "on." (Adults can feel this way too, of course.) For teens who struggle with self-regulation, it can seem difficult to find a time to be "off" and create the opportunity to think, process, and reflect on their own. In today's world, we default to thinking that increased access to technology is directly correlated to improved learning outcomes, and in some cases there are definitely benefits. But, it can also have the counter-effect: challenging students' ability to think up solutions for themselves and process information—whether that information involves thinking critically about a social issue, an academic problem, or a personal values issue. Not every issue has an answer that can be googled, and this lack of internal and external solitude can have negative long-term repercussions. In her well-researched best-seller *Quiet*, author and noted introvert Susan Cain explains how many successful inventors, thinkers, and scholars have found "solitude to be an important key to creativity," yet our society is not built to encourage time for removed reflection.[28] Adolescence is a particularly crucial time for the foundational development of talents, and Cain notes that "teens who are too gregarious to spend time alone often fail to cultivate their talents" because the development of talent often requires a level of solitude and reflection that makes them feel uncomfortable.[29]

The on-all-the-time mentality also creates an underlying level of undeniable exhaustion and increases stress and anxiety for all involved. Students no longer have the ability to leave social drama in the classroom, in the cafeteria, or on the playground. Being social is now all-encompassing—blink and you might miss out on something important. For teachers, the multiple avenues of communication create added stress, no longer giving them a needed break from the daily stresses of teaching and managing a classroom of students. Parents' interactions with teachers, once limited mostly to back-to-school nights and parent–teacher conferences, now have the potential to be nonstop. Many parents I speak with become frustrated when a teacher doesn't respond to an email immediately, not fully realizing that designing lesson plans and managing a classroom and grading papers or exams can require levels of solitude that don't always allow for a quick reply. In reality, answering and addressing each of these emails adds hours to a teacher's potentially jam-packed schedule. It is not hard to see why many teachers feel an increased level of burnout and exhaustion, especially as the school year progresses.

There are certainly benefits to our multiple avenues of connectedness, once we find the appropriate boundaries and ways to manage our communication that are both responsive and allow for appropriate breaks and distance to recharge. In *Quiet*, Susan Cain also discusses the power of social media to create another avenue of socialization and interaction for introverts who might not always feel comfortable in large social settings, explaining that "introverts . . . welcome the chance to communicate digitally. The same person who would never raise his hand in a lecture hall of two hundred people might blog to two thousand, or two million, without thinking twice. The same person who finds it difficult to introduce himself to strangers might establish a presence online and then extend these relationships into the real world."[30]

So it's not always the actual social media that is the issue, or the interconnectedness it brings—rather, it is the fact that we can easily fall into a trap where we can't (or don't) feel as though we can turn it off. This issue exists for parents, educators, and students: The teacher who stealth-posts late on a Sunday night sends the message that she thinks students should be checking their online homework portal at all times, and the teacher who answers student emails at 11 p.m. is unconsciously sending the message that students should be up at that hour working on homework for his class.

In her 2014 book *It's Complicated: The Social Lives of Networked Teens*, Microsoft Research principal researcher danah boyd concludes that much of teen online socialization is merely a result of teens wanting to create and maintain connection and friendship with others. Through her interviews with teens around the country, she is "convinced that the greatest challenges facing networked teens are far from new."[31] She likens socializing online to teens hanging out in public spaces, explaining that teens in many communities have fewer and fewer safe public spaces to see one another in person, and so online conversations provide connection that might otherwise be lacking.

There *are* fewer and fewer public spaces for teens to safely spend time. In areas noted for high crime rates, teens hanging out in groups quickly garner unwanted attention. But, I would take danah boyd's argument one step further: In many ways, today's teens are not only short on public spaces to congregate, but they also lack the open time to communicate freely. By "open time," I mean the afternoon free of obligation or the weekend morning spent lounging, or having brunch at a diner or coffee shop, or running into a friend casually and organically. That's why the Power Down Day had such an intense effect on the students at the high school—the on-all-the-time mentality had made it feel as though there was no real down time.

danah boyd calls spaces where teens can work to find a place within society online "networked publics"[32] and compares them to a town square, downtown area, strip-mall parking lot, or local diner where kids might have congregated in the past. To her, these networked publics are online spaces where teens socialize, but they are different than traditional public spaces because they are more persistent and sticky, meaning the content created lives on long past the interaction. Also, the experience is more visible, because more people can see the conversation or interaction than just the individuals involved, and these interactions are more spreadable, meaning that posts, messages, and videos intended to be personal in nature can quickly go viral, causing a host of unexpected secondary issues.[33]

Using danah boyd's idea of networked publics, I compare giving a child a smartphone to allowing him or her to go downtown and hang out with friends. Except for one thing: Most parents wouldn't let their twelve year olds hang out downtown after midnight or at two in the morning on a school night. When parents allow teens to keep their phones in their bedrooms at night, in many cases, they are doing just that. In that way, the on-all-the-time mentality is the most ongoing threat to overall wellness, because there is no time to relax and regroup. Even a tween tucked safely into bed is still "on" if he or she is texting witty sayings to a new friend or romantic interest. A survey of 13–17 year olds suggests that teens don't want to be online all of the time, as 43 percent of respondents answered that they wish they could unplug sometimes and over one-third of them said that sometimes they wish they could go back to a time before Facebook.[34] Many young people have a desire to put down their devices, but that desire competes with their fear of missing out (*fomo*) and a burgeoning ability to self-regulate.

To promote social media wellness, we have to understand the academic and social pressures that lead to the on-all-the-time mentality, and we also need to provide appropriate structure for kids to be offline in a way that is consistent, meaningful, and relevant. I've noticed that many of the students I work with (adults, too) want permission to be "off" but need help figuring out their own best balance of socialization and self-regulation. Instead of waiting for a burnout or crisis, we have to be decoders and help students identify their own appropriate sense of balance, while at the same time empowering students with tools to build their self-awareness around their own social and emotional needs. In the upcoming chapters on wellness, I highlight strategies that encourage structure and on/off time within a daily and weekly routine.

"ALL ABOUT THE LIKES"
PERSONAL VALUES DEVELOPMENT

In April 2016, eighteen-year-old Ohio teenager Marina Lonina and a seventeen-year-old classmate went to the home of twenty-nine-year-old Raymond Gates, whom they met the day before at a shopping mall.

When Raymond Gates began sexually assaulting her friend, Marina Lonina allegedly began livestreaming the rape on Periscope, the app acquired by Twitter in 2015. Instead of calling 911 to alert authorities, Lonina is heard laughing and giggling in the background of the ten-minute live feed. Authorities were contacted by one of Lonina's followers, who was watching the feed from another state. Franklin County prosecutor Ron O'Brien maintained that, though Lonina might have initially started filming the event as a way of providing evidence, "she got caught up in the likes" and feedback she was receiving from viewers of the video, and that the external validation clouded her judgment and decision-making skills. Both Lonina and Gates were charged with kidnapping, rape, sexual battery, and pandering sexual matter involving a minor.[35]

Let's stop and think about this for a moment. A young woman allegedly gets "caught up in the likes" and laughs and giggles while videotaping her friend being raped. What's more, she never contacts authorities or actively tries to stop the assault. We would like to think that something as heinous as livestreaming and giggling while a high school classmate is pinned down and sexually assaulted is beyond the realm of possibility. But, we underestimate how tweens and teens are affected by the confluence of unique forces in their lives. A teenager is still in a precarious phase of brain development, one in which the all-important prefrontal cortex, which weighs decision-making, makes judgments, and provides impulse control, is not fully developed. The combination of social media pressure and an underdeveloped prefrontal cortex can lead to rash decision-making and regrettable choices that have a long-term impact. And although parents and adult role models still play an important part, tweens and teens are at inarguably the most crucial time in their lives when it comes to their own personal identity development.

In 2012, a research study found that tweens wanted to be famous more than they wanted to have any future profession, financial success, or career.[36] This inherent desire for fame, combined with constant likes and comments, adds complexity to an already complicated adolescent experience. The potential for a wider global audience and Internet fame keeps teens and tweens creating and posting content, because today's social media spawns a new type of celebrity—one whose fame is defined more by number of friends, followers, and viewers than by notable achievements. And that fame can be monetized. The most recognizable social media celebrity is arguably Kim Kardashian, who, with the guidance of her mother and manager, Kris Jenner, has built herself into a global brand. In November 2016, Kim Kardashian had 86.6 million followers on Instagram and 48.9 million followers on Twitter, and her reported 2015 earnings were $53 million (up from $28 million in 2014).[37] Celebrities use social media channels like Instagram and Twitter to increase interaction and engagement with their fans, and companies use it to promote engagement and loyalty with their brands. At the same time, each post, like, and online interaction can have an incremental influence in the identity formation of an impressionable tween or teen.

In noted developmental psychologist and psychoanalyst Erik Erikson's stages of psychosocial development, or stages of life, adolescence (between ages twelve and eighteen years) is seen as one of the most formative times in a person's development. Adolescents often experience confusion juggling concern about what others think of them with figuring out their own identity. This identity formation is both occupational ("What am I going to do with my life?") and sexual ("Who am I attracted to?"). During this time, adolescents can experience "identity confusion" and "role confusion" as they try to figure out their beliefs and place within the world, and they may experiment with different identities, ideologies, and affiliations. Erikson argued that a healthy, well-adjusted adolescent develops his or her sense of self and the virtue of "fidelity—the ability to sustain loyalties freely pledged in spite of the inevitable contradictions and confusions of value systems."[38] In many ways, Erikson's theories are relevant when thinking about today's adolescent experience and social media use. In theory, social media is a great tool for experimentation during identity confusion, if and when it is used in safe and developmentally appropriate ways. Anonymous and ephemeral apps allow adolescents to try out different identities and belief systems temporarily, though we know there are potential risks and opportunities for things to backfire. Therefore, if we want adolescents to use their time of developmentally appropriate exploration effectively, we need to change our approach to how we think about social media and its role in students' lives and in their development of personal values.

Much of today's educational programming about social media is rooted in fear rather than in values development. For example, most schools have a police safety officer or lawyer inform students about the consequences of making poor decisions related to social media use. That is not necessarily wrong, but in the coming chapters, I discuss how we can also help students using social media to think critically about their own values and choices and use their online experiences as another tool in their quest to have a healthy, well-adjusted sense of self.

Much of today's educational programming about social media is rooted in fear rather than in values development.

For the sake of clarity and brevity (there are entire books on personal values development), I distill personal values development down to three main concepts:

1. How we treat others (including, but not limited to, family, friends, and community members)

2. How we treat ourselves

3. How we engage within our community

I am not interested in passing moral judgments on what is or is not appropriate, but it is highly relevant to examine behaviors that cause social, emotional, and physical harm. Among active technology users, social media has become a new form of groupthink that results in questionable, dysfunctional, and potentially dangerous decision-making toward ourselves and others. In early 2014, Vine, the now-defunct video-sharing tool once owned by Twitter, had videos invoking the phrase "Do It for the Vine!" in which adolescents and young adults performed dangerous stunts in short-form video clips. A quick search on YouTube offers a bevy of compilations of failed "Do It for the Vine FAILS!," including one young man who tries to jump over a moving car and instead ends up in an ambulance, cautioning, "Don't Do It for the Vine!"[39] Though Vine was shut down in October 2016, "Do It for the Vine!" remains a great example of how basic common sense goes out the window in the search for likes, and how some individuals experience an overpowering desire to be part of a viral challenge that has gained momentum. Worldstarhiphop.com, known by users as Worldstar, is an aggregate video blog founded in 2005 that has become known for posting videos of violent fights and crude sexual acts. The founder of Worldstar deemed his website, which targets black youth, to be "the CNN of the ghetto."[40] In one early scene in the critically acclaimed television show *Atlanta,* spectators watching a fight about to break out begin pulling out their phones while proclaiming, "This is going on Worldstar!" as a way of indicating something terrible is about to happen that will be recorded and later posted.[41]

It's important to step back and remember, as I've noted earlier, that many of these underlying issues have always been prevalent. Bullying, meanness, drug and alcohol use, addictive behavior, unhealthy sexual relationships, sexual assault, self-harm (emotional and physical), and other utterly unfortunate decisions all existed long before the creation of the Internet. Social media and increased technology use provide an avenue through which these issues *persist* or become markedly amplified. The consistent content, wider audience, and longer shelf life combine to form a powerful influence on tween and teen behavior, and on how young people come to view their relationship with themselves and others and create their place and purpose in the world.

To be sure, there are many ways that social media use can promote and encourage kindness, compassion, empathy, and generosity. According to Pew Research, 69 percent of teens using social media believed their peers were mostly kind to one another online, with 65 percent of teens using social media reporting having an experience online that made them feel good about themselves, and 78 percent having at least one positive outcome from an experience on social media.[42] Even so, 95 percent of teens say they have witnessed cruel behavior online and are most likely to ignore it or defend the person being treated cruelly.[43]

We all (it is hoped) want tweens and teens to develop a healthy sense of self and establish personal values so that they become well-adjusted adults. In some ways, personal values development has become a controversial topic (more so in certain regions of the country and depending on political affiliation), but helping tweens and teens be healthy, resilient, and well-adjusted is an overarching goal I am sure we all share. During the middle school and high school years, having conversations that encourage students to realize that they have choices, and to help them think about whether their choices reflect their values, can be far more powerful and effective than simply telling them what to do. I've spent the past fifteen years helping adolescents think about how their personal values are reflected in their daily decisions and what they can do to shift their behaviors to align with their own life goals. When I encourage them to think about how long-term success is all about incremental choices around how we spend our time and energy, I've found adolescents to become far more intrinsically motivated to make positive and proactive changes. To be sure, adolescents need structure, but we're being short-sighted if we think structure in the form of rules and policies is the only step. In the next chapters, I address how schools can incorporate personal values development into their conversations about social media use, and how parents can incorporate it as part of their conversations about making everyday choices on what to engage in and disengage from—online and in real life.

SUMMARY

Adolescence has long been a period fraught with insecurity and indecision, and social media and technology use adds a layer of complexity to an already complicated time of life. When we think of social media and how it affects socialization, self-regulation, and safety, there are five main side effects tweens and teens experience on social media. Students experience their own heightened expectations after constantly processing amplified versions of how things should look, feel, and be—academically, socially, and otherwise. They currently receive mixed messages from parents and other adults on how to behave and interact, in part because everything is so new and ever-changing that we have yet to step back and reflect on our own behaviors and choices. The amount of content posted to online social media networks can quickly be overwhelming, and the concept of a crushing level of content highlights tweens' and teens' inability to self-regulate and make decisions about how and when they spend their time on each thing. Without proper filtering and compartmentalizing, many people feel as though they are "on" all the time with no time to be "off" and simply process, reflect, and regroup. Solitude has been shown to be a hallmark for creativity and social and emotional processing, which lends itself to the importance of creating opportunities to power down in our daily lives. The staggering amount of content and the on-all-the-time mentality can also contribute to personal values development that becomes all about the likes, in which standards are developed through the filter of likes and feedback. As more and more teens today equate celebrity and fame with success, we have to find ways to encourage personal values development that promotes a healthy sense of self within the classroom and greater community. If we want to find ways to authentically encourage healthy socialization, self-regulation, and safety, it's crucial that we prompt tweens and teens to think about how their own personal values affect their daily choices and habits, and what changes they can make to redirect their time and energy toward things that are more of value to them. The coming chapters will discuss how to do so.

CHAPTER 4

Conversations

How to Talk About
Social Media

In the fall of 2007, *New York Times* education reporter Alan Finder flew out to the Silicon Valley to follow me around for a few days and hear more about my work with disorganized tween and teen boys. We had connected initially when he reached out to interview me for a piece about employers checking the online profiles of potential hires. During that first interview, he asked what I did for a living and was a bit surprised by my then-standard reply, "Basically, I clean out boys' backpacks." Eighteen months later, he came back to find out more about my work with binders, planners, and crumpled papers at the bottom of backpacks.

On his second day in the office, Alan expressed a bit of befuddlement, observing, "These kids all show up early for their appointments, and they seem genuinely excited to be here." Those who were early either sat patiently in the waiting room or got to work at one of the empty tables in the office, which he would later describe as "cozy." Alan's own son was a teenager at the time, and he likely had a difficult time imagining his son showing up carly and being enthusiastic about becoming more organized and cleaning out his backpack.

When Alan met with several of the students, he recognized that these tween and teen boys (and girls) were not all straight-A students, nor were they all necessarily intrinsically motivated to do better in school (and life) before coming to our office. He met students who had improved from a 2.8 GPA to a 3.6 GPA and who had gone from being known as a class clown to being a class leader and role model. In my conversations with students, I talked with them about (then comparatively nascent) social media, texting, and online distractions in addition to study strategies, focusing on improving sleep and stress management. Alan openly wondered what made them so excited and genuinely engaged in their academic and extracurricular potential, as well as their learning in general.

My work with tweens and teens on organization, time and energy management, personal purpose, social media management, and wellness all has a common thread. Quite simply, I am positive and enthusiastic, and, most important, I make it all about them. We know that, developmentally, adolescents are in a time of their lives when they are trying to find their place in the world, and they can become overwhelmed trying to figure out their own personal identity and values when so many different voices are telling them how they should look, act, and be. So much of tween and teen life is about consciously and subconsciously navigating the expectations of others—whether parents, siblings, relatives, teachers, friends, or coaches. Over the years, my work has become centered more and more around helping students identify what is important to them and allowing them to identify what makes their time and efforts more valuable and purposeful. Our conversations plant the seed for them to (1) realize they have choices about how they spend their time and (2) recognize how their daily habits and interactions, online and in real life, all contribute to their energy levels and intrinsic motivation.

In Chapter 1, I shared the story of Danielle, who listened to my presentation at her middle school and decided to delete her Ask.fm account. She decided to do that on her own. At no point did I tell her and her classmates to get off social media or delete their accounts. I didn't even espouse the many dangers of being online, choosing not to spend my time with them sharing stories of tween and teens getting kidnapped, arrested, assaulted, or killed. I also didn't tell them how spending time on social media might prevent them from getting good grades, or that if they wanted to attend a "good college" (*what does that even mean?!*) they should make better choices about how to spend their time. Finally, I didn't mention that if they did something inappropriate on social media they could get in really big trouble. I figured that creating a culture of fear and anxiety would make students more likely to tune me out rather than tune in to my larger message. Instead, I started my presentation with a simple question, one I thought would grab their attention. I began by asking, "How many of you would like seven to ten extra hours of free time per week?"

Nearly all of us are desperate for more time in our always-on, always-going worlds. When I ask that question of my audiences, I usually receive an enthusiastic response as well as a bit of genuine curiosity—from parents, educators, and students alike. When I ask students how they would spend that extra free time, most proclaim, "Sleep!" Typically, I start a discussion around daily habits and choices that add up to minutes and hours of time, energy, and draining distraction. Most tweens and teens can relate to the concept that some of our daily experiences can be energizing, and other interactions can feel draining. For example, getting into an argument with a sibling on the way to school or realizing you forgot to complete an assignment can be draining. Having a fun conversation with friends in the quad before class or receiving positive feedback from a teacher, by contrast, can be energizing. At the same time, even though we don't always have a choice in how we spend our time, we do have a choice in how we react to experiences and how we choose to let them affect us. In this chapter, I highlight some of the ways I approach talking about social media and overall wellness with tweens and teens. The goal is to help them feel in control about how they spend their time online and in real life, and to understand that every interaction—anonymous, ephemeral, or ever-lasting—contributes to their overall energy levels and feelings of well-being.

These conversations can happen with parents, mentors, or educators. The key is understanding the perspective of your audience, and recognizing *how* to have the conversation is just as important as having the conversation itself. Approaches that might resonate with some young people might not work at all with others. There's no one-size-fits-all approach. Regardless of whether your audience is a single student or an entire grade level, the most crucial step for encouraging engagement and intrinsic motivation is helping them realize they have more choices than they might think, and that their incremental daily choices and consciousness around simple habits add up to greater opportunities and experiences.

UNDERSTAND THE
LANGUAGE AND THE LINGO

In the preceding chapters of this book, I provided a broad overview of social media, because I recognize how crucial it is for parents and educators to understand and be able to speak the same language that young people are speaking. I realize that things are shifting constantly and that what is important in one geographic area or grade level may have very little relevance in another. As well, by the time you read this, some of the social media apps highlighted in earlier chapters may have lost favor with the tweens and teens in your community. No problem. The best way to understand the language and the lingo is to listen and allow tweens and teens to be your best source of information. Speaking the language certainly doesn't mean that you need to understand every little nuance of social media, but being genuinely intrigued and asking open-ended questions with wonder and curiosity goes a long way. I can't tell you how many times I have found out about some new app or issue simply by listening carefully and asking strategic follow-up questions. For instance, when I worked with focus groups of junior high girls as part of my research for my second book, I watched an entire season of the reality show *The Bachelor*—all thirteen episodes—back-to-back after the girls told me they turned to *The Bachelor* for relationship advice. I often joke that those are thirteen hours of my life I am never getting back, but it was also intensely valuable for me to see how these young girls were evaluating how to build and maintain social and romantic relationships based on a heavily edited reality show that involved twenty-five women vying for the attention of one man. I learned more about VSCO, an app with high-quality photography editing tools, when I talked with teen girls who were spending more and more time on the app in the hopes of making their permanent posts look professional. They loved the extensive editing tools and filters, which were designed for the use of professional photographers, and how they were able to have a profile without worrying about others' validation. (As noted in an early profile piece in *Fast Company*, VSCO bills itself as an "anti-social social network: You can't leave comments. You can't click a heart icon or 'like' something."[1]). As of December 2016, Instagram now also lets users disable comments if they so choose.[2]

> The best way to understand the language and the lingo is to listen and allow tweens and teens to be your best source of information.

In terms of social media, I use nearly all the apps students tell me they use as well as others that I find out about through my own research. Apps are being updated continually, and, as a point of conversation, I ask students to explain their favorite features and what they like about different apps or websites. I've been intensely curious about online games, video games, and interactive sites in a way I never before would have imagined. Many times, the conversations are a way to segue into something students have seen or experienced online. Sometimes, I'll ask what their friends or classmates are using, and what issues they are seeing online, because students sometimes initially feel more comfortable talking about friends' behavior than their own. Parents and educators occasionally tell me they tried to use an app but gave up because it didn't feel intuitive. In that case, I encourage them either to have a tween or teen become the teacher and explain all the features of the apps they use or to do what the kids do: search online for "How to use [social media app]?" and watch the related how-to videos.

EXERCISE

Download and use three of the apps popular among tweens and teens in your community. Parents, ask your kids to identify apps they use most and have them teach you how to use them (again, if they are unwilling, feel free to use online videos and learn). Educators, find out which three apps are most used by students in your grade level or school and become comfortable with the unique features of each app. Spend a week using them daily. You will find the increased awareness can give you added perspective in future conversations around values, habits, and daily choices.

USE THE FRAMEWORK OF SOCIALIZATION, SELF-REGULATION, AND SAFETY

The fine points of social media use are changing constantly, and, indeed, by the time this book is published, some new app or website might come along and trump the popularity of nearly all the social media and technology tools to date. When talking about social media, I encourage shifting the conversation to focus on using the three Ss (*socialization, self-regulation,* and *safety*) as guideposts to how you think about social media wellness and related policies and guidelines you might create in your home or classroom. Throughout the next few chapters, I will focus on wellness in the form of these three Ss, and it's important to understand how each contributes to social media wellness.

Socialization relates to how students treat others and themselves, and how they can decide whether or not to engage or disengage online (and in real life). *Self-regulation* refers to how we can provide structure and guidance around compartmentalizing and filtering the many potential online distractions that make it difficult to complete work, and how we can build consistent opportunities for reflection and single-tasking (instead of multitasking). *Safety* covers both personal safety as well as group and community safety, and it focuses on physical safety in addition to social and emotional safety. We want to give tweens and teens the skills needed to recognize potentially unsafe situations for themselves and others, and to feel comfortable reaching out to any number of resources if something doesn't go as planned. The key here is realizing what safety nets and support mechanisms work for each individual tween or teen—some might feel comfortable going to a parent or school counselor, but others might not—and it's crucial to make sure every student has resources they feel comfortable reaching out to in times of need.

RECOGNIZE THE IMPORTANCE OF ATTITUDE AND APPROACH

Many parents call my office exasperated, and I can hear the frustration through the phone line. Some teachers and administrators I've met sound as though they need a year's sabbatical or at least a very long vacation, and their stress and frustration prevents them from stepping back and seeing the full picture. Social media and technology use (including video games) isn't all good or all bad. We can't change the fact that these different apps and technology options exist, so our job is to help students find solutions that encourage them to become engaged, enthusiastic members of their school and greater communities. Tweens and teens are in a time of self-discovery and are trying to figure out and feel out what works for them— and what doesn't—in their daily lives. The best way to support that process is to ask open-ended questions without judgment. Words matter. So, "Don't you realize you're wasting your time on Snapchat?" is probably not going to get anyone anywhere. "You should have been doing your homework, but now it's 10 p.m. and you've spent all your time texting. If you don't get an A on that history test, there will be consequences!" will likely be equally unsuccessful. Those examples may sound extreme, but they are actual quotes from parents of students I've worked with.

> The best way to support teens in the process of self-discovery is to ask open-ended questions without judgment.

When parents or students first come into my office, I can quickly get a fairly good sense of their openness to making changes. The same goes for when I meet faculty at schools. Being skeptical is not necessarily the same as having a bad attitude, but being vehemently judgmental and asserting that everything is hopeless ends my job before it even begins. For me, the most important indicator of the potential for change and wellness is rooted in attitude and approach. If you think something is going to work, then it probably will, and if you think it won't, well . . .

Tone matters. Check your own frustration and anger before starting any conversation around technology and social media use. Asking an open-ended question without expectation encourages tweens and teens to authentically reflect in a judgment-free environment and allows them to reach for their own truths, rather than saying what they think others want to hear. In the classroom, and at home, it can be easy to be frustrated with how social media and technology seemingly have the potential to interrupt in-real-life interactions and experiences. But the way to find a balance that works is to be open to conversations, to be curious, and to provide a safety net when things don't go as planned. Part of providing a safety net has to do with the attitude and approach you take—if a culture of fear has been created (in school or at home), tweens and teens are more likely to hide issues until they become too much to handle. But if young people know that in times of confusion they can seek assistance from multiple people, then the entire community becomes stronger.

Some readers may think that I'm being overly optimistic and perhaps lack the reality check that comes from working with kids who may be tougher to reach. But I've worked with students of all skill levels, academic abilities, socioeconomic backgrounds, and ethnicities, and I know that all tweens and teens want to do well. Some may not want the adults in their lives to know it, and others would rather fail than ask for help. Think about it from a student's perspective. It's so much more promising, inspiring, and invigorating to work with someone who cares about you *and* believes in you. That's of cornerstone importance in thinking about our attitude and approach toward social media and technology use.

MAKE IT ALL ABOUT THEM

When students first come into my office, I usually spend our initial conversation asking lots of questions. I ask students what they like to do for fun and how they would spend a free afternoon. Sometimes I get the typical response of "Hanging out with friends" but, more often than not, something interesting or a little different will come out, sparking a deeper conversation about interests and intrinsic motivation.

Most important, I ask students how they would like to improve or excel in their lives. Simply asking these questions plants the seed of possibility and helps them understand that I see their potential and believe they have the power to change their habits if they choose to do so. Nearly every tween or teen I've talked to (and adults, too) has something they want to change, improve, or alter in some way. When I talk with tweens and teens, I hear some version of the same five things over and over. Most want to

1. Do well in school

2. Excel in sports or extracurricular activities

3. Have more time for friends/family/pets/hobbies

4. Develop stronger relationships with friends/family and/or make new friends

5. Get more sleep

Generally speaking, at least one of these five areas is applicable and relevant in the lives of nearly every tween or teen (there are exceptions, of course). Understanding what is important for each student individually provides the opportunity to talk about daily habits and choices, and what small, incremental changes can be made to get them closer to their own personal version of success.

With social media and technology use, it's important to help students ask their own questions. Who are they communicating with? What apps do they prefer to use? Where and when are they often online (waiting for the bus, walking home from school, waiting to be picked up)? Why do they want to use social media? What have been their biggest challenges online (and in real life) in relation to their technology and social media use? Some use social media to socialize with others: to make friendships, build a network, or maintain relationships. For others, social media can be used as an escape from others—for example, walking into a room where there isn't a familiar face can be nerve-wracking, and whether it is at a party or in the school counselor's office, the new default has become staring at the phone. I've walked into the waiting area of my office to find four teens, all about the same age, deeply engrossed in their phones in part because they are too shy or hesitant to start a conversation and don't want to appear awkward. Sometimes I break the ice for them, and then they start chatting with one another.

You may think the idea of making it all about them is obvious, but it's not typically what we do with tweens and teens today. More often than not, we—and by "we" I mean parents, educators, peers, and the media culture in general—tell tweens and teens, whether consciously or subconsciously, that they should act and/or behave in a certain way. When I work with students, I tell them that our work is *not* about their parents, teachers, siblings, friends, or anyone else they think they're supposed to impress or be beholden to. Instead, our work is all about *them*. The most common reaction I receive is one of relief and enthusiasm.

EXERCISE

Here are a few open-ended questions to start the process of self-reflection. A quick note: Asking too many questions is just as ineffective as asking no questions at all. Know your audience and their capacity for reflection. It may be that one, two, or three of these questions are all you need to use:

1. What went really well for you last (month/quarter/semester)?

2. What would you like to do differently this (month/quarter/semester)?

3. If we were at the end of the (month/quarter/semester) and it went really well, what would that look like to you? How would that feel?

4. What are your biggest distractions?

5. When are you most focused? What do you need to do to maintain that level of focus?

HELP THEM IDENTIFY THEIR VALUES

Step back and think: We rarely take the time to ask tweens and teens to think about what is personally important to them, allowing them to reflect on their own beliefs, priorities, and values. More likely, parental figures and role models share what is supposed to be of importance. There's nothing wrong with that—except, we hope our next generation comprises intrinsically motivated critical thinkers, and we're missing a great opportunity to encourage self-reflection and personal expression when we neglect to ask tweens and teens what they value and how their behaviors support those values.

Values and belief systems change over time, particularly among those in the middle of adolescence. At the same time, simply having the opportunity to identify issues of personal importance gives young people a sense of power, because each person's values and beliefs are unique to them and may be specific to the issues they are currently facing in their lives.

Asking students to identify their values provides an opportunity for self-reflection and greater understanding and offers a valuable conversation starter when used in conjunction with open-ended questions asked without specific expectations. I use this exercise regularly with adolescents and young adults, and it usually garners active responses. Many young people tell me they haven't really thought about or identified their personal values or, even if they have, they have yet to examine how their daily choices reflect those values.

EXERCISE

This exercise can easily be modified for a classroom or home setting, and it's often most effective if everyone gets involved as a way to provide perspective for conversation. Provide students with a list of 25–30 values (I've included a sample list of values here, but feel free to modify the list based on your audience). Ask them first to identify the 3–5 values that are currently most important to them and ask them which of their current daily habits and choices are helping them live up to those values, and which habits are not. Then, ask them how their current social media use contributes to or hinders their ability to live up to the values they identified as personally important.

SAMPLE VALUES		
Abundance	Emotional health	Joy
Altruism	Environment	Leadership
Appreciation	Family	Personal growth
Authenticity	Flexibility	Physical health
Commitment	Freedom	Privacy
Communication	Friendship	Respect
Community	Fun	Service
Compassion	Gratitude	Spirituality
Connecting to others	Humor	Trust
Creativity	Integrity	Vitality

Note: Modify the list of values as needed for the intended age group and audience.

When I did this exercise with an eighth-grade girl whose family had recently moved cross country, her previously sullen face lit up and she started writing energetically. It gave her the time and space needed to recognize that she wanted to make new friends and to participate in activities that were meaningful to her. We were then able to come up with strategies to help her achieve both of those goals.

ENCOURAGE THEM TO "GET REAL" ABOUT DAILY CHOICES AND HABITS

It's not hard to empathize with the difficulties of what I call the incremental creep of multitasking. It commonly occurs when students are working on a paper or project and every so often double-check their phone for incoming texts or notifications from social media apps (*Did someone reply, like, comment, or re-tweet?*). They genuinely believe they are working productively on the task at hand, but every time they pick up their phone or see a notification pop up on the side of the computer screen, their brain switches focus—even for a second. Research shows that even three seconds spent focusing on something else—say, turning attention to a text message—can double the chance of making a mistake.[3] And the switching back and forth requires time and energy—and quickly leads to exhaustion. For example, a student who is trying to complete an English paper while carrying on a text conversation with a friend will find that the constant switching back and forth makes everything take longer. Most of the time, though, students don't realize or fully understand how their daily choices and habits around social media use affect their personal outcomes.

Students aren't completely to blame for their allegiance to a multitasking way of life. As a society, we've unknowingly embraced this notion that multitasking is the key to success in school and life, with educators and employers often inadvertently creating systems that encourage multitasking. None of the research supports this notion. In fact, research suggests the opposite is true: We can make only so many decisions at once, and multitasking wears us out and decreases our productivity.

For students, trying to complete an assignment on an iPad or tablet, which forces them to toggle between the online text and the assignment sheet (both stored on the tablet), creates the need for multitasking abilities that not only make everything take more time but also require more energy. In Chapter 5, I'll talk more about tools and strategies to encourage more single-tasking or monotasking. For now, one of the most important conversations to have with tweens and teens is to help them identify their personal energy levels: What choices are energizing, and what choices are draining?

> One of the most important conversations to have with tweens and teens is to help them identify their personal energy levels: What choices are energizing, and what choices are draining?

When I talk about the idea of energizing versus draining experiences, I encourage students to think about how we only have so much energy every day, and simply having to be at school early in the morning five days a week requires a certain amount of energy. I ask students to identify some of their daily choices and habits and how those choices and habits affect their energy. For some, going online and socializing, and hearing positive messages from friends, can certainly be affirming and energizing. But scrolling mindlessly through social media feeds over and over again can start to become draining and without purpose or meaning. Encouraging students to build awareness and get real around their daily choices enables them to make greater connections with their seemingly small choices and their greater overall sense of being. It also allows them to identify the draining nature of negative online experiences, an often overlooked issue that I discuss in more detail in Chapter 6.

In terms of social media, I ask students to identify what online choices they are making that energize them and what choices feel draining or exhausting. For example, many students (and adults) pick up their phones at every opportunity. In a way, it quickly becomes a secondary reflex. I've asked students to take the time to be more conscious about their reasons for picking up their phones and going online whenever they have a spare moment.

I've seen the simple exercise of increasing awareness have a profound impact on greater choices and decision making. Middle school and high school girls have told me they decided to remove certain social media apps from their phones during the week because they found the ease of opening the app made them more likely to become distracted. They enjoyed interacting with friends and realized they would be more conscious of their online socializing if they removed those apps Monday–Thursday. Teen boys have proactively decided to delete the YouTube or ESPN apps from their phones or tablets during the week because they believed that little change would increase their daily consciousness about their overall use. When one sophomore told me she was planning to give up playing the clarinet (an activity she truly enjoyed) because she didn't think she had enough time, I encouraged her to download the Moment app on her iPhone and take a close look at how much time she was spending on her phone. Moment is an iOS app that allows users to track how many minutes a day they spend on their iPhone and iPad, and there's even a family plan that allows all family members to track use.[4] For Android phone users, an app called QualityTime serves a similar purpose. Sure enough, she was spending at least 180 minutes on her phone every day, some of it between classes but most after school and in the evenings. She realized she could find the needed time more easily than she thought and decided to "transfer" 25–45 minutes of those moments spent online to practicing the clarinet.

In none of these instances did I tell students what they should be doing—instead, my focus was on helping tweens and teens to truly understand the impact of their daily choices and allow them to make connections between their personal values and how they are spending their time on a daily basis. In some ways, using social media and technology contributed to values they considered important, though students were also able to identify areas in which their excessive use or always-on mentality hindered their overall performance.

EXERCISE

Encourage students to spend a week being more conscious of how and when they are picking up their phones or visiting sites that are distracting. If students have an iPhone or iPad, have them download the Moment or Quality Time app to track their time spent on the device, and see how well it matches up with how they want to be spending their time. What activities do they want to do that they currently don't feel they have time for? How much of that time was productive, and how many moments were spent surfing mindlessly? All that mindless surfing takes energy, and sometimes simply reducing it and raising overall awareness of time as a commodity can be incredibly liberating.

WORK COLLABORATIVELY TO COME UP WITH ACCEPTABLE USE POLICIES

When I presented to the camp directors mentioned in Chapter 1, I asked how many of their camps had acceptable use policies for their counselors, campers, and parents. Many looked surprised, as few had any acceptable use policies in place, and none had thought about bringing parents and families (who often are not on camp grounds) into the conversation. I reasoned that parents were a key part of the conversation, and oftentimes the disconnect between camp policies and (a lack of) home policies can lead to potential discrepancies. Online resources from sites such as Common Sense Media can help schools and families to come up with acceptable use policies, and I highly encourage those sample agreements to be a starting point for collaboration.

Consider the following questions: For an acceptable use policy that incorporates socialization, self-regulation, and safety as important markers, what are appropriate and inappropriate manners of online socialization? What behaviors would result in consequences, and what would those consequences be? When thinking about self-regulation, what structure can be devised at a school or family level to build in opportunities to "power down" or have time offline on a regular basis? For example, one Silicon Valley high school requires students to put their school-issued tablets and personal phones away while they are out on the quad during lunchtime. The policy is in place to encourage face-to-face conversations, and if students want to work online, they can do so in the library. School administrators have found the policy to be effective because it offers students a choice—and more and more students choose to sit outside and have face-to-face conversations.

In terms of safety, schools and parents can brainstorm with students to find multiple avenues of support to utilize when things don't go as planned. What are the different resources—family, friends, school counselor, outside support, clergy members, extended family? An effective collaboration also helps students realize that they are part of a greater community and that safety nets are in place for them to report or discuss when they see or read something that makes them feel uncomfortable.

In the Schools

I've seen many of the acceptable use policies that schools have students and parents review (and realize that some schools don't have acceptable use policies yet). Many policies are filled with legalese that makes students' and parents' eyes glaze over when they read them. For schools, addressing potential legal issues and concerns is crucially important, but the language should be fully decipherable and easily understood. There should also be a staff version of acceptable use, especially as it pertains to student–teacher communication and classroom phone use. I encourage schools to come up with an advisory committee of parents, educators, and students that meets at least two times a year to review acceptable use policies—after all, technology changes on a seemingly daily basis. This committee can bring up suggestions and amendments based on current school technology trends and overall media culture. Diversity of perspective is important, and although the school (and legal counsel) should come up with the final version, parents, educators, and students should collaborate and provide input. Schools also should provide guidelines for parents so that the work at home is in sync with the policies at school—in many instances, parents don't know where to start and can become frustrated and send their children mixed messages. At the end of this chapter, I provide sample acceptable use policies, and more resources can be found online.

In the Home

Before collaborating with children on an acceptable use policy, parents can start building their own awareness around how their children spend their time online. Understanding the language around social media use, identifying main sources of distraction, and using a school's acceptable use policy as a conversational starting point for household policy can be important initial steps. Sample family technology-use agreements can be found online, and I provide one at the end of this chapter as well. In the upcoming chapters on wellness, I provide some guidelines for potential topics to address in home policies, so parents may want to review those chapters to figure out what is most important to include (see also Table 4.1). Above all, parents should use this time for collaboration to spark a conversation around appropriate and acceptable use and find a way to make sure their children have numerous safety nets they feel comfortable reaching out to if things do not go as planned online or in real life.

TABLE 4.1 Top Five Parental Control Apps for Computers and Mobile Devices

APPS FOR IOS AND ANDROID	WHAT IS IT?	PROS	CONS
OurPact (ourpact.com)	Highly recommended app, designed and developed with child professionals and parents as a parental control and a way to teach responsibility and time management to children. Remotely blocks sites and apps, tracks activity, and schedules usage.	Free. Mobile-based; can customize device use for recurring schedules; allows additional time on devices if parent unlocks; easy to set up and use.	iOS users may have issues with hidden apps that reappear on the home screen; a patch has been created to fix this bug.
Screen Time (screentimelabs.com)	Popular app that lets parents manage both time and content on smartphones and tablets. Blocks designated apps (but allows others, educational, etc.) tracks usage and can time out kids from devices remotely. Can create checklists for children to incentivize less online time.	Flexible; allows parents to add bonus time on devices as reward; comprehensive and mobile based; uninstall of app is password protected; 14-day free trial offered.	$3.99/month; premium features cost more. Can be worked around if child creates a widget, which will allow access to blocked apps through the home screen; impairs apps' effectiveness.

(Continued)

TABLE 4.1   (Continued)

APPS FOR IOS AND ANDROID	WHAT IS IT?	PROS	CONS
Family Time (familytime.io)	Solidly rated app that allows parents to block apps and sites and to limit child's screen time. Tracks usage and also child's location and arrival and departure time.	Provides geo and location tracking; can install protection to prevent deletion of app; child data protected; beta testing of text message monitoring in progress; mobile based.	$2.25/month plus annual fee for installation on one child's device; premium features or adding devices costs more. Continuous use of GPS can drain battery life.
Net Nanny (netnanny.com/mobile)	Highly rated parental control for its ease of use and effective and sophisticated blocking and filtering abilities. Provides a complete picture of what your child does online. Parent can block apps, manage devices remotely, and disable devices during sleeping hours.	Can mask profanity and will block games based on rating system or specific content.	$69.99/year for 7 computers or devices. Cannot capture keyboard strokes or desktop images; browser based (users must block other browsers and adjust settings).
Curbi (curbi.com)	Versatile app that tracks screen time, blocks content, and manages device usage remotely; provides weekly report of child's device usage.	Can set device restrictions (no camera, no Safari, etc.); built-in content filter; permanent Google "safe search" feature; 14-day free trial offered.	$6.99/month. Easy for child to turn app off in settings; app can cause device to crash.

SOCIAL MEDIA WELLNESS

A WORD ABOUT TECHNOLOGY ADDICTION

Every so often, parents will come up to me after a presentation and talk in hushed tones about their son or daughter who becomes angry or threatens or engages in violent behavior whenever technological device use is limited. I've heard from parents whose children break furniture in order to gain access to video game consoles or throw raging fits and punch holes in the wall when their devices are taken away. In most cases, these parents are sad and ashamed, and having such rage in their home has become exhausting. Other times, parents will call our office, describe behaviors that suggest an addiction to technology, and express the hope that our organization and time-management strategies can help. I discuss the signs of technology addiction in Chapter 7, but, in general, addiction to technology (or anything, for that matter) is a serious issue that goes beyond the scope of organization and time-management strategies. It can require work with a counselor or behavioral therapist, as well as support for the entire family.

Much of the work in this book revolves around creating proactive ways to promote wellness in the hopes of *preventing* addictive behaviors, but as with any form of addiction, there are often several social and emotional issues going on that need to be addressed in the face of an addiction to technology. As such, the strategies in this book may have little to no immediate effect when a student is struggling with serious technology addiction.

SUMMARY

The way we talk with tweens and teens has the most powerful impact on their ability to make proactive and prosocial decisions about their social media and technology use. Attitude, approach, and tone all make a significant difference on whether or not a message is received, and taking time to step back and understand your audience can be crucial to long-term social media wellness. It can be helpful to start by having tweens and teens identify their values and then think about how well their incremental daily choices are reflecting those personal values and helping them to achieve their personal or academic goals. By encouraging young people to identify their values, parents and educators can plant the seeds needed for incremental changes in behavior that lead young people closer to the goals they identify as important. Acceptable use policies, both at home and at school, should be worked on collaboratively with tweens and teens and should be written in clear language that everyone understands. The focus of acceptable use policies should be to provide students, parents, and educators with the tools needed to encourage positive and proactive socialization, self-regulation, and safety.

Middle School Student Acceptable Use Media Agreement

Socialization

I will be a good online citizen and work to create a positive, respectful online and in-real-life community.

I will respect others' privacy and will not intentionally act in a way that harms, embarrasses, excludes, or hurts another person online or with my phone.

I understand that I am leaving a permanent "digital footprint" behind, and I will not post anything online or send anything with my phone that could embarrass me or jeopardize my security or privacy.

Self-Regulation

I will think about the consequences of my actions before I post, message, text, or send images.

I will be conscious of how much time I am spending online, on my phone, and on other devices, and I will continue to enjoy the other activities and people in my life.

I will not use my phone, computer, or other devices after 9 p.m. on school nights, and all electronics should be out of my bedroom at that time.

I will be aware of how technology and screens are affecting my school work, friendships, and relationships with my family.

Safety

I will not create accounts or give out any private information, like my full name, phone number, address, or birthdate, without my family's permission.

If I see something, I will say something. I will tell my parents about any uncomfortable situations, bullying, or any kind of inappropriate behavior I experience or witness online.

I will not share my passwords with anyone except my parents, and I will use privacy settings on all email and social media accounts.

I understand that all of my devices belong to my parents, who trust my judgment and respect my privacy. If they are concerned about my online safety, I will answer their questions honestly.

Student Social Media Acceptable Use Agreement for Main Street High School

Socialization

I will follow Main Street High School's code of conduct when posting online and work to create a positive, respectful online and in-real-life community.

I will respect others' privacy and will not intentionally act in a way that harms, embarrasses, excludes, or hurts another person online.

I understand that I am leaving a permanent "digital footprint" behind, and I will not post anything online that I wouldn't want my family, teachers, college admissions officers, or future employers to see.

Self-Regulation

I will do my own work and not copy and paste others' work, as this is a copyright violation.

I will make sure that I have permission for any images I use or that they are part of the Creative Commons.

When I link to websites to support my own ideas, I will read the articles thoroughly to be sure they are suitable for school use.

I will be aware of how much time I am spending in front of screens and on social media, and how that use is affecting my school work and grades.

Safety

I will not give out any private information, like my full name, phone number, address, or birthdate, without my family's permission.

If I see something, I will say something. I will tell my teachers or parents about any uncomfortable situations, bullying, or any kind of inappropriate behavior I experience or witness online.

I will not share my passwords with anyone but my teachers and parents, and I will use privacy settings and read privacy agreements wherever possible.

If I do not follow these terms and conditions, I may lose access to online tools in the future.

Staff Social Media Acceptable Use Agreement for Main Street High School

Socialization

I will follow Main Street High School's code of conduct when posting online and will work to create a positive, respectful online community.

I will respect student and staff privacy online, and I will not share any personal or confidential information or images or write about students or colleagues without their permission.

I will share my expertise online in a way that adds value to the conversation in terms of information and perspective and is accurate to the best of my knowledge.

Self-Regulation

I am aware that lines between public and private and between personal and professional are blurred in the digital world and acknowledge that what I do online needs to be consistent with Main Street High School's best practices and professional standards.

I will be respectful of the fact that social media is intended to create dialogue and that people will not always agree on an issue. I will remain calm if I disagree with someone's opinion and also own and correct any mistakes I make when needed.

I will respect copyright and fair use guidelines online and ensure that any sources or links I post are appropriate.

Safety

I will be cautious about sharing too much personal information online, and I am aware that if I post anything inappropriate, such as sexually explicit messages, use of alcohol or drugs, or provocative photographs, I may be subject to review.

I understand that establishing a personal relationship with any student online, via text message, or through phone calls is inappropriate, and I will not include any students in my personal social media activities or outside school-approved activities.

I will report bullying or any other inappropriate behavior I experience or witness online.

Parent Acceptable Use Media Agreement

Socialization

I will get to know the websites, games, and apps that my child uses, and I will use them myself to get a better understanding of what my child is doing online.

I will recognize that media is a large part of my child's life, and I will work to understand the pros and cons of technology, including having my child show me how to use his or her favorite sites and apps.

I will help my child find media that are useful, safe, and fun.

Self-Regulation

I will be conscious of how much time I am spending in front of screens myself, and I will continue to enjoy the other activities and people in my life.

I will be aware of how technology and screens are affecting my work, friendships, and relationships with my family.

I will let my child make some mistakes regarding technology and help him or her to learn from them.

I will create and discuss reasonable rules and guidelines for my child's daily screen time, including limiting phone and Internet use while doing homework.

Safety

I will talk to my child about any concerns I have about his or her media use or behavior before simply saying "no" to visiting sites or using apps or devices.

If my child tells me about a problem he or she is having online, I will not overreact. We will work together to find a solution and prevent it from happening again.

I will respect my child's privacy, but I will ask my child to provide me with a list of his or her passwords.

I will not access my child's accounts without his or her knowledge, and I will do so only if my child's safety or the safety of others is at stake.

Family Acceptable Use Media Agreement

Socialization

We will be good online citizens and work to create a positive, respectful online and in-real-life community. We will respect others' privacy and will not intentionally act in a way that harms, embarrasses, excludes, or hurts another person online or with our phones.

We understand that we are leaving a permanent "digital footprint" behind and will not post anything online or send anything with our phones that could embarrass us or jeopardize our family's security or privacy.

Parents will recognize that media is a large part of their children's lives and work to understand the pros and cons of technology, including having children show them how to use their favorite sites and apps.

Self-Regulation

We will be conscious of how much time we are spending online, on our phones, and on other devices, and we will continue to enjoy the other activities and people in our lives.

We will not use phones, computers, or other devices during family meals or during other designated technology-free time.

We will be aware of how technology and screens are affecting school work, friendships, and relationships with family, and we will come up with solutions to curb technology use as needed.

We will create and discuss reasonable rules and guidelines for child daily screen time, including limiting phone and Internet use while doing homework and at bedtime.

Safety

Children will not create accounts or give out any private information, like full names, phone numbers, addresses, or birthdates without a parent's permission.

(Continued)

(Continued)

We will not share our passwords with anyone except family members, and we will use privacy settings on all email and social media accounts.

If we see something, we will say something. Children pledge to tell their parents about any uncomfortable situations, bullying, or inappropriate behavior they experience or witness online.

Parents will respect their children's privacy, but parents will need a list of passwords for all children's technology and social media accounts. If parents are concerned about safety, they have permission to access these accounts as necessary.

CHAPTER 5

Academic Wellness

Organization, Compartmentalization, and Energy Management in the Age of Distractions

The high school's information technology (IT) specialist looked at me with a mixture of amusement and bewilderment. He was a somewhat reserved gentleman, with a distinguished stature and the efficiency of someone who had spent years in corporate America. Now, in semi-retirement, he had become the person in charge of managing IT at a local high school that had recently decided to implement a one-to-one tablet program.

The school he worked at was about to start the second year of the program, and his most recent task was to refurbish the 1,500 or so tablets that had been turned in after the first year. The school essentially owned all the tablets, and students turned them in at the end of the year, much the way a student in past years would have returned textbooks. As anyone working with high school students can attest, there is normally significant wear and tear on any item after a full year's use.

By the end of the summer, after several hundred hours of work, the IT specialist had refurbished all the tablets, making sure they were updated with the latest software, so that on registration day (also known as school picture day), students could pick up the slim, light-weight tablets that would now house most of their textbooks and note-taking applications.

"What was the most surprising thing you found when you went through all the tablets?" I asked, expecting that most of his time was spent fixing broken screens and replacing missing covers.

"Well," he said slowly, "when I went through all the tablets, some were in far better shape than others. But, one thing that surprised me was that some of the students, and I went back and figured out they were mostly freshman boys, had tablet screens completely covered with documents. It was as if they just saved everything to the home screen of their tablet *for the entire year*."

In other words, these students had never learned or appreciated the simple genius of digital folders.

He went on to describe the overall physical condition of these tablets—they were also, unsurprisingly, somewhat of a mess. It didn't take long for me to realize the scope of this newfound problem: For years, I dealt with students' crumpled papers, usually discovered at the bottom of backpacks or spilling out of binders. Now, those crumpled papers were digital, quietly hidden within the confines of a sleek tablet that itself might be stuffed at the bottom of a backpack. When the school principal had called me a few weeks earlier, she noted that there had been an overall drop in students' grades during the first year of the one-to-one tablet program, and they were trying to figure out why. The lack of physical signs of disorganization was one reason many teachers and administrators were unaware of the root cause of the problem. Another reason, I would find out later, was that students using tablets were typically much quieter in class, usually because they were absorbed in surfing the web or on an Internet site unrelated to the task at hand.

Over time, I realized that although the school went to great lengths to make sure students knew how to use key programs, such as Notability and Microsoft OneNote (which help with note-taking and information retention), they had done nothing to help students come up with strategies for organizing files and managing workflow. They may have assumed students would figure these things out on their own, and in some cases, students did. In many cases, though, students did not—and often didn't understand exactly why they felt so overwhelmed. The school also had not provided clear guidelines for faculty on how and where to announce assignments and exams, and how to distribute and collect assignments and essays. As a result, students were juggling standards and expectations from six or seven different teachers. Some teachers preferred Google Docs, others used Dropbox or Box to manage file-sharing, and still others used apps that are now unavailable. In essence, the school's failure to streamline the location of assignments turned what had previously been as simple as turning in a piece of paper into a far more complicated process, which left many kids completely confused. The new standards around tablet use created an entirely new language, but in many cases students were left without a dictionary.

THE NEW LANGUAGE OF TECHNOLOGY IN SCHOOLS

Just as social media has created a new language that causes a rift in understanding between many adults and adolescents, so too has the use of technology in classrooms. In the same way that adults over thirty-five years old didn't experience an adolescence filled with apps, notifications, and viral video loops, teachers and administrators over thirty-five years old haven't been a student in a classroom where one-to-one tablets and computers are used to manage classroom assignments and teacher communication. Many times, school administrators, teachers, and counselors haven't stopped to think about the full impact of new online tools and apps on students' overall learning experience.

I recently presented an in-service workshop to teachers and administrators at an independent middle school. The teachers were incredibly engaged and forthcoming, and they truly believed technology had made their lives—as well as the lives of their students—much easier. I casually asked one teacher about how he communicates homework to students, and how students were asked to turn in their assignments. As he shared his method, another teacher from the other side of the room blurted out, "Wow—I do it completely differently!" Within a minute, chatter erupted as teachers began to compare methods, and we had an "a-ha!" moment. Within each department, many teachers had similar strategies for managing workflow, but across the school, there was no consistent strategy for sharing information or for distributing and collecting assignments.

Seizing the opportunity, I suggested gently, "Now, let's pretend you're an eighth-grade boy who has a regular course load. How does he go through his day?" By now, teachers were quickly recognizing how difficult it would be for a student to manage all the different workflow strategies—before even starting on homework. Some teachers put homework online, some shared homework only on the board, and one math teacher required all work to be done with graph paper, while a Spanish teacher insisted that his classroom was "paperless" and went to great lengths to maintain that standard. Until that moment, the teachers did not realize the potential for confusion and frustration as students simply tried to navigate the school's one-to-one tablet program.

I then shared results from a survey given to their students just a few weeks prior. Over half the students said it took them at least thirty minutes every day to *figure out* their assignments. After the school instituted an online learning management system, many teachers no longer announced assignments in class, believing they were saving valuable time by telling students to check the school's online portal. In reality, students would attempt to navigate said portal from home, and were at times faced with spotty Wi-Fi connections or glitches with the portal or homework assignments that hadn't been updated. Even when things went smoothly, students were easily distracted from recording homework simply by being online. At the same time, teachers weren't consistent. Some teachers used the online portal diligently, whereas others would forget to post altogether but figured that mentioning an assignment out loud at the end of class was sufficient. Some posted online every day, some posted once a week, and others rarely, if ever, posted assignments online. Sitting there talking about all the discrepancies and differences made my head hurt. ·

The teachers realized that students who used a half-hour or more per day to figure out all their assignments were spending almost three hours of potential work time (or more) every week simply to manage workflow. In that way, technology had made things more complicated, in part because a streamlined system was lacking. I've found it most productive when all teachers within a school or a grade level try to standardize their respective systems in some way, so that students aren't juggling wildly different expectations. For an easily distracted student, going online to "figure out the homework" often leads to other distractions that can last an hour or more. Many of these middle school students also wrongly assumed that figuring out the homework was time actually spent on homework. When I spoke with the students, I used a baking analogy with them and countered that tracking down all the ingredients at the supermarket doesn't contribute to the baking time of cupcakes. Students who spend a great deal of time completing work often don't have good strategies in place for organizing their materials and managing their time and workflow.

This school, like many of the schools I visit that have adopted tablet or computer programs, also stopped giving students written planners. Eliminating written planners provided a substantial cost savings, but administrators hadn't tried using online task-management options like myHomework. If they had, they might have realized that many of the online options don't help students who want to plan out their entire week in advance (including appointments, extracurricular activities, sports practices, and family obligations). My students repeatedly told me how much they benefited from keeping their tasks and schedule all in one place, and how they felt infinitely less stressed after spending a week of tracking their assignments, activities, and to-dos in a paper planner. Writing everything down offline encouraged compartmentalization and allowed them to identify tasks that needed to be focused on individually. When students go online to figure out a homework assignment, they are inevitably tempted by the Internet's endless possibilities. Using a written planner helps to prevent that.

Students have long struggled with issues around organization and time management. Educators don't always fully appreciate the importance of teaching *and reinforcing* daily organizational habits with tweens and teens. In implementing technology programs without addressing the considerable side effects, they also often overlook the fact that increased technology can unintentionally make daily tasks more complicated. Teachers may have autonomy to develop specific strategies for use in their own classrooms, but it might be more effective to collaborate and develop systems that are consistent throughout the school or at least the grade. For students, needing to use different methods for each class can feel the same as having six or seven different bosses, each of whom has differing expectations and ways of doing things. Such a situation could easily become overwhelming for an adult, much less a tween or teen juggling a host of academic, extracurricular, familial, and social obligations.

In later sections of this chapter, I highlight specific organization and time-management strategies for teachers and students. For now, it's helpful to take a moment and reflect on how and when information is shared and processed in the daily classroom and school experience.

EXERCISE

Take a moment and reflect on how assignments and workflow are managed.

For school administrators and teachers: Do you (in your classroom, department, grade level, or school) have a set standard for how assignments are shared with students? How far in advance are assignments posted online? How are assignments turned in—are there several options, or only one way? Take a moment and imagine that you are one of your own students, and try to figure out what the daily and upcoming assignments are. How long does that take? How easy is it to manage? Does the school provide a written daily planner?

For parents: Take on the role of your child, and figure out how assignments are shared and how to turn in assignments for each class. How many different procedures, apps, or methods are used? How long does it take you to break down and understand all that is required or asked?

For students: How long does it take you to figure out all your assignments and upcoming exams, essays, and projects? Where do you write them down or track them? What do you do once you have completed them? How are they turned in? For each class, write down how you track and turn in assignments. Then, for the next three days, record how long it took you to figure out the day's work and think about what could be done to make that process less time consuming.

HOW SOCIAL MEDIA AND TECHNOLOGY AFFECT ACADEMIC WELLNESS

Tania came into my office somewhat preoccupied. "I got my history research paper back today, and [my teacher] gave me a C+." Tania was a high school junior who worked diligently, but writing research papers was difficult for her. She was warm and gregarious, had a bubbly personality, and was easily distracted. As we were talking, Tania's phone made four or five notification buzzes before I asked her to put the phone on silent, and she complied without a second thought. Though she had spent some time completing this long-term assignment, she left a good deal of the work until the last minute, so I wouldn't have been surprised if she made small grammatical or formatting errors that resulted in missed points. I asked if she had looked over her teacher's comments and general feedback.

"I skimmed her comments, and she wrote a lot of comments, but I talked with my friends and a lot of people didn't do so well so I am not worried. I am going to email [my teacher] and see what the class average was, because I don't think most people did that well."

I stopped and thought for a moment before proceeding. "Tania," I asked, "what does the class average on the paper have to do with your own writing? How is spending time figuring out the class average going to help you become a better writer? Wouldn't going over the teacher's comments be a better use of your time?" I watched her squirm a bit, because she didn't really have an answer to my questions.

"Well," she started, "I figure if other people didn't do that well either, then I shouldn't be that concerned. Like, if everyone got Bs and Cs, then that's okay."

In Chapter 3, I highlighted altered expectations as one of the side effects of social media and technology and shared the story of Nick, who became upset with his own SAT scores after seeing his friends' postings of their high scores. The comparison culture that has developed works both ways—students certainly experience heightened expectations when they see others' performance and compare those accomplishments relative to their own. Conversely, students now alter their expectations to focus on how they are doing relative to others. Instead of concentrating on their own learning process and experience, many students are increasingly focused on where they fit in.

These altered expectations and the comparison culture aren't entirely a result of social media and technology use—students have long compared themselves to their peers. Because so much is shared and compared in our always-on world, it becomes natural for students to share and compare academic results. The constant comparison and on-all-the-time mentality (signaled by Tania's constant phone buzzing) results in a focus on the comparison rather than on personal growth, self-improvement, and personal purpose and potential. For students like Tania, there are missed opportunities for personal growth, because of the emphasis on how one does relative to others rather than relative to themselves.

What is lost in this share-and-compare environment? There are certainly many ways to benefit from collaboration; however, looking to external factors for internal growth can be counterproductive. Ultimately, it becomes easy to miss personal strengths and areas for growth when a student is consistently swayed by the crowd.

At the same time, we've created a classroom and school environment that sends a whole host of mixed messages around learning and productivity. There's conflicting evidence on whether or not bringing technology into the classroom improves learning and retention, and research suggests that writing notes by hand improves retention.[1] If we want to maximize learning and productivity, that doesn't always mean using technology—and that issue isn't always fully addressed. For instance, many schools encourage students to use a device that serves as a main source of distraction, without first giving students the skills they need to organize, compartmentalize, and prioritize. Many school administrators pursue the noble, environmentally conscious goal of having their schools go "paperless," without realizing that many students are stressed out by some of the side effects of the paperless culture. Nearly every school I've visited that has a tablet or computer program has at least one extremely tech-savvy teacher who insists that his or her classroom is completely paperless. Generally, that teacher's system is one of the most complicated, with elements that make it stressful for students when there is no flexibility.

For example, students using a tablet to complete an assignment that requires access to their digital textbook often find themselves toggling between their textbook and a worksheet that's also on the tablet. The seconds spent toggling might as well be spent multitasking, as far as the brain is concerned, and the switching back and forth quickly leads to exhaustion (or, in my case, headaches). There are simple alternatives to toggling, of course, that require a bit of flexibility. Some programs allow for a split screen, which might work for some students but won't for others.[2] Tablets, computers, and related technology can be excellent tools, but we also need to help students to develop organizational skills *and* recognize that everyone learns differently. Technology provides more opportunities for varied methods of learning and engagement, but it should not be seen as the only way to improve learning outcomes.

The insistence on going paperless in a classroom can disproportionately affect students who might not have reliable access to a computer or the Internet once leaving school grounds. For a student who relies on the school or public library to access online documents (versus being able to store paper documents in a binder), there may be an added hurdle to completing assignments that can double or even triple the amount of time spent on homework. Most schools I work with that have tablet or computer programs believe that if the school issues a tablet or computer, then the student should be fine. In reality, lack of Wi-Fi access can also be a barrier to success and is another reason for needed flexibility.

As I noted in Chapter 3, students now experience information overload when they are bombarded by the results of a simple Internet search. Type something as vague as "2016 presidential election" into a search engine, and the Internet blesses you with millions upon millions of web pages worth of information from a variety of sources—some factual, and others completely made up. This quick access to content is both helpful and paralyzing, and the top results might not be the most useful or accurate. Students now need to learn how to effortlessly filter information and to identify reputable sources from a sea of possibilities.

Parents and educators play an important role in setting standards around compartmentalizing work, fun, and rest. We often underestimate the subtle clues we send with our seemingly innocuous daily choices. For instance, parents feel conflicted when children are up late using a computer or tablet to complete assignments. They might want their children to have technology-free time before bed but not if the child is going to be penalized academically for not completing an assignment, and so they direct their anger toward the school for giving too much work. In reality, students know that completing homework is an acceptable excuse for being online, and they may play off their parents' fear of academic failure in an effort to gain more screen time.

Making assignments due at midnight also contributes to the on-all-the-time mentality. Teachers offering a midnight turn-in time might be trying to help students who are overscheduled and overwhelmed, but instead they are sending the message that it is normal and acceptable for students to be up until midnight completing schoolwork. Ashley Hill, a longtime San Francisco Bay Area high school teacher, has a different approach. She tells students at the beginning of the school year that she doesn't answer email past a certain hour and often replies to students' evening emails encouraging them to get to sleep and come see her the next day to discuss an assignment or exam without penalty. She reasons that responding to emails about a homework assignment at 11 p.m. or midnight subconsciously sends the message that it is normal and acceptable for students to be up that late completing work when they likely could benefit from being asleep.

The strategies I provide in the upcoming sections have worked for many of the students in my office and at schools I've consulted with in the past. I include this information on organizing assignments and managing workflow because much of academic wellness is centered on learning better ways to navigate and self-regulate our always-on world. Some of the solutions may seem obvious, but sometimes simple fixes are the most effective. I've always been of the mindset that what works well for one person might not work for another. To that end, take what works and leave the rest. The ultimate goal is increased happiness, good health, and wellness within our schools and greater communities.

EXERCISE

What are some ways to navigate information overload? How can a source be deemed to be factual? What is "fake news," and what are the effects of inaccurate stories being spread widely without second thought?

For parents and teachers: provide students with three to five search topics that would potentially return a great deal of information and ask students how they would mentally filter and choose what to use as resources. Sample topics could include the 2016 presidential election, the civil rights movement, Hurricane Katrina, laws related to combating climate change, or the fall of the Roman Empire.

OPTIMIZING ORGANIZATION WITH VIRTUAL FOLDERS AND IN-REAL-LIFE (IRL) BINDERS

When students came to see me fifteen years ago, we would go through all their papers—*every single one*—and put them in binders, one for each subject, with five-tabs: "Notes," for notes taken in class; "Homework," for assignments (those recently completed and ready to be turned in on top, with returned work underneath); "Handouts," for any useful information a teacher might provide; "Tests/Quizzes," for study guides and returned assessments; and "Paper," for extra loose-leaf paper. Everything was hole-punched, and the front and back pockets of the binder were to remain empty. Within this framework, students adjusted as needed: My usual advice was that, since it was their binder, *they* could figure out what would go where. For instance, for a science class, a student might choose to file returned lab write-ups as homework assignments or handouts. The central goal was for them to be able to find things quickly and effectively, and to minimize crumpled papers. If their teachers had a specific way they wanted the binders to be organized, we used that approach instead. It was, and is, a flexible system.

Today, things are a bit more complicated. Students at schools with one-to-one tablet or computer programs usually store the majority of their files on their computer or, more recently, in the cloud, using a file-sharing and content management system. Many students still have a few papers and need some sort of physical binder system, though one binder for each class seems somewhat excessive. Still, the same tenets hold true: Students should keep files organized so that they can quickly find and retrieve the files with little effort. My rule of thumb is this: An organized file system means you are able to hand over your computer or tablet, and, with minimal instructions, someone else can find a needed file or document in under a minute.

Today, I encourage students to create a file folder on their tablet's home screen or desktop for each of their classes and to create sub-files within the individual class folders titled "Notes," "Homework," "Handouts," and "Test/Quizzes." Some students might want to break down those folders further by topics, chapters, or sections of information studied, but again, that is optional. Essentially, we take the physical file system and transfer it to a digital one. This file system can be used within cloud storage systems, and it can be adapted to a specific teacher's standard. If a teacher doesn't have a specific system, then "Notes," "Homework," "Handouts," and "Tests/Quizzes" is a great default. The goal should be for there to be no "papers" stuffed in the pockets of the binder (i.e., hanging out on the home screen or desktop).

> An organized file system means you are able to hand over your computer or tablet, and, with minimal instructions, someone else can find a needed file or document in under a minute.

Teaching kids how to organize and file documents may seem mundane, but as someone who has seemingly filed over a million papers in my lifetime, I have witnessed the relief conveyed on the face of a child whose 892 pieces of loose-leaf paper now have a designated home. That same relief is apparent when I make students sit in my office and create digital file folders and file every digital document.

It's not enough to simply have students create virtual folders and physical binders—there also needs to be time for a daily or weekly regrouping to help them stay organized. Nearly all students are well-meaning, starting out with the greatest of intentions around organization, only to fall off track. Building in a daily or weekly regrouping can be done easily at home or in the classroom, and it can make a world of difference. At home, a half-hour on a Sunday or Monday night can make regrouping a family activity where everyone takes time to clean out binders, briefcases, backpacks, and home screens. In the classroom, regrouping can be built in to homeroom or advisory, or within a class period. I've seen teachers build it in to class time on a Monday or Friday, giving students 15–30 minutes to clean out their binders, organize papers and files, and write in their planners (more on planners in the next section). After several weeks of offering regrouping time, teachers tell me that students seem more relaxed and become insistent that they have their regular regrouping time. For teachers, the win-win becomes easy to see: Those minutes spent helping students to proactively organize saves the time and energy that otherwise would be spent tracking down missing assignments and dealing with stressed-out students (and/or parents).

EXERCISE

For teachers: Think about how you promote organization in your class. Are your students required to have a virtual or IRL organization system? Do you check it regularly or allow them to take time in class to regroup and reorganize? What simple things can you do that will promote organization (and ultimately save you time) in your classroom?

For parents and students: Set aside a weekend afternoon—preferably scheduled in advance, with all the materials on hand—and create virtual and IRL folders and binders. Go through every single digital file and every piece of paper and recycle, trash (literally or virtually), or store it. Come up with a file-naming system that works for you (see sidebar on page 120).

MAPPING OUT ASSIGNMENTS AND ACTIVITIES

Over the past decade, I've seen many schools with tablet and computer programs stop distributing paper planners—and then slowly realize their mistake. Many administrators reasoned that planners, which often end up lost, ripped, or unused, are a waste of paper and resources. They might not always be used, or kept in ideal conditions, but there are a number of reasons why schools should rethink that decision—and why students should think about continuing to track assignments and activities with a written, visual planner, even if the school doesn't provide one.

I fully appreciate the ease and simplicity of digital calendars and notes and believe that schools that use an online learning management system (such as Haiku, Schoology, or edline) should continue doing so. However, I also encourage students to use online learning management systems as a backup to keeping daily assignments and activities in a written planner.

A written, visual planner enables students to keep all of their assignments and activities in one place, ideally with ample room to record assignments, projects, and exams, as well as track activities, family events, and appointments. A written planner allows for the stress-relieving brain dump that happens when students write and track everything in one place, without having to toggle, type, or click between different sections. Students can easily number their assignments and prioritize, and they are potentially less distracted by the possibility of going online. Sometimes the coolness factor takes effect, and students, particularly those in middle school, feel uncomfortable being the only one with a written planner. In essence, written

A WORD ON NAMING FILES

It seems simple and self-evident, but students often "lose" a file because they forget what it was named, spending stressful minutes trying to locate it. I encourage students to come up with a naming system that includes the class name, section of information, assignment type, and date. Some examples:

- USHChap4.1ReviewQuestions111516 (United States History Chapter 4.1 November 15, 2016)

- BIOPhotosynthesisUR030517 (Biology Photosynthesis Unit Review March 5, 2017)

- ENGChaucerEssay011517 (English Essay on Chaucer January 15, 2017)

planners are a simple way to encourage monotasking and compartmentalization.

I encourage teachers to normalize the use of written planners by creating time and space for students to bring out their planners in class and write down their assignments. For teachers who believe there isn't enough time to do so, I suggest thinking of the time as a preventive measure: Three minutes spent daily prevents hours of dealing with missing assignments, school counselor inquiries for failing grades due to missing work, and parent conferences due to low performance.

In an ideal world, teachers would give students their assignments in class (writing them on the board as well as giving a verbal reminder) *and* post assignments online. Students benefit most when teachers are able to post the upcoming week's assignments and exams on the online learning management system by the previous Friday afternoon. This ideal schedule is not always possible, but this simple shift encourages students to become more proactive in managing their upcoming week. Students who live in two households, or who have extracurricular activities that require a significant evening and weekend time commitment, can use weekends to get ahead so that they feel less overwhelmed during the week. (Some readers may argue that children shouldn't be so overscheduled, and although I generally agree, that really is a discussion for another book.) Some students benefit from previewing information before it is introduced in class, so knowing what information will be covered in the upcoming week can be beneficial as well. One high school senior with significant learning disabilities found that simply previewing the information for the upcoming week greatly increased his comprehension and retention. Once he began spending two to three hours every Sunday going through upcoming math, English, and history lessons with a tutor, he felt more confident in class and was more willing to participate. Within six months, his GPA improved from a 2.3 to a 3.4, and his classroom anxiety decreased dramatically.

In my office, I use a version of the following five-step process for managing tasks on a written planner—students can do this at home or in class as part of a regular homeroom or advisory activity:

1. Write down all the upcoming assignments for each class available on the night assigned.

2. Add any tests, long-term projects, or essays by writing them at the top of the day they are due.

3. Add in any sports activities, family events, doctor's appointments, and social happenings.

4. Schedule in blocks of time for homework (more on that in the next section).

5. Number assignments in order of priority and check them off when completed.

EXERCISE

For educators: What do students at your school use to map out assignments? Are students using written planners or an online system? Is it working? Do they have time in class or advisory to schedule out their week and figure out how to manage tasks? What could be done differently?

For students: Think about the benefits and drawbacks of using an online planner versus a written one—what would work best for you? Spend a full week trying out the strategies for a written planner and also perhaps trying out an online app or tool separately. Then think about which method maximizes your productivity.

MANAGING TIME AND ENERGY

When I was working on my second book and ran several focus groups of seventh- and eighth-grade girls from different middle schools, every single girl admitted that homework took them far longer than they wanted it to. I wanted to get a sense of how and where they were completing their homework, and what potential distractions were interfering with their ability to get their work done. Most said they spent hours every night completing work in their rooms, and a few admitted that their increased workload, combined with athletic and extracurricular activities, caused them to get less than six hours of sleep per night. At that time, the girls weren't attending schools with one-to-one or one-to-many tablet or computer programs, but they all used computers to complete their assignments.

As I began to work with the girls on finding organizational solutions, I helped them realize that their once-overwhelming workload could become more manageable if they were able to eliminate distractions and compartmentalize work into smaller blocks of time with short breaks in between to maximize productivity. I had them put their phones on silent in the other room during their designated homework time, sign out of all social media sites, and block messaging on their computer or other devices. They used the *Pomodoro Technique,* which is a simple method of doing twenty-five minutes of focused work followed by a five-minute break. Regardless of how much homework was assigned for the evening, they agreed to complete a full two-hour work block every day (except Friday), comprising four twenty-five minute Pomodoro blocks. After completing assignments due the next day, they used any extra time to get ahead on longer-term work or projects. Over the following weeks, some of the girls were able to cut their homework time in half—*in half!* They completed their work in the dining room, living room, kitchen, or local library instead of in the bedroom, and they began to see their bedroom as a place for rest and relaxation.

These girls recognized that the line between working and socializing was increasingly blurred, especially when it came to collaborative projects and integrated learning. A group video chat with three friends about a school project ostensibly turned social, so the collaborative group project took longer than expected. One girl felt especially guilty for being offline during her homework block and not immediately answering a friend who needed help on an assignment. She reframed her thinking to recognize that she would be better able to help her friend once her own work was completed.

Our draconian measures of compartmentalization motivated the girls after they saw the benefits of putting the habits and structure into place in their daily lives. They began to better understand the law of diminishing returns: That is, their ability to complete work productively waned after spending a few hours online, and they became more easily distracted when they were tired. I encouraged them to think about our work like a game to maximize productivity, with the ultimate goal of having more time for things they enjoyed (including sleep). They realized that, for most of them, two hours of focused work was equivalent to more than four to six hours of work with distractions—except that with distractions they were also more likely to make mistakes. Within weeks, they all seemed more cheerful, open, and engaged—and they were motivated to find even more strategies to encourage self-regulation and compartmentalization.

EXERCISE

For educators, parents, and students: What are your (or your students') biggest distractions? Are specific apps or online sites more distracting than others?

STRESS: THE ART OF MONOTASKING AND ENCOURAGING PERSONAL PRODUCTIVITY

My younger sister, Dr. Allia Griffin, teaches social justice, ethnic studies, and theatre classes to college students. As a teenager, Allia was admittedly easily distracted and quickly bored in classes, so as a lecturer, she goes to great lengths to keep things interesting—thoughtfully weaving videos, short reads, and interactive projects into classroom discussions in which everyone actively and openly participates. Her classes are usually oversubscribed with a waiting list.

One thing Allia doesn't allow in her classes are phones or computers—she puts this requirement on the syllabus and reminds students at the beginning of every class. The topics they discuss in class are nuanced and challenging, and she knows that a student who's texting in the middle of class will quickly become lost. So, in the rare event that she does see a student on his or her phone, she skillfully, without missing a beat of her lecture, reminds the student to put away the device. She does this without interrupting her train of thought, and her students, for the most part, quickly get used to the tech-free classroom environment. On a recent teacher evaluation, a student remarked she had never had a teacher be so stringent about maintaining a tech-free classroom, and the student really appreciated the way it changed the classroom dynamic.

I am clearly not arguing for all classes to be tech-free. But one of the most important things teachers can do is to be explicit about expectations and tell students when technology is to be used in class and when it is to be put away. Students with learning differences should, of course, always be allowed their accommodations to help them thrive in the classroom. Regardless of whether or not students are using computers or tablets, each teacher should work to create some structure and expectations for learning inside and outside of the classroom.

Today's students live in a world of mini-multitasking. Merely scheduling time to do work using a written planner, or hoping students pay attention in class, doesn't do much when a student has seven different screens up and is being bombarded with different messages and notifications. Students who are listening to a lecture while managing two text conversations, checking social media, and seeing if the shoes they want are now on sale aren't able to process any of those things properly, and the mini-multitasking results in decreased productivity and increased exhaustion.

Much of this book is about how to help students compartmentalize and monotask, or focus on one task at a time. My goal is for students, teachers, and parents to recognize how compartmentalizing can increase productivity and decrease stress. For many people, compartmentalization and monotasking are underdeveloped skills that need to be developed over time. At first, it can feel uncomfortable, in a skin-crawling kind of way. But, I've had students with diagnosed attention-deficit/hyperactivity disorder (ADHD) tell me they use the same strategies learned as a teenager in my office at their full-time job years later. There are certainly long-term benefits to learning these techniques early.

Consider the following simple study and workflow strategies:

- *Use dual screens.* Having dual screens for "work" and "social" can create a mindset of compartmentalization. On a work screen, all social media and other related sites are signed out of and potentially even blocked. The ultimate goal is to use the work screen to help maintain a sense of focus. Variations can be made for individual needs. For instance, some students put all potentially distracting apps in one digital folder. Most schools that issue tablets to students block the download of certain games and other distractions (this is by no means a foolproof solution, but it does provide some structure). Having students identify their own distractions and their best solutions for compartmentalization is an important first step.

- *Try the Pomodoro Technique.* I generally recommend that middle school students spend ninety minutes to two hours per day on homework, and that high school students spend around two hours per day on homework (as with everything, this varies depending on many factors). For some students, two hours of homework seems like an extreme amount; for others, it seems like not nearly enough time. More often than not, though, when students start using monotasking and compartmentalization strategies, their homework gets done more quickly. The key is to work ahead on days when there isn't much homework that needs to be done immediately.

  For some students, it can seem overwhelming to work for a ninety-minute or two-hour block. Using the *Pomodoro Technique* and spending twenty-five minutes of uninterrupted, focused time on one task, followed by a five-minute break, seems far more manageable. During the five-minute break, students should get up, walk around, go to the bathroom, get a snack, or the like, but should stay off social media and refrain from checking messages. Otherwise, those five-minute breaks can quickly become forty-five-minute breaks without so much as a second thought.

- *Use technology to encourage compartmentalization.* Even though much of this book focuses on the ways social media and technology can provide students (and adults) with some of their biggest distractions, there are also wonderful tools to encourage compartmentalization. I often use the Forest app on my phone when I am writing because it helps me to stay focused for a set amount of time. While my phone remains untouched, a digital tree will grow. If I try to use my phone, I'm given a reminder along the lines of "Go back to the Forest immediately to avoid killing the tree!" It really works. Many writers use Freedom to block out distractions while they're trying to work on the computer. I turn off my Wi-Fi as a simple solution. Table 5.1 lists several productivity apps. By the time you're reading this book, some will likely be defunct and new ones will be available. The key to any app that encourages compartmentalization is simplicity: It should be easy to use and ideally encourages a single-task focus.

- *Evaluate online versus paper study methods.* Online websites and apps such as Quizlet enable students to create digital flashcards and quizzes that are portable and easily accessible. Students can type in the information they are trying to remember, and the online tool will come up with a quiz to test their memory. This system works well for some students, but for others, writing down the information on an index card or taking the time to come up with their own review sheet may be more effective for their comprehension and retention.[3] Research indicates that writing down information can improve retention, so it truly comes down to what works best for each student.[4]

- *Find ways to avoid toggling.* One of the benefits of using a tablet is that it's a lightweight alternative to lugging around four to five heavy textbooks. It enables students to store most of the information they need on one device. At the same time, when assignments are also stored on the tablet and students start toggling between the textbook and, for example, an online worksheet, the repeated mini-multitasking quickly becomes exhausting. Finding ways to avoid toggling is a key to encouraging compartmentalization and decreasing the stress associated with technology use. Sometimes split screens can be effective, but other times there is not enough space for either within the tablet screen, and another solution might be more effective. Printing out the worksheet, writing out the answers, and then scanning or taking a photo of the completed worksheet is one possibility. Keeping a physical textbook at home to use for homework (if possible) is another. The key is to find solutions to the literal and figurative headaches that come from nonstop toggling.

- *Create physical barriers to distraction.* Yondr is a lockable pouch that snuggly holds phones and completely blocks users from accessing and using them.[5] It was originally designed for concerts, theatrical performances, weddings, and other events that were to be designated cell phone free (musicians and Broadway actors are never happy to have a performance disrupted by a cell phone's notification sound or camera flash). The pouch is now used by schools that want to create a cell-phone-free environment, and for students, it could be a way to self-regulate when trying to stay free of distractions while getting work done.

EXERCISE

For educators, parents, and students: Look at Table 5.1, and pick two productivity apps that might be useful for your (or your students') needs. For instance, the Forest app can be used to focus on one task in a fun way, and Freedom can be used when you are working on a paper or an assignment that needs your full concentration but not an Internet connection.

TABLE 5.1   Apps to Help Students Manage Time, Increase Productivity, and Reduce Stress

APP	WHAT IS IT?	PROS	CONS
Forest (forestapp.cc)	Use to stay focused; set timer and the app grows trees while you work	Keeps you locked out of your phone for a time period you designate	Can be disabled by restarting phone
Freedom (freedom.to)	Disables access to the Internet to allow focus on an essay or for studying	Takes away the option of using the Internet to procrastinate	Does not work if access is needed for research; can reset by rebooting

(Continued)

TABLE 5.1 (Continued)

APP	WHAT IS IT?	PROS	CONS
Hocus Focus (Mac) (hocusfoc.us)	Makes inactive windows disappear from view, leaving the current window as the only one visible on the screen	Helps concentrate focus on current window because the inactive screen vanishes quietly from view	Not good if user needs to toggle between screens constantly
Moment (inthemoment.io)	Automatically tracks how much you use your iPhone and iPad each day; can use individually or Moment Family	Can set daily limits on use, set notifications when you exceed limits, and even force yourself off your device when over your limit	Over-limit notifications block screen if you've forced yourself off your phone; can still take phone calls
myHomework (myhomeworkapp.com)	Student-friendly all-in-one planner for school	Lots of useful features: tracks homework, sends reminders of items due, syncs information, tracks class schedule	So many features, app can be overwhelming
Research Project Calculator (rpc.elm4you.org)	Helps students create a schedule for completing an assignment or project based on the start date and due date	Gives concrete dates for when parts of a project need to be done; helps break down a large assignment into simple phases	Each phase can be too general; for example, if creating a video project, it doesn't give a breakdown of when each step should be done
SelfControl (Mac) (selfcontrolapp.com); Cold Turkey (PC) (getcoldturkey.com)	Blocks websites that a user designates as blacklisted	Great for those who are disciplined or have someone who will add the blocked websites (i.e., a parent)	Setup can take a while, as adding websites is a manual process

APP	WHAT IS IT?	PROS	CONS
Tomato Timer (a simple Pomodoro timer) (tomato-timer.com)	Use the Pomodoro Technique (25 minutes on, 5 minutes off) to alert users of when to focus on work	Easy-to-set timer; helps regulate the periods of productivity	None; choosing timer is a matter of individual interface preference
ZenFriend (zenfriend.com)	Use to track daily meditation; helps to build a daily practice	Meditation reduces anxiety and stress, while helping a person's overall ability to focus	None; easy to use and good for you!

FINDING FLEXIBILITY FOR DIFFERENT LEARNING STYLES

The beauty of today's technological advances in learning is that we have increased opportunity for personalization, and for individualized learning plans. To that end, the ideal learning environment is one in which students are encouraged to find and use the strategies that work best for them, and those best practices may or may not involve the latest and greatest technological innovations. For example, some students prefer to read and underline in physical textbooks rather than in digital versions. Others find it most reassuring when they can have all their assignments and related reading stored in one easily transportable tablet. I still read most books in physical form, underlining and annotating, and then store all my notes electronically. I prefer to outline much of my writing by hand before typing up the more detailed drafts. Each person has a style that works best for him or her, and learning and tinkering and discovering different styles of learning should be a celebrated part of the academic journey.

Promoting academic wellness with a student-centered philosophy focuses on giving students tools and allowing them to develop their own set of best practices. The strategies in this chapter work well for students with different learning styles and challenges, as well as for those diagnosed with ADHD and processing speed challenges. There are great alternatives that now blend the benefits of handwriting with the benefits of cloud storage. Moleskine's Smart Writing Set, for example, allows individuals to write and draw by hand and then instantly create online images and share them through a smartphone or tablet. Some students benefit from being able to listen to textbooks and other books instead of reading them, while others find that reading and listening at the same time improves their retention.

> The ideal learning environment is one in which students are encouraged to find and use the strategies that work best for them, and those best practices may or may not involve the latest and greatest technological innovations.

Our role as parents and educators is to empower students to use technology as a resource and to realize that it isn't the only resource. The ultimate goal should always be for students to maximize their own personal potential and figure out how they best learn, filter, and retain information. There is no one-size-fits-all approach, and there doesn't have to be. Flexibility may mean using a physical textbook and a piece of paper rather than toggling on a tablet, or creating virtual flashcards for foreign language class and using handwritten notes for math class. Some classes may benefit from online discussion groups where more introverted students might feel more comfortable sharing and discussing ideas. Recognizing how and where technological innovations work best for students, and reflecting on when and where low-tech options might be more effective, is one of our most challenging and pressing needs.

EXERCISE

For teachers: What is the role of technology in your classroom? In dinner parlance, is it the main course or a side dish? Is it used as an appetizer or dessert, or is it the entire meal? Do you provide options for those who may not want to do everything online? What high-tech and low-tech accommodations are available?

For students: Think about each of your classes. What are your most effective ways to learn and retain information for each class? Do you have a preference for digital or physical textbooks (if both are available)? How can you avoid toggling between screens?

THE CHEATING DILEMMA

Educators have long dealt with issues surrounding academic integrity, and new smartphone technology and cloud storage services, combined with an increased focus on collaborative class projects ("group work"), create new layers of complexity. If students are working on a project together, for instance, what type of collaboration is appropriate, and what is considered an academic violation? As the lines become more blurred, educators and administrators spend an increasing number of hours dealing with academic integrity issues. One high school expelled students who used an intricate Google Docs system to share homework and test answers. Another school discovered that homework answers were being copied when the dean of students accessed student email accounts to investigate unrelated harassment claims.

"There's now a copy/paste/screenshot culture," the dean of students explained to me, going on to describe how students use their school-issued email addresses (which can be monitored by administrators) to share answers, divide and conquer longer assignments that are not meant to be collaborative, and share screenshots of test questions with classmates taking an exam later in the day.

Though the more blatant acts of academic dishonesty seem fairly straightforward, the sheer volume of available information now creates new opportunities for misunderstanding and unintentional violations. It seems nearly impossible for a high school student to come up with a completely new and radical thematic understanding of books like *Pride and Prejudice* or *The Scarlett Letter*—both frequently found on my high school students' reading lists. Software programs like Turnitin focus on finding papers that plagiarize the words of others, but how do we help students understand the subtleties surrounding the use of others' ideas? When is it deemed inappropriate to do so? Schools need to proactively help students understand what constitutes plagiarism and cheating beyond the most basic principles, and understand that information overload might make it seem more challenging for a student to develop a completely independent thought around certain texts (even more of a reason for teachers to teach less-known readings). I've come to learn two things through my experiences: One, we all need to do a better job of identifying up front what constitutes academic dishonesty and, two, schools need to create an ongoing dialogue with students about what they deem appropriate and inappropriate. Even though there are likely some pull-through similarities, each school and teacher may have differences on what is considered appropriate, and that needs to be clear to students.

There are no easy answers for questions surrounding academic integrity, and the range of academic, social, and emotional issues that encourage cheating is far beyond the scope and focus of this book. At the same time, some of the issues relate to the way in which we approach our conversations with students, highlighted in Chapter 4. Why do students choose to cheat? What is the intention (e.g., to save time, to get good grades)? Do they think it is no big deal? Are they tempted by the thrill of risking getting caught? What are their own values around their own learning and abilities? Students often justify their decision to cheat with a host of excuses, some of which are rooted in fear, shame, and security. Some do so simply because of a brazen "just because I can" mindset. Other times, students may not believe their behavior constitutes cheating. Some of the stress around altered expectations, and the mixed messages students receive around the focus on grades and scores rather than overall learning, comprehension, and good habits, can also play a role. At the core, when students feel overwhelmed because they don't have adequate systems in place to process and learn information, they may feel as though the ends of getting good grades justify and excuse the means.

As schools work to build guidelines around appropriate use, providing guidelines on what is and is not defined as cheating, establishing a clear set of consequences, and creating an overall focus on learning, process, and good habits can help to promote academic wellness.

EXERCISE

For educators: What are your school's guidelines around academic dishonesty and cheating? What are the consequences, and what is the difference between an appropriate collaborative exercise and an inappropriate violation of academic integrity? Do different teachers have different rules, or is academic integrity interpreted similarly across academic departments? In terms of papers, are guidelines for appropriate and inappropriate citations and use given to students?

For students: Why do students at your school cheat, and what do you think the main factors are that encourage them to do so? If you cheat, what motivates you to do so? What are your school's guidelines around academic dishonesty and cheating? What are the consequences, and what is the difference between appropriate collaboration and academic dishonesty? In terms of writing a paper, what are the guidelines around appropriate citations?

SUMMARY

Academic wellness incorporates how students organize tasks and manage workflow in a world full of potential distractions. The many components of academic wellness include the following:

- *Organization.* Encouraging students to learn how to create digital folders and physical binders, and how to track assignments using a written planner

- *Daily/weekly regrouping.* Giving students a regular structured time each day or week to help them go through all assignments, file and store information as needed, reflect on the previous week, and plan out the upcoming week

- *Time and energy management.* Allowing students to focus on where work is completed, how it is completed, and what distractions can affect productivity

- *Productivity hacks.* Using apps such as Pomodoro, Forest, or Moment to encourage students to manage distractions

Helping students build organization and time- and energy-management skills is the foundational first step to encourage them to focus, manage distractions, monotask, and find solutions for the mundane tasks that typically build up stress. Use Table 5.1 as a resource to identify potential solutions, and take time to research new productivity apps that may have become available since this book's publication. Work with students to figure out their individualized learning styles, and help them find solutions for how to organize their work, identify when and how they work best, and understand what tools they need in order to focus on their own growth and development.

CHAPTER 6

Social and Emotional Wellness

Encouraging Students to Be Healthy Online and in Real Life

A few days after Sara's knee surgery for her torn ACL, I called to check up on her progress and recovery. Sara was a diligent student and star soccer player, and I knew she was concerned about how the surgery might affect her academic performance and athletic prospects. Highly motivated and ambitious, Sara devised a full plan to catch up on all her missed work, working with a tutor to make sure she understood calculus despite missing class and maintaining a strenuous physical therapy regimen to get herself back on the field as soon as possible. I also wanted to make sure she rested and took care of herself.

"How are things going socially and emotionally?" I asked her mom, Cathy, knowing that Sara was not a young woman who liked to rest.

"She's doing okay," Cathy replied, "though last Sunday was rough. She shed more than a few tears." Cathy went on to explain that the tears were not from residual knee pain, but rather from friendship pains.

"Her friends told her they would stop by on their way to the Festival of Lights Parade," Cathy explained, referencing the huge holiday parade that envelops the streets outside my office every year on the Sunday after Thanksgiving. The parade is old-fashioned community fun, attracting over 30,000 spectators to our small downtown area as floats, high school marching bands, and holiday characters like Santa Claus and Frosty the Snowman parade down the street. "A half-hour before the parade was set to start, one of the girls sent her a text and said they decided not to go [to the parade] and wouldn't be stopping by after all. Sara was disappointed, but teenage plans change."

She paused. "An hour or so later, Sara saw the girls' posts on Instagram. They *had* gone to the parade. Sara was pretty devastated." I could feel the hurt in Cathy's voice as she continued, "Sara considers these girls to be close friends, and to find out they lied by seeing the Instagram posts—I felt so sad for her. I didn't know what to say."

I don't believe the girls intended to act maliciously toward Sara. More than likely, they were teenagers who were running late, had trouble finding parking, ran into people they knew, and suddenly felt as though they didn't have time to walk over to Sara's house. Of course, their decision lacked empathy (and basic civility). The girls probably chose to send a quick text to cancel instead of calling and potentially hearing the disappointment in Sara's voice. The simple truth may be that sophisticated digital tools (social media apps, cell phone cameras, and the like) don't take teenage behavior and decision-making skills into account. In all likelihood, Sara's friends just didn't think about anything other than themselves at that moment. While her friends' behavior was disheartening and disappointing, Sara also needed help to keep the incident in perspective so that it didn't seem bigger than it actually was—which can seem nearly impossible when endless hours of social media interactions provide fodder for nonstop interpretation.

One of the key issues for social media wellness is helping tweens and teens decide what they should and should not spend time worrying about. In the end, some things are not worth agonizing over, even when social media provides the opportunity for constant reminders.

As well, we underestimate how much seemingly small pings of communication—making last-minute changes, chronicling events instead of simply enjoying moments—combine to redefine socialization as we know it. Smartphone apps and text messaging make it so easy to get in touch (and stay connected) with others, but there's a rarely considered downside to how easy it has become to change or cancel plans. Social media socialization redefines how tweens and teens develop and maintain friendships and intimate relationships. In many ways, everything is experienced twice—there's the online experience, which can be presented a certain way, and the in-person experience, which may or may not correlate. For tweens and teens, this navigation of dual experiences affects social and emotional wellness, often in ways we don't fully appreciate and address.

To be sure, social media socialization can enrich friendships by allowing for a wider sharing of ideas and information. For adults, asking a question on Facebook or Twitter could potentially crowdsource ideas from the friend you haven't seen since the third grade or the former neighbor who moved away five years ago. I've seen journalists and authors gather research online for upcoming stories and books, and seen apartments rented and jobs filled through online friends-of-friends connections that combine to make the world seem that much smaller and friendlier.

> Social media socialization redefines how tweens and teens develop and maintain friendships and intimate relationships. In many ways, everything is experienced twice—there's the online experience, which can be presented a certain way, and the in-person experience, which may or may not correlate. For tweens and teens, this navigation of dual experiences affects social and emotional wellness, often in ways we don't fully appreciate and address.

At the same time, it is important to understand how social media can prevent tweens and teens from experiencing crucial social and emotional growth and development. The latest real-time apps provide increased opportunities to make careless and reckless choices without consideration of longer-term impacts, and an expectation of instant gratification can undermine patience and incremental progress. With so much going on at once, today's tweens and teens struggle to make sense of it all.

As Cathy shared Sara's experience with her friends, I wondered if anyone would talk to those girls about the bigger impact of their decision that evening. Would Sara tell them how she felt when she saw the photos on Instagram? Would Cathy mention the incident to the girls' parents, who likely had no idea what transpired? Unless Cathy or Sara spoke up, the girls might never fully realize the impact of their choices, and their parents wouldn't be able to use the incident to initiate a greater conversation around kindness and civility. At the same time, should Cathy or Sara devote their time and energy to addressing this issue, or should they simply move on? There are so many ways to see this incident—and there's not necessarily one right or wrong approach. Similar to the academic issues discussed in Chapter 5, we haven't fully addressed how to promote social and emotional wellness within the new culture of online socialization, and how to do so in a way that doesn't blow everything out of proportion. Indeed, the Golden Rule of treating others as we want to be treated seems to have become unnecessarily complicated, but it doesn't have to be.

THE NEW LANGUAGE OF SOCIAL MEDIA SOCIALIZATION

While writing this book, I presented a keynote talk entitled "Social Media and Our Own Wellness" to a group of three hundred mothers and their teen daughters. I often hear from students who feel as though they are constantly "lectured" about the negative effects of social media, so in this talk I chose to take another approach.

I started out by sharing stories about how social media has positively impacted my life. I started with the story about how I was once about to board a Sunday evening flight and checked Facebook to find an urgent message from an Associated Press reporter who had sent me the message after failing to hear back from my book publicist. The reporter wanted to interview me and was on a tight deadline, so I sat in the boarding lounge for a few extra minutes and completed the interview before the flight. Within thirty-six hours, an article about my first book, *That Crumpled Paper Was Due Last Week*, and my related work was distributed to hundreds of newspapers and digital sites—a pleasant surprise, and something that might not have happened had I not quickly returned her message.

After sharing a few more stories (including the time I was featured in a *New York Times* piece after tweeting to a parenting columnist), I felt as though I had been successful in engaging the entire audience.

"But," I continued, "and you knew there was a but coming, right?"

The mothers in the crowd laughed as I continued. "There's more to our social media world than meets the eye. It affects all of us more than we realize. . . ." I went on to dissect some of the ways social media socialization affects our social and romantic relationships, as well as our familial ties. Our connections can certainly be potentially positive and energizing, like the personal stories that I shared. At the same time, there are more opportunities for toxic, nonstop, draining experiences. I use the term *filtering* to describe two very different aspects of social media socialization: one, how people can literally filter out the seeming imperfections of everyday life in their online postings and, two, how we can choose to proactively engage in ("filter in") positive prosocial experiences *and* disengage from ("filter out") toxic, draining, and potentially humiliating conversations and experiences.

Today's tweens and teens haven't been given adequate social and emotional tools to deal with the negative feedback, shame, and humiliation that can be part of social media socialization. When someone sends a nasty and mean message, it can have an insidious effect on an entire day. This feeling is not limited to tweens and teens—how many times has a curt email or brusque online comment felt a bit jarring? Even the smallest misinterpretation has the potential for unintended side effects. Without having the tools needed to avoid, address, process, and move past potential hurt and humiliation, students can turn to negative compensatory behaviors to try to anesthetize the very real hurt experienced online and felt in real life.

As I spoke with the mothers and daughters about how time online impacts real life energy and wellness, I felt an uncomfortable silence envelop the room. Every mother and daughter seemed to be collectively sharing a knowing, painful acknowledgment. The underemphasized truth is that our online and in-real-life worlds are far more interconnected than we've been led to believe. Social media is *designed* to be addictive, and it creates a secondary cultural language that affects norms regarding what we consider appropriate, thus consciously and subconsciously affecting how we treat others and how we treat ourselves. We've become so fixated and hooked on the addictive qualities of social media—the dopamine release that happens when we receive a text message or our photo is liked—that we don't always realize we have a choice in how and when to engage— and how and when to disengage.

At the end of my talk, a mom in the front row blurted out, "Wait, what is a Snapchat streak?!"

That question reaffirmed the critical cultural divide that we have yet to address effectively. It might not seem like a big deal that the mom didn't know what a Snapchat streak was, but nearly every one of the hundred and eighty or so teen girls in that room had at least one ongoing Snapchat streak. Of course, it could be argued that by the time parents maintain a few of their own Snapchat streaks, their children might be off Snapchat altogether. There's probably some truth to that, but even so, that shouldn't prevent parents from being better informed. Although cultural divides have nearly always existed between one generation and the next, the vast quantities of content and the multitude of new ways in which information is accessed and disseminated make the current situation critically different.

Today's tweens and teens try to navigate questions like, "What does that emoji mean?" "Did he mean to send me that emoji?" "Does it mean what I think it means?" and "Why didn't she respond to my text yet?" These sorts of questions reveal today's newly blurred lines between what defines friendships and romantic relationships that are healthy and those that are not. Young people who believe their parents have no idea what today's modern courtship entails reflexively look to their peers (and the Internet) for advice. And good outcomes rarely result from a sixth grader asking another sixth grader or an anonymous bevy of YouTube or Tumblr users for advice about potential romances or sex.

There is a great deal to be gained—and lost—in today's culture of social media socialization. To address tweens' and teens' social and emotional wellness, we must wholeheartedly accept and appreciate that there can indeed be positive benefits to using social media. Now, more than ever, it is easier to connect with others around the world, and it is easier to access information about local, national, and global issues. There is also an expanded opportunity for a greater sense of community and support. Many online communities provide supportive reassurance to others in a way that is meaningful and transformative, regardless of whether users have ever met in person or even know others' true identities. Tweens and teens experiencing issues related to sexuality, divorce, or health and wellness may feel more comfortable being vulnerable within an online community, particularly anonymously, than in person with classmates they see every day.

At the same time, the online experience opens up tweens and teens to a plethora of experiences they may not be socially and emotionally prepared to handle. The new lines of messaging communication create confusion around what values and qualities constitute healthy communication within friendships or romantic relationships. For instance, many preteens and teens use the term *talking* to constitute an exploration of a potential romantic relationship ("Jimmy and Alana are talking"). During discussions with high school students, I often pose this question: Are you really "talking" with someone if you only send text messages or Snaps to one another, and never communicate face-to-face when you see one another in the hallway at school? Students are typically somewhat split on this question, without a clear consensus of opinion. Some students readily believe they can be in a healthy, intimate relationship with a person who walks by them without even exchanging a basic greeting—as long as there was consistent online communication. I am not convinced.

Perhaps most simply, a world focused on social media socialization misses the spontaneity and seeming magic of free-flowing face-to-face conversation. In *Reclaiming Conversation*, Sherry Turkle describes how text messaging may seem quicker and more efficient, but it also has the potential to make everything more transactional and less personal.[1] Two individuals conversing over video chat carry themselves differently than those sitting next to one another in a coffee shop or on a park bench. Stream-of-consciousness conversations usually rely on a combination of tone, expression, and body language, all of which are severely limited or nonexistent in text messages, photos, and even video chat. As a result, social media socialization has the potential to become more transactional in nature. Many of my students increasingly express anxiety and concern about having in-person conversations with friends, teachers, or parents when the topics might feel awkward or uncomfortable, and over the years, I've had to role-play more and more conversations with parents, school counselors, and teachers. Some of this stress results from the lack of regular, daily practice in the art of conversation, as a great deal of communication has now transferred to the written or visual world. There is a big difference between receiving a smiley-faced emoji and having a friend look into your eyes and say, "Thank you so much for all your help. I appreciate you." There's a certain beauty to the in-person, fully present conversation that is now seemingly becoming a lost art, and needs to be intentionally rediscovered.

HOW SOCIAL MEDIA AFFECTS FRIENDSHIPS, RELATIONSHIPS, AND PERSONALITY DEVELOPMENT

When Jamila described her "huge" fight with Amy, I needed clarification that all the insults and full-blown condescension (*Amy to Jamila:* "You have to realize that no one really likes you, and I now realize why") occurred over Snapchat messaging. Amy and Jamila were once middle school classmates, and when Jamila's family moved away, the two kept in touch by sending photos and messages on social media. They were now high school freshmen and hadn't seen each other in person for over eight months. The girls used Snapchat to "fight via messaging" in an argument that went on for an hour and left Jamila restless and unable to sleep. I was unclear exactly what the fight was about, though I knew they had an "explosive friendship" filled with drawn-out arguments and draining drama. To Jamila, this fight had ended the friendship.

So, imagine Jamila's surprise the next morning when Amy had sent her a Snap.[2] Understandably confused, Jamila soon realized Amy's motivation: their sixty-two-day Snapchat streak.

Social media can make it more difficult to let go of friendships that have run their course—unfriending or unfollowing someone can seem extreme, so the trickle effects of communication continue long after a friendship has ended, morphing into a form of "friendship bloat," a term I use to describe the misappropriated time and energy. Not every person is destined to become a lifelong friend, and research indicates that most Americans have three to four close friends (and hundreds or thousands of Facebook friends).[3] An ongoing Snapchat streak with someone barely considered an acquaintance is a terrific example of friendship bloat.

"Amy didn't want to be the one to break our streak," Jamila explained. Snapchat streaks encourage friendship bloat and social media addiction: As the streaks become longer, the stakes feel higher and no one wants to break the streak.

The confusion increases dramatically when it comes to romantic and intimate relationships, as today's tweens and teens (and young adults) are forced to navigate far more potential minefields. Many tweens and teens are desperate to know how to appropriately and safely experience intimate relationships online and in real life at a time when anything sent privately can easily become public. Greater access to sexually explicit material and pornography challenge perceptions around healthy relationships and sexuality, and it is easy to underestimate how much that affects social, emotional, and physical health. Much has been written about the effect of online pornography on intimate relationships and expectations around sexual performance, and how explicit images and videos affect tween and teen views on relationship development and physical intimacy. In her 2016 book *Girls and Sex*, journalist Peggy Orenstein notes, "The Internet has made porn more prevalent and accessible than at any time in history, especially to teens."[4] She cites research suggesting that over 40 percent of children between the ages of ten and seventeen have been exposed to online pornography, many times accidentally.[5] Parents and educators are often dumbfounded when tweens and teens send explicit photos or watch online pornography as a source of sex education. It is difficult for many parents to understand and accept that the desire for intimacy, belonging, and connection is often at the root of many questionable decisions to send explicit personal photos.[6] There is also a focus on promoting fear around potential consequences to encourage better decision making. After all, the viral nature of explicit photos can cause shame and humiliation (more often for girls), and depending on the jurisdiction, tweens and teens can be charged with trafficking of child pornography for sending explicit photos of themselves and others. This is a much more complicated legal issue than most parents realize, and law enforcement officers who deal with child pornography often advise that parents have an *obligation* to randomly check photos on their child's cell phone.

Parents often worry about invading their child's privacy, but proactive work to avoid the potential lifelong consequences of sending or storing explicit photos is well worth the downside. In California, taking a photo, sending a photo, and storing a photo (in an app or on a phone's storage device) are all separate potential felony counts of child pornography,[7] and those convicted are typically required to register as sex offenders. At sleepovers and get-togethers, kids might think posing and taking photos in compromising situations is funny, but there can be long-term legal repercussions. My tip for parents is to gather all the phones and store them away in a basket at the beginning of any sleepover.

Some parents believe they should be able to trust their kids until they have reason to believe otherwise, but that can sometimes come too late. For instance, parents often don't realize that explicit photos are typically stored in hidden apps and that there are a number of apps that look like and function like calculators on a phone (including Private Calculator, Calculator+, Secret Calculator Folder) but that are actually password-protected hidden vaults for photo storage.

It seems straightforward to provide tweens and teens with guidelines and rules for online behavior and social media use, and for some tweens and teens, having that framework of understanding is enough to influence their daily behavioral choices. At the same time, parents need to help kids develop their own definitive reasons for not getting drawn into bad situations as a result of peer pressure. Parents often overlook the importance of having regular discussions with their kids about feelings, intimacy, and prosocial and compassionate decision making. Unless we take the time to help tweens and teens to identify and understand their own whys for social media use—which I discuss in the next section—and help them develop their own critical thinking skills, we are missing the opportunity to help students create a strong foundation for long-term social and emotional wellness.

Research suggests that teens' increased time spent online contributes to increased narcissistic behaviors and potentially affects healthy personality development.[8] The exploration of identity and self is a healthy and normal part of the developmental process, and tweens and teens generally create profiles and share photos and other posts as a way of experimenting with their own evolving identity development. These behaviors become unhealthy when developmentally appropriate identity formation is hijacked by a tween or teen's addiction to feedback and craving of likes, loves, and (positive) comments, and he or she becomes reactive to what generates the most favorable response, rather than what reflects his or her own values and interests. If we want to help our next generation become more empathetic, understanding, and purposeful, we need to address social media socialization in a way that focuses on socialization, self-regulation, and safety in the context of social and emotional wellness.

HELPING STUDENTS
FIGURE OUT THEIR "WHY"

Students juggling multiple online social experiences—trading messages via Instagram and Messenger while sending and receiving Snaps and communicating via WhatsApp—creates the internal experience of having twenty-seven screens open on a computer and not knowing where to start. In short, an overwhelming amount of information is bombarding them at once, and they don't know how to process it. The on-all-the-time mentality doesn't allow students to step back, reflect, and prioritize their friendships and relationships, and they quickly fall into the trap of thinking that everything needs to be answered or responded to or consumed right away. Being on all the time leads to exhaustion, which, combined with a fear of missing out, contributes to a lack of impulse control and diminishes a young person's ability to self-regulate.

Tweens and teens have few guideposts to decode the increasingly blurred lines and confusing nuances around friendships and intimate relationships. Does being a good friend mean being constantly available to answer Snaps? What constitutes a friend emergency? Can someone be a friend if you've never met in person? Some video gamers consider their closest friends to be gamers they play with online everyday but have never met in person. Many gamers hold their responsibility to their teammates in high regard. Lucas, an avid high school gamer, explained that he would feel as though he let his friends down if he wasn't online and ready to play as planned. "They're counting on me," he reflected empathetically, with a sense of loyalty that would often be seen as a value in a deep-rooted friendship.

I always encourage students to step back and figure out their "*why*" when it comes to social media use. Why are they spending time on their phone or online in general? Is it for fun, to make friends, or to feel a sense of belonging? Are they going online out of boredom, anxiety, fear, or a need for a break from real life? When they go into a room or stand in a line and don't know anyone, why do they pull out their phone? (Everyone does this, by the way. I turned around in my local coffee shop to find a line ten people deep, and every single one of them was on their phone.) Is it out of habit? Loneliness? Fear of standing alone and not knowing what to do? Many tweens and teens want to feel included, and they don't always realize how their daily choices and behavior can reduce their ability to make and maintain meaningful connections. A few minutes spent quietly in line can be reenergizing, whereas checking a phone constantly to pass the time can quickly become draining—especially if the messages received or news consumed is fraught with conflict.

As Sherry Turkle notes in *Reclaiming Conversation*, research suggests that the mere presence of a phone on the table decreases the empathy between individuals sitting together.[9] And because social media likes and approval have been shown to result in an addictive dopamine release, checking your phone to see who has liked or commented on a photo or posting can quickly become addictive.[10] Consequently, stepping back to identify "why" is so crucial, as is figuring out ways to prevent addiction.

Simply encouraging tweens and teens to ask themselves "why" every time they pull out their phone helps them become more intentional and conscious of their behavior. Some phone settings allow users to see how much time is spent on any one app, and that also helps increase awareness. Over time, I've seen many tweens and teens resisting the urge to check their phone every two to three minutes, simply by asking themselves "why?"

In my office, I regularly see how increased awareness, combined with relevant data, can encourage behavioral change. For instance, students who want to improve their academic performance to get their parents "off their back" become motivated to use the Forest and Moment apps to complete their work more efficiently. Not having to listen to their parents nagging and lecturing is an added benefit that one student described as "priceless."

EXERCISE

Ask students to download the Moment app and for three to seven days track their "why" for each time they pick up their phone. Have students note when they picked up their phone to avoid doing a homework assignment or task, or to procrastinate in general. When did the phone or computer act as a safety blanket?

ENCOURAGING STUDENTS TO DEFINE QUALITIES OF HEALTHY RELATIONSHIPS

The One Love Foundation was founded to honor Yeardley Love, a University of Virginia student-athlete who was murdered in May 2010. One Love's mission is to educate young people about relationship violence and to encourage young adults to develop four qualities that Yeardley exemplified: service, kindness, humility, and sportsmanship. To that end, the foundation created a curriculum and workshops focused on preventing relationship violence and developed related social media campaigns. The foundation's first widespread social media campaign, #ThatsNotLove, focuses on defining what qualities are and are not part of healthy relationships. Although the One Love Foundation's main focus is on preventing relationship violence, its underlying mission is to promote healthier relationships.

Melanie Sperling, program coordinator at the One Love Foundation, explains that many times a teen's decision to send an explicit sexting photo is not the result of a one-time inquiry.[11] Often, teens are asked repeatedly and badgered several times until they give in and send the explicit photo. One of the key takeaways of the One Love Foundation curriculum is that receiving pressuring messages that don't respect boundaries can be a sign of an unhealthy relationship. The One Love "Escalation" film shows how seemingly innocent, flirty text messages can quickly turn unhealthy and abusive. When One Love runs workshops at secondary schools and colleges, they often find that students—male and female—are desperate and excited to talk about these issues, in part because the defining qualities of healthy and unhealthy relationships—romantic or otherwise—have become blurred in our always-on, always-more world.

EXERCISE

Ask students, either individually or in groups, to think about the qualities of healthy and unhealthy friendships. What examples of social media or in-real-life behaviors can be seen as healthy or unhealthy? Who are the people they can turn to when they feel a friendship or relationship has potentially become unhealthy?

RECOGNIZING NEGATIVE COMPENSATORY BEHAVIORS

In my book *The Myth of the Perfect Girl*, I describe negative compensatory behaviors as anything that takes attention away from an issue instead of addressing it directly. For instance, individuals can turn to drinking, drug use, cutting, unhealthy sexual relationships, video games, and Internet/social media addiction instead of dealing with issues involving anxiety, fear, depression, and academic and social insecurity.[12] Even seemingly healthy choices like exercising or eating well can turn into negative compensatory behaviors when there is an unhealthy focus or need for control. For example, a student who feels overwhelmed by his schoolwork and his parents' impending divorce could avoid dealing with those concerns by spending hours every day playing video games. Playing the video games by himself or with other gamers provides him a temporary escape from the pain he would rather ignore, makes him feel powerful and in control of his online domain, and gives him a sense of community he might not feel at school or at home.

I am not saying that all students who use video games are engaging in negative compensatory behavior, though most addictions develop as an escape from or compensation for something else. Our culture has made Internet and social media obsession an acceptable compensatory behavior, even though it can mask feelings of loneliness and emptiness just like alcohol or drug abuse.

In addition to helping tweens and teens understand their "why" around social media use, it is also important to help them recognize when social media and Internet use becomes a negative compensatory behavior, and help them instead proactively identify appropriate resources for when they need assistance. A student who doesn't understand a homework assignment could spend hours on Instagram and Snapchat instead of finding ways to better understand the material. Another student could spend hours playing video games when he feels depressed about a relationship breakup.

When students understand the difference between proactive and reactive behaviors, they realize that they always have choices about how they respond to setbacks and disappointments. Over time, increased awareness encourages them to proactively address issues instead of hiding behind negative compensatory behaviors.

UNDERSTANDING CONNECTION VERSUS ISOLATION

Friendships and relationships shift and change for a variety of reasons, and maintaining multiple clusters of connection enables us to find different ways to feel a sense of belonging and inclusiveness. These clusters of connection provide students with multiple opportunities to develop a crucial sense of engagement and belonging. For instance, one teen could find supportive friends on her club soccer team, in her church youth group, at her school service club, and among her cousins who she sees once a month. Even if something goes awry with the friends on her soccer team, she still has three other clusters of connection to turn to for support and validation. Teens with only one close friend or friend group may feel isolated when the lone friend moves away or a friend group disbands or starts to do things without them. Ideally, at least a few of the communities where a tween or teen finds connection would be in real life, but that may not always be possible. In many cases, online groups or communities, or communicating with friends who have relocated elsewhere, can provide a sense of connection that might otherwise be missing. At the same time, online and in-real-life experiences should complement one another. An obsession with being online that keeps someone from having in-person experiences can be socially and emotionally damaging.

Schools of thought vary on whether or not increased social media use gives a feeling of more connectedness or one of isolation. In my experience, either can be true, depending on the context and the content.

In *It's Complicated*, danah boyd argues that increased social media use is more likely to give teens an increased sense of connection.[13] In some cases, that can certainly be true. In a recent research study of social media use among teen girls, 56 percent of girls surveyed felt more connected to some friends and 44 percent of girls believed they made new friends through their use of various social networking platforms.[14] In line with these findings, 48 percent felt as though they could be more honest with one another online than they could in face-to-face interactions.[15] For students living in geographically isolated areas, or not attending a conventional school because of illness or other reasons, social media can serve as a lifeline. This is not to say that online exploration is completely safe or that it doesn't leave them vulnerable in some way. It simply means that some social media platforms can give some tweens and teens a sense of belonging where it once didn't exist.

At the same time (and sometimes within the same social media platform), increased social media use can easily make teens feel more isolated. There is a voyeuristic quality to liking and commenting on an Instagram photo of a friend who lives cross-country, and even though it may provide a sense of connection, absent is the shared intimacy that might be felt during a quiet lunch conversation or a lakeside chat. Scrolling through photos of classmates at a pool party might spark a heightened sense of isolation if a teen wasn't invited and/or couldn't attend. A report by Common Sense Media found that 57 percent of girls and 28 percent of boys tend to feel left out when seeing photos of others online. This preoccupation with social involvement can affect personal and educational development in ways we have yet to fully recognize or address.[16]

In a study published in *Developmental Psychology*, Stanford researcher Clifford Nass and his team found that for girls between the ages of eight and twelve, there seems to be a correlation between girls' multitasking, social media use, and overall well-being. According to his research, girls who spend more time online multitasking, and switching between different apps or programs, as well as those who spend time socializing and watching videos, tend to feel less overall social success and are less likely to feel "normal."[17] The antidote to alleviate this social anxiety was found to be fairly straightforward. Spending less time online and more time having face-to-face conversations and interactions helps students interpret others' social cues, which can remedy the frequent misinterpretations or misunderstandings that occur during an extended online conversation and can contribute to feelings of loneliness and isolation.

CLOSING THE EMPATHY GAP AND CULTIVATING COMPASSION

Early in her book *Reclaiming Conversation*, researcher Sherry Turkle describes how today's digital communication has led to a "crisis in empathy" among young people and adults.[18] Parents and educators rightfully worry about how increased time in front of a screen affects social and emotional intelligence. Research suggests that communicating from behind a screen decreases empathy toward others, which suggests why some people feel emboldened to say things online that they would never say in person.[19] Many observers argue that this crisis is linked to research showing that more time spent using media leads to increases in depression and anxiety and, in many cases, also decreases productivity.[20] It's the dark side of the potential benefits that Susan Cain describes in *Quiet:* It can be wonderful for students to have a new way of communicating, unless they feel emboldened to behave in a way that lacks civility, humanity, empathy, and compassion.[21]

FIGURE 6.1 Sample Cluster of Connection

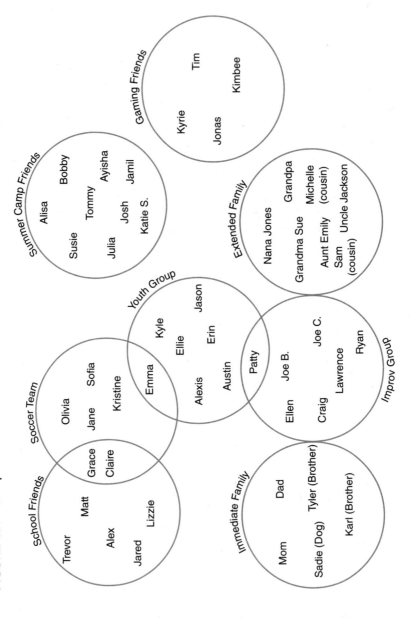

It is important to highlight the difference between empathy and compassion. Empathy is defined as the ability to share and understand the feelings of another person and is often developed by seeing a person's face and reaction—looking at emojis and abbreviations rarely evokes the same reaction as seeing tears rolling down another person's face or hearing a warm-hearted laugh. Compassion not only focuses on understanding the suffering of others but also incorporates a desire to alleviate that pain and suffering. When students are using more technology in the classroom and at home, what can we do to encourage them to develop empathy and compassion for others online and in real life? The first step is to encourage students to make time for quiet self-reflection and self-compassion. Self-reflection is often most powerful when removed from the rush of noise and content, preferably outdoors. For some, getting out into nature and hiking, or spending time by a lake or the ocean sans selfie stick, may do the trick. For others, taking fifteen minutes every morning and using an online app like Headspace to encourage meditation can plant the seeds of change. Self-compassion generally happens best when we take time away from noise and obligations to identify and address our own self-care needs.

One of the most critical and simple actions we can take involves our own modeling of behavior and choices. If we want students to be organized, how do we organize our own daily and weekly online and in-person communication? If we want them to pay attention, how do we respond to breaks at home or in class time? Do we rush to our phones to check our own email, or do we start conversations with teens to see how their day is going? Parents who want their children to be fully present have to model their own version of being fully present—while driving, at breakfast, or after dinner. Educators who want students to be active participants have to model the same sort of enthusiasm—even when they think none of their students are watching. Are times for face-to-face, technology-free conversations built into a daily or weekly routine? Is there time set aside for self-reflection and self-compassion in the classroom and at home? Our own simple choices make a big difference.

In this time of new language and social norms, sometimes a lack of understanding is mistaken for a lack of empathy. Many tweens and teens have a difficult time identifying which conversations are better suited for in-person interactions, and which ones can be handled via online messaging or email. What is often cited as a lack of empathy and compassion is actually an inability to identify the appropriate way to respond to different situations. Many students don't really know when they should pick up the phone and when they should strive for an in-person conversation, or what type of email or messaging communication is appropriate. Not long ago, one of my high school students sent me several brusque emails that lacked basic greetings and appropriate tone. He also took a week to respond to one of my emails that required a timely response. At first, I was annoyed, and it would have been easy for me to write off his faux pas as the result of a lack of empathy. Upon reflection, I realized that he simply needed instruction in appropriate communication. The next time we met in person, I explained how his email manner could be misconstrued as abrasive and rude. I guided him on how to appropriately compose a professional email and on the appropriate response time for certain issues (within 24–48 hours, given that he checked his email once a day). He immediately changed his style, and now all his emails to me have an appropriate header, greeting, and response time.

In a school setting, having designated structured time like Power Down Days (described in Chapter 3), combined with schoolwide activities and technology-free conversations and interactions, can make a difference. Schools that are able to create a regular outdoor education component—whether it is a daylong, technology-free field adventure or a weeklong backpacking trip that is a required part of the curriculum—will see benefits. Researchers at the University of California, Los Angeles, found that sixth graders who spent just five days at an outdoor camp without access to electronic devices were better at recognizing human emotions and nonverbal cues than peers who had spent five days with their typical access to devices.[22] The short length of time—five days—suggests that it doesn't take much to improve social and emotional recognition. I encourage parents and students to work together at home to set up a structure for technology-free, social-media-free time and space.

Recultivating empathy and compassion in an age of social media socialization isn't difficult, but it does take time and intention. It requires all of us to understand and appreciate that even though our world may be ever changing, many of the underlying notions around kindness, civility, compassion, and respect remain the same.

EXERCISE

We know that face-to-face communication encourages increased empathy and compassion, as some of the most important communication is nonverbal. Encourage students to identify situations in which face-to-face conversations are more appropriate than online messaging. Have them consider conversations with three groups of people: parents, teachers or other adults, and peers. Ask students to identify what conversations for each of those groups are best had in person, and what conversations can be handled online.

PROMOTING APPROPRIATE SOCIAL AND EMOTIONAL BOUNDARIES

One of the pitfalls of an adolescent's desire to be wanted and liked is the potential for overexposure to the cruelty of others, amplified in an online world that is sometimes filled with miscommunications, misunderstandings, and lapses in judgment. Tweens and teens who share selfies and video chats publicly leave themselves open to the stinging commentary of anonymous trolls, without the social and emotional reserves needed to adequately process and move past such meanness.

Earlier in this chapter, I mentioned the importance of tweens and teens learning how to "filter in" and "filter out" online experiences as they choose how to engage or disengage with others. It goes back to asking tweens and teens to identify and reflect on their "why" in relation to social and emotional boundaries. What are they choosing to share? Who are they sharing with? Why are they choosing to share or engage online? One of the most essential ways to encourage the cultivation and development of tweens' and teens' empathy and compassion toward others is to give them the time and space to appreciate appropriate self-care and self-compassion. After all, it is nearly impossible to truly care for others if they are unable to recognize and address their own needs. The most effective way to help students develop their own sense of self-compassion is to help them develop and implement appropriate social and emotional boundaries online and in real life.

Tweens and teens often fail to realize that they can—and should—proactively choose how to engage online with others. In essence, they have more control than they think about how and when they engage online. For instance, tweens and teens tell me they post photos and videos publicly, and allow for anonymous comments, so that they can gauge how others "really" feel about them, not accounting for how negative, anonymous cruelty can leave them feeling anxious and unglued. Nearly every social media app—including Facebook, Twitter, Instagram, and Snapchat—has features for reporting, blocking, unfollowing, or other forms of personal filtering. In December 2016, Instagram announced the ability for users to disable comments.[23] The key is to empower students to see proactive and reactive filtering as a normal part of developing healthy social and emotional boundaries online.

Students sometimes don't know how to figure out what they should filter, block, and avoid. Encourage students to think about what energizes them and what drains them. If following or engaging online with someone or something (whether an individual person or an online community) feels draining and overwhelming, perhaps they can think through their personal choices and decide whether they want to adjust their online boundaries to reflect those choices.

Even when students feel secure online, there can always be too much of a good thing. Too much time spent online can quickly impinge on social and emotional boundaries, and simply setting aside time each day to be offline can be a way of rebalancing. For some students, it can be important to establish appropriate boundaries when it comes to responding and reacting to messages—for instance, all messages do not require an immediate response. Building in time daily for what I like to call an oasis point—a mini-reflection or vacation that provides for an emotional check-in, reflection, and regrouping—can be an effective way to maintain social and emotional boundaries that otherwise can quickly be overlooked. An oasis point can be as simple as taking ten minutes to have a cup of tea or spending twenty minutes writing in a journal free from technological devices and distractions.

Finally, it is developmentally appropriate for tweens and teens to want to explore romantic relationships. However, given the abundance of online pornography and media-driven hypersexuality, it can be easy for young people to conflate emotional intimacy with nudity and sexual intercourse. Tweens might mistakenly believe that sending a nude photo of themselves is a way to establish intimacy with someone they like, and it may make them underestimate the potential negative repercussions if that photo goes viral. And it's not just immediate negative repercussions—the photo may never be removed from the Internet . . . *ever*. Depending on where the photo ultimately lands, the photo may always be searchable. Parents often have no idea why their son or daughter decided to take and transmit explicit photos (for a sense of intimacy? belonging? connection?) and are left reacting and dealing with the aftermath.

As a society, we tend to focus on the consequences for teen girls of taking and sending explicit photos, yet most teen boys have little guidance on how to evaluate, reflect, and identify what feels healthy and appropriate to them (and why). Rarely do we give students the opportunity to actively reflect on healthy social and emotional boundaries in a nonjudgmental environment. Today's increased access to pornography and the ease with which photos and videos are captured and shared to wide audiences make it all the more important for parents and educators to help students proactively develop social and emotional boundaries when it comes to intimate relationships as well as social ones.

EXERCISE

Ask teens to develop a mission statement around appropriate social and emotional boundaries online. What type of behavior do they feel warrants blocking and reporting users? What type of filtering will they use to maintain comfortable social and emotional boundaries? How will they respond if they see someone being bullied or mistreated online?

DEVELOPING A PLAN FOR GUIDANCE AND SUPPORT

In the fall of 2012, fifteen-year-old Audrie Pott committed suicide in Saratoga, California, a leafy suburb a short drive from my office. Audrie attended the local public school, and after her death, her parents traced her phone and email records and discovered that Audrie had been at a party eight days earlier where she was sexually assaulted by at least three classmates after she became drunk and passed out; the classmates purportedly took compromising photos of her.[24] Those photos were then shared with others, and it was later reported that Audrie was bullied by classmates as a result of the incident. Her parents blamed the sexual assault and resulting humiliation for her suicide.[25]

There are many things that can potentially go wrong online (and in real life), and it is critical for students, parents, and educators to proactively work together to develop a plan for guidance and support. I encourage families and schools to include in media use agreements (see Chapter 4) a section on identifying supporters and clarifiers—those people a student feels comfortable turning to in an emergency when their social and emotional welfare is at stake. Supporters can be defined as individuals who are positive and supportive—I usually give the example of friends or peers who can be counted on in a time of need. Clarifiers are adults who can provide clarity and guidance when issues seem confounding and overwhelming. I encourage students to identify three supporters and three clarifiers they can reach out to if something doesn't go as planned. Parents can certainly act as clarifiers, but there are times when students might not feel comfortable reaching out to their parents, and it is helpful to identify teachers, extended family members, counselors, clergy members, or coaches who might be potentially valuable clarifiers.

In addition to in-person supporters and clarifiers, students might find an online resource valuable as well. More and more social media apps are putting safeguards in place so that users are sent a message when one of their posts might signal something worrisome. For example, the app After School offers access to a trained online counselor to users who post something troublesome. Beginning in October 2016, Instagram let users anonymously flag photos and postings if they think the poster might be at risk for self-harm. Whenever a photo or post is flagged, the original poster receives a message stating, "Someone saw one of your posts and thinks you might be going through a difficult time. If you need support, we'd like to help," along with tips and online resources.[26] In her highly acclaimed TED talk entitled "Texting That Saves Lives," Nancy Lubin shares how text messages have a "100 percent open rate" by teens and may in some cases be the best way to communicate with teens during a crisis.[27] She notes that a teen might not answer a phone call but will open a text message (even if he or she doesn't respond). Lubin is now the founder and CEO of Crisis Text Line, which is a free, 24/7 crisis text line staffed by volunteers who work anonymously with those in crisis. According to a profile in the *New Yorker* magazine, "Each day, on average, Crisis Text Line instigates at least one active rescue of a texter who's thought to be in immediate danger of suicide."[28] Regardless of how, where, or when a student seeks support, it is critical for each student to proactively identify the individuals and resources that would work best for that student in a time of need.

EXERCISE

Have students identify their supporters and clarifiers. How can they best reach those individuals in a time of need? Encourage them to collaboratively research and discuss which online resources, like Crisis Text Line, would work best, and have them develop their own personal action plan to deal with a crisis situation. Have students think through several scenarios related to being depressed, anxious, having a photo or posting shared online without permission, or feeling harassed or bullied, as well as appropriate ways to respond to a friend in need.

ACKNOWLEDGING AND VALIDATING THE BYSTANDER EXPERIENCE

We don't always recognize and appreciate how jarring it is to see or read something uncomfortable online—even more so if it is about someone we know or something we care about. Over time, we as adults may learn to block, avoid, ignore, or sometimes become anesthetized to our feelings. In many tragic cases where students have harmed themselves after being bullied and harassed online, other classmates and peers witnessed the online happenings. They have seen the photos and videos that were shared and have read the vicious comments. Live-feed videos that capture violent crimes and self-harm can trigger feelings of sadness and rage, especially when not appropriately acknowledged and processed. One of the most crucial roles for parents and educators is helping students understand that the in-real-life and online worlds are more socially and emotionally intertwined than they might think. Within your family or school community, there is value in acknowledging and validating the importance of the bystander experience, and it can be as simple as a phrase like, "If you see something, say something," and encouraging students to think of someone they already know and trust who they would feel comfortable approaching for help.

EXERCISE

Within your family or school, have a conversation about what students can do if they see something online that makes them feel uncomfortable or seems inappropriate. What are the potential resources? Have students identify which peers and adults they would feel comfortable approaching if something were to occur. Are there ways for students to report their concerns anonymously?

SUMMARY

Tweens and teens are navigating dual online and in-real-life social experiences, and they need the appropriate guideposts to do so. One of the most important things parents and educators can do is build their own awareness around what students are doing online, and why they are choosing to do what they do. Tweens and teens need guidance that addresses the long-term impacts of daily choices around messaging, photos, and video usage in a way that is supportive, loving, and effective. Students should be motivated to proactively identify their clusters of connection and resources for support for when things don't go as planned so that a small incident doesn't morph into something that is more detrimental and so that they feel their experiences online are acknowledged and validated. Our work in promoting social and emotional wellness is critical to raising teens who are compassionate, empathetic, and resilient young adults.

CHAPTER 7

Physical Wellness

Finding Balance in an Unbalanced World

When I encourage students to think about their own physical wellness, I suggest they think beyond the common assumption that people often share: that looking healthy and feeling healthy are one and the same. In my work, I emphasize that physical wellness should focus on *feeling* healthy and making daily choices that promote overall wellness. I want students to realize that focusing on better physical wellness habits around nutrition, sleep, stress management, and functional exercise is crucial to their overall well-being, and to achieving their academic and personal goals.

But I also realize how difficult it can be to maintain a focus on physical wellness when there are so many competing priorities. It's hard enough wanting to do well in school, sports, and extracurricular activities while maintaining social and family obligations, and the creep of technological distractions can easily upset the delicate balance of physical wellness. It can start slowly, with a few texts or Snaps sent after "lights out" or an all-day video gaming marathon, and it doesn't take long for both boys and girls to struggle to maintain physical wellness in the face of such challenges.

THE TEETERING IMBALANCE

Many tweens and teens who come to our office for help with organization and time management are motivated to become better organized by the prospect of gaining an extra 7–10 hours of "free" time per week simply by doing their work more efficiently.

When Margo first called our office about her son, Jay, I thought he sounded like so many of the high school sophomore boys I talked about in my first book, *That Crumpled Paper Was Due Last Week*. Margo described Jay as a "sincere slacker," a term I used to describe boys who genuinely think they are putting in a great effort when the reality is quite different. According to Margo, Jay once loved playing basketball more than anything in the world, but his efforts had become lackluster over the past few years.

"He doesn't go to the open gym practices or early morning workouts. He does the bare minimum," she said. "He used to talk about his dream of making the high school varsity team and now no longer seems motivated or excited at the prospect of playing with his teammates." I sensed that something was missing from the picture, and it didn't take long to understand what else was going on.

"My son loves playing video games, especially *Call of Duty*," she explained. *Call of Duty* is one of the most popular action-style military video game series today. She went on to explain that she created incentives for him to do his chores by offering him a half-hour of game time for every set of chores completed. "I know I am probably doing something wrong," she reasoned, "but I am not sure what else to do."

I empathized with Margo, and with the additional challenge that parents today face around all sorts of distractions—and underlying disordered screen use—that can have very real social, emotional, and physical implications. Video games, like social media apps and websites, are designed to be addictive, and adults don't fully appreciate and understand how challenging it can be for teens to pry themselves away from something that makes them feel, even for an instant, like a master of the universe. In a national sample of youths ages 8–18, nearly one in ten video game players demonstrated pathological (or addictive) signs of play, answering yes to questions like the following:

> "Over time, have you been spending much more time thinking about playing video games, learning about video-game playing, or planning the next opportunity to play?"
>
> "Do you become restless or irritable when attempting to cut down or stop playing video games?"
>
> "Have you played video games as a way of escaping from problems or bad feelings?"[1]

Most of today's video games have the added element of being a tool for socialization, and many tweens and teens see their game playing as a way to spend time with friends. Like so many other behaviors that are unhealthy in excess, playing video games is considered socially acceptable in moderation. Nonetheless, game use can quickly morph into an unhealthy imbalance, and sometimes addiction, with little warning.

In talking with Margo about Jay and his dependence on video games, I inferred from the clues she gave me that something was unbalanced: For example, he was no longer interested in things he used to enjoy, like basketball. He was also no longer exercising or even moving the same way he once did (even walking the dog took great effort), and he isolated himself socially in his quest to spend more time playing video games. His self-imposed isolation affected his relationships with his parents, siblings, and peers. In addition, once he started playing, it was hard for him to stop. He would easily have played for twelve hours or more if his parents didn't put limits in place. His video game habits affected his sleep patterns, which made him incredibly sleep deprived. His irritable and surly mood would subside almost immediately if he knew he would soon be able to spend time with his beloved game console.

I think about Jay's unbalanced state in relation to video game use when I think about how we approach physical wellness with today's tweens and teens. Physical wellness, in essence, is all about having some semblance of internal balance. It is about feeling good and recognizing how easy it can be to feel unbalanced in our always-on digital environment. What works well for one person may not work for another, but in most cases, it requires extra effort to help teens and tweens develop self-awareness around the effects of their behavioral choices on their ability to maintain and enhance physical wellness. At the same time, one of the most important antidotes to disordered screen use (and related issues) is to help tweens and teens find what I like to call seeds of purpose, or ways to be purposeful that are meaningful to them. The crux of my work is all about helping tweens and teens find their own sense of engagement through learning new skills; creating, building, or collecting something; or finding time for a simple pleasure or hobby like gardening, cooking, or playing music or promoting a certain cause. Oftentimes, disordered screen use begins from an internal emptiness and lacking of some sort—after all, simply being a tween or teen can be an incredibly disjointed experience, and there's always a struggle to find a sense of engagement and belonging. When that is missing, the easy filler and temptation of more and more time online can lead to disordered screen use, which can have unhealthy social, emotional, and physical ramifications.

Ultimately, there are many ways to think about physical wellness. When I talk to parents and students about screen-based media use and physical wellness, I focus on sleep, functional exercise, and stress management as key factors. I continue to use the framework of socialization, self-regulation, and safety to find ways to promote a sense of balance, provide structure to reduce the potential for unhealthy behavioral choices, and allow the opportunity for regrouping and getting back on track when things seem to go sideways.

PROMOTING SLEEP

A few months after the very first iPhone came out in 2007, the parents of one of my high school juniors came into my office for a meeting. They confided that their son's first cell phone bill was a stack of papers so thick that it essentially fit in a shirt-sized box. Why? Well, their cell phone service provider had tracked every single text message their son had sent over the month (and, yes, he clearly sent a lot of text messages). But most surprising to these parents was that most of the text messages were sent between midnight and 3 a.m., to his new girlfriend. No wonder he was so irritable in the morning.

Whenever I ask audiences of parents if they have ever dealt with an irritable tween or teen, I am generally met with unrestrained laughter that gives me the answer I already know. Sleep deprivation is one of the first signs of imbalance. Exhausted, sleep-deprived teens often tell me they stay up late on social media or playing video games because they can't pry themselves away. And students who are asleep quickly awaken when their phone lights up with a text message or other notification. A study of college students found that 47 percent of students awoke after sleep onset to answer text messages and 40 percent to answer cell phone calls.[2] In the study, greater levels of tech use during sleep time resulted in lower sleep quality, which can increase the likelihood of symptoms of depression and anxiety. It's safe to assume that most high school students have similar habits and outcomes. In their quest to be social, they struggle with self-regulation, and it affects their overall well-being and safety.

Sleep deprivation is one of the most harmful side effects of our always-on digital world. According to the Centers for Disease Control and Prevention, teens need between 8.5 and 9.25 hours of sleep a night, though many teens get fewer than 6.5 hours of sleep per night.[3] Over the course of the school year, these students are deprived of so many hours of sleep that it would add up to about fifty missing nights of sleep per school year—nearly two months of missed sleep is an easy explanation for students' irritability, inability to focus and concentrate, and feelings of depression and anxiety. If there is a single thing that gets students' attention during my presentations and workshops, it is those fifty nights of missing sleep.

> Many students miss up to fifty nights of sleep per school year due to technology use.

When Robert's mother first called my office, she was worried about her son's lack of sleep and how it was affecting him academically, socially, and emotionally. Robert was a junior in high school and taking all honors and AP classes—so I assumed it was his intense course load that was causing him to stay up late at night. His mother politely but forcefully disagreed, explaining that her son could handle the workload academically but was a severe procrastinator who would sometimes wait until midnight to start work due the next day—including long papers. Robert became easily anxious, and the procrastination fed the anxiety, which led to more procrastination, which led to . . . more video watching.

In our first session, I learned that Robert spent four or more hours *per day* after school on YouTube—usually before starting his homework. Watching YouTube videos was his way of unwinding, and he would watch videos related to something he was learning in school, humorous clips from television shows he liked, and new content uploads from people whose YouTube channels he subscribed to. The YouTube app was on the iPad he used to complete his schoolwork, so it became easy for him to toggle between trying to complete homework and watching videos. When I asked if he thought it was possible for him *not* to visit the YouTube website or use the YouTube app on his phone and iPad for a few days, he became visibly uncomfortable.

I immediately shifted my approach and suggested finding ways for him to compartmentalize his video watching until after his homework was completed. Robert's obsession with watching videos began as a result of the ultimate paradox: He watched videos from academic resources like Khan Academy to help with his schoolwork, but he became distracted by comedy clips and music videos. His obsession with YouTube affected his ability to complete his work, get sleep, and maintain healthy habits. Something had to change.

To get Robert to reduce his YouTube viewing to a level that let him complete his work and get to sleep at a reasonable hour, I helped him come up with mini-goals that he felt were attainable. He first decided to delete the YouTube app from his iPad, which he used mainly for schoolwork. He would keep his phone (which still had YouTube access via the web and the app) in the other room when completing his work and also gave the phone to his mother starting at 10 p.m. He made these choices because he didn't like being sleep deprived, and his mother started actively taking away the phone in order to create structure. Over six months, Robert changed his routine so that he was slowly able to bring some healthy habits back into his life.

Many students will say they stay up late doing homework, but a closer look helps them realize that much of their homework time was spent media multitasking, and so they end up trading seventy-five messages with three different friends while trying to complete a math assignment. A recent study of young adults found that those who spent the most total time on social media throughout the day were twice as likely to experience sleep disturbances.[4]

There are three key ways to help students with sleep deprivation: (1) Encourage them to monotask rather than multitask, (2) create structure to help with self-regulation around late-night phone use, and (3) encourage them to have a bedtime routine that promotes restful sleep. Research suggests that adolescents and young adults who use multiple electronic devices are more likely to sleep less at night and to be more tired during the day.[5] There are strategies throughout this book, especially in Chapter 5, that help to encourage monotasking, or ruthless prioritization, and the way to get students to buy in is sometimes as simple as making it a game and having them see how much faster work gets done if they aren't multitasking.

Research also suggests that adolescents who use their cell phones after the designated "lights out" time reported being more tired and were more likely to experience some form of sleep disturbance.[6] According to the National Sleep Foundation's 2006 Sleep in America poll, nearly every adolescent has at least one electronic device in their room, including televisions (57 percent), video game consoles (43 percent), and phones (64 percent).[7] For tweens and younger high school students, it can be as simple as requiring all technology (phones, tablets, laptops) to be out of the bedroom after a certain hour. This requires consistency on the part of parents, because an emerging body of research suggests that many adolescents already experience behavioral addiction to screen-based media that prevents them from changing their daily choices.[8] A 2009 research study in *Pediatrics,* entitled "Adolescents Living the 24/7 Lifestyle: Effects of Caffeine and Technology on Sleep Duration and Daytime Functioning," found that teens used an average of four technological devices after 9 p.m.[9] The teens who did the most multitasking with technological devices were also the most likely to be sleep deprived.[10]

Sometimes parents argue that they want their kids to learn how to self-regulate on their own. As much as I would like to agree, I also know that it is difficult for students to always make good choices, especially given how quickly screen-based media use can become addictive. In fact, students often tell me how relieved they are when their parents take their phones or make a nightly charging station a requirement, because it relieves them of the social pressure of potentially having to be "on" when all they want to do is go to sleep. Chapters 4 and 5 address the different ways that students can be motivated to make good choices for themselves, and many students simultaneously benefit from structured downtime. I encourage parents to think of it as their way of preventing disordered screen use simply by coming up with daily and weekly opportunities for tweens and teens to have structured offline time. This is particularly important for older teens, who are dealing with conflicting priorities. As students move through high school, they often get their driver's licenses at the same time that they become more sleep deprived. "Drowsy driving," or driving while sleep deprived, can have the same effect as driving under the influence of alcohol.[11] Essentially, students appreciate being able to blame their parents for being unable to return a late-night text (though they are unlikely to ever openly admit that to their parents).

Finally, the repetition of certain tasks at the end of our day—putting on pajamas, brushing our teeth, washing our face—works as a sort of winding down at the end of the day, and over time, this repetition of tasks consciously and subconsciously slows us down to prepare for rest. I suggest students read a physical book (avoid screen-based reading) or take a few moments to write in a journal to get anything pressing off their mind and on paper before trying to rest.

> ## EXERCISE
>
> Have students track their sleep—and their late-night technology use—for five days. How many hours did they sleep? On a scale from 1 to 10, what was their sleep quality? How many minutes before going to sleep did they cease technology use? Did they get up after falling asleep for any reason? What was their bedtime routine? Are there changes they would make to their bedtime routine? Was the phone in their bedroom? How did that affect their sleep? How could they improve their sleep quality?

ENCOURAGING STRESS MANAGEMENT

A study of young adult cell phone users found that users spend, on average, over five hours a day using their phone.[12] Over half the time (55 percent), the cell phone was used for less than thirty seconds, likely as the user was checking notifications to see if any likes, comments, messages, or notifications had come through.[13] This frequency of use is significant, because constant checking of a phone can be a form of multitasking and potentially increases stress and anxiety as each little noise or notification distracts the user from processing information.

Many parents have no idea how often their children actually use their cell phones—and because most children spend a majority of their time away from home (at school or engaged in sports and after-school activities), it is sometimes difficult to gauge or monitor. One high school dean encourages parents to look at their children's phones to see which apps are being used most often and which ones drain the battery most quickly. She also recommends that parents look at how often children send and receive text messages (and at what time during the day) to get the big picture on what their children's cell phone use really looks like.

When it comes to phone use and functional exercise, research suggests that those who use their phones a great deal are less likely to be physically fit and active.[14] Teenagers especially benefit from moving around as a way to improve social, emotional, and physical well-being. Researchers have noted that teenagers who are physically active feel an improved sense of well-being, elevated mood, and improved cognitive performance, whereas teenagers who have increased involvement with screen-based media tend to have poorer physical health, quality of life, and quality of family life. Simply put, moving around helps lift moods, which happens less and less when students spend more time online.[15]

In our office, we ask students to identify five *healthy* ways they can deal with stress. For some students, coming up with five healthy ways to deal with stress seems like a lot, and most can't come up with much after one or two ideas. I encourage them to think about at least one activity that involves movement, like walking the dog or shooting hoops, and at least one that is quiet and technology-free, like writing in a journal, reading a book, spending time with a family pet, meditating, or taking a bath. I may list a few strategies other students have identified as helpful, including talking to a friend, parent, or sibling; listening to music; and spending time outdoors.

Sometimes students tell me that scrolling through Instagram or sending Snaps is their way of finding relief from daily stress, and I respond by explaining how watching, scrolling, liking, and commenting can also be seen as passive ways of numbing stress, and I encourage them to think of proactive ways of managing stress. As we discussed in earlier chapters, social media can cause fomo (fear of missing out) and thus create more stress from viewing certain posts or seeing photos about events to which they weren't invited.

A number of useful apps and fitness trackers can be used to increase movement and decrease stress. As mentioned in Chapter 6, mindfulness and meditation apps such as Headspace and ZenFriend can encourage students to build in moments of reflection each day. The Color Therapy app is an online coloring book that allows users to take a few moments out of their day to mindfully relax.[16] Even using timer apps like Forest or a Pomodoro app can encourage students to spend a designated time (even simply 15–25 minutes) writing or reading, without being tempted to pick up their phone and check notifications or messages.

FOCUSING ON FUNCTIONAL EXERCISE

When I talk about movement, I use the term *functional exercise* to describe exercise that is inherently stress-relieving, because for many student-athletes, playing high-level sports is rather stressful as they juggle different issues related to engagement and performance (*Am I starting in this game? Will I make the traveling team? Why is the coach not playing me? What if I fumble?*). High-level club and traveling teams create additional expectations, and the amount of stress on developing bodies has led to an increase in repetitive stress injuries and related issues.[17] I encourage many of the athletes I work with to identify some form of movement that is stress-relieving for them—it could be walking, running, swimming, or shooting hoops outside of their club or school athletic endeavors. For some, using an app to track performance can be motivating and inspiring. A friend of mine wanted to run more for both stress relief and physical fitness. He had spent his time playing sports but was never much of a runner, so he began building on his new healthy habit by using the Nike+ app to record each of his runs. Currently the app helps him record the time and distance for each run, and with it he takes photos either during or after the run to serve as a background for a social media post to help him remember the run. He travels a great deal for work and pleasure, and the app has helped him record and remember his runs all over the world. Other fitness trackers, like Fitbit and Jawbone UP, can also help track movement in ways that can be motivating, and many have a social aspect that enables users to connect and share with friends. This built-in socialization can provide inspiration and motivation for those seeking to move more.

To be clear, the same activity that is stress-relieving to some may be stress-producing for others. Some students hoping to move more might find using a fitness-tracking device like a pedometer (or a fancier Fitbit or Jawbone) to be motivating, while others might slip into unhealthy obsessions with daily performance. The key is helping students find what works for them and encouraging a sense of balance with physical wellness.

UNDERSTANDING ADDICTION

More and more families are struggling with the challenges of adolescent screen-based media and video game addiction. Part of the issue is that both activities are socially acceptable. Addiction to (anything) is generally rooted in an underlying desire to escape from daily reality, and screen-based media and gaming provide an outlet for socialization and a feeling of total control and life mastery. What follows is an inability to self-regulate as a result of the incredible sensation or "high" that comes from a "hit"—whether that "hit" is moving to a desired next level on a video game or getting a certain number of likes and comments on an Instagram photo.

It's true that not all video game users are addicted, and not all gaming is necessarily bad. In fact, there are many ways that gamification can enhance learning and understanding. At the same time, I encourage parents and educators to put preventive measures in place so that daily and weekly digital detox can happen. It's also important for educators and parents to help students find ways to make their own personal realities more appealing than the online experiences, which often stems from helping students find ways to become purposefully engaged in their school and greater communities in a way that acknowledges their own values and interests. Many parents barely notice how quickly their child's use begins as a novelty and transforms into an obsession with social, emotional, psychological, and physical consequences. In most instances, parents do not realize there is an issue until the habit has turned to disordered use, as screen addiction can easily be masked, especially when a child uses some type of screen device to complete work for school. For adolescents who are most susceptible, it doesn't take long for an addiction to form and begin to damage family, social, school, and psychological functioning. For many parents, online addiction is such a new form of addiction that they have a difficult time accepting and understanding that it is a mental health issue, even though the effects are just as devastating as those of any other illness.

> It's also important for educators and parents to help students find ways to make students' personal realities more appealing than the online experiences.

An eighth-grade boy who we worked with admitted that he would get up around 4 a.m. on Saturday mornings to play six or seven hours of uninterrupted video games. He had been diagnosed previously with ADHD (research suggests that pathological gamers are twice as likely as moderate gamers to have been diagnosed with an attention disorder) and used his time online to socialize and escape from the perceived stress of his home life.[18] In the course of the week, he counted over forty-two hours playing video and online games, even though his mother thought he was limited to two hours per day. His mother was initially adamant that she wanted him to learn how to self-regulate and understand the consequences of his choices ("How well is that approach working?" I remember asking her). She didn't realize her son had an addiction until it affected his school performance, relationships, and overall mood. He broke furniture when he was denied access to his game console, and he lied about completing his schoolwork and chores in order to sneak in a few more hours of gaming. Research suggests that three main factors contribute to pathological levels of video and online game use: "the use of games to escape daily life, the use of games as a social outlet, and positive attitudes toward the steady accumulation of in-game rewards."[19] Gamers who have a social component—that is, they feel as though they have online relationships they want to maintain or develop—are more likely to exhibit addictive behaviors.[20]

KNOWING THE SIGNS AND GETTING HELP

Teen cell-phone addiction, Internet addiction, social media addiction, and gaming addiction are all behavioral disorders in which teens are disengaged from daily living and unable to interact with others because of obsessive habits. Many times, the inability to self-regulate, combined with concerns around socialization, can cause students to form imbalanced attachments to screen-based media or video games. When parents are trying to determine if their child has some form of addiction, I encourage them to reflect on a few questions related to their child's screen-based media, online gaming, or video game use (these same questions can be modified and asked directly to a teen as well):

1. If the phone/Internet/social media/online or video games were unavailable for an hour/day/week, how would your child react?

2. What would happen if the phone/Internet/social media/online or video games were suddenly (and without warning) unavailable? If your child would become upset, how long would it take for him or her to refocus efforts elsewhere?

3. Has your child lied about his or her phone/Internet/social media/online or video game use?

4. Has your child's academic performance been adversely affected by his or her phone/Internet/social media/online or video game use?

5. Does your child occasionally or regularly forgo sleep for phone/Internet/social media/online or video game use? (Occasionally can be once or twice a week; regularly would be more than twice a week.)

6. Does your child occasionally or regularly forgo food or personal hygiene for phone/Internet/social media/online or video game use? (Occasionally can be once or twice a week; regularly would be more than twice a week.)

7. Has your child ever hidden his or her phone/Internet/social media/online or video game use? How so?

8. Has your child's phone/Internet/social media/online or video game use affected his or her friendships or family relationships in a negative way? How so?

9. Has your child forgone social events in favor of spending time with the phone/Internet/social media/online or video games?

10. Has your child ever been explosively angry or violent at the prospect of not having access to the phone/Internet/social media/online or video games?

These questions should serve as starting points for conversation and reflection. Many different variables are involved; however, if the answers to most of questions 3–10 are yes, it would be a good idea to seek the advice of a mental health professional. In many cases, family therapy is helpful for understanding the unique dynamics and unusual forces at play.

PROTECTION FROM PHYSICAL HARM AND DANGER

An important aspect of physical wellness is physical safety from harm and danger. Whenever I talk with parents about social media use, the underlying fear is that their child will potentially meet a sexual predator online using an app or in a chat room. That risk certainly exists, but the reality is that tweens and teens spend the majority of their time online communicating with friends and classmates, and researching ideas and topics of interest. It's somewhat common for teens to stop midconversation in order to check the veracity of a claim or look up a fact or statistic related to the topic of conversation.

Unfortunately, we do hear of and read stories involving tweens and teens meeting sexual predators or violent criminals online, and then setting up in-person meetings with disastrous or deadly results. Teens who struggle with developing and maintaining in-person friendships or who are psychologically vulnerable and experiencing depression or anxiety are more likely to seek and maintain potentially risky online relationships. In middle school and high school, the fluidity of friendships and relationships can be a daily source of anxiety—for students as well as their parents.

The most important first step is recognizing what tweens and teens are sharing online. A survey of teens revealed that 72 percent of them have a social media profile, and 47 percent have a public profile with information that can be viewed by anyone.[21] Some of the information shared online includes photos of themselves (62 percent), the city they live in (41 percent), the school they attend (45 percent), and their cell phone number (14 percent).[22] Some teens also use location trackers on their devices, so that when they post something, their exact location is also shown.

It's also crucial to understand that while older teens (ages 14–17) might be more likely to receive unwanted sexual solicitations online, they are also more likely to be seeking a relationship online, and not all online sexual solicitations are unwanted. Until the dating app Tinder banned teen users in June 2016, nearly 7 percent of registered users were teenagers (that, of course, does not include the teens who lie about their age).[23] Spotafriend, an app marketed to teen users ages 13–19, has the same overall premise as Tinder—users look at photos of others and decide whether or not they want to be connected; if both parties agree, they can begin private messaging.[24]

So, how do we keep tweens and teens safe? Many parents struggle with the notion of respecting their adolescent's privacy versus maintaining his or her safety, and I believe that both can be achieved through open, honest communication. Parents should think through what they feel comfortable with their teens sharing online and publicly, and also recognize that privacy settings never mean total privacy. Parents should also proactively establish guidelines for tweens or teens who want to meet in-person with someone they initially meet online. It's easy to scoff and say that adolescents should never meet anyone in person whom they meet online, but the reality is that the Internet is used as a means of communication and information, and opportunities arise. When parents are forthcoming about strategies and family policies, tweens and teens are more likely to think twice before lying and sneaking around. Will adolescents still lie and sneak around? Yes. But they are less likely to do so if parameters are in place.

> Many parents struggle with the notion of respecting their adolescent's privacy versus maintaining safety, and I believe both can be achieved through open, honest communication.

In the debate over privacy versus safety, a question often arises related to parents' access to tween and teen passwords. Safety needs to be the first priority, working in tandem with building and developing trust. So, for a middle schooler who is still learning his or her way around good decision making and phone use, parents should feel fully comfortable having 24/7 access to the child's phone and passwords. As a student gets older and develops a history of making good choices, parents should still maintain that they have access to the phone in a way that also builds trust and responsibility. For example, older high school students can put all passwords in a sealed envelope, to be used only in case of emergency.

I've been asked about parents enabling technology-tracking devices on their children's phones, and I absolutely understand that it can be a complicated and very personal decision. As with many things involving social media and technology, much of it comes down to approach. When parents ask for my opinion, I often ask them why they feel the need to use such devices. Is it because they are concerned for their children's safety, or because they don't trust their children? Those are two very different issues. In general, I've found tweens and teens are more receptive to and understanding of the use of tracking apps when it is included as part of a family use agreement to promote safety, rather than for potential reprisal and punishment. There is so much going on in our world—from natural disasters to violent crimes to routine traffic accidents—that it is easy to approach tech tracking from the perspective of safety and love rather than fear and punishment. For instance, I work with several families that live in dense urban areas and use the Find My Friend app to keep track of their kids' whereabouts—and it has been useful more than a few times, from both the parents' and kids' perspectives.

Of course, some parents and educators argue that parents' use of tech-tracking devices amounts to parental stalking, and tweens and teens can turn off their phones when they are in a place they aren't supposed to be. Again, it is all about approach, how the family use agreement is devised, and understanding that what works for one family might not work for another. I come from the perspective that children's physical well-being and safety is of paramount importance.

SUMMARY

Parents and educators play an important role in helping students think about physical wellness and safety. The desire to be more social can create temptations that counteract the importance of self-regulation and safety, and we all have to work together to find solutions that are both effective and realistic. Encouraging students to prioritize sleep, create opportunities for functional exercise, and proactively address stress management can help to avoid screen-based media addiction.

CHAPTER 8

Moving Forward

Implementing the Strategies at School and at Home

The end of a book sometimes begs the question, "Now what?" How do we begin to put this all together? In many ways, I hope the end of this book is just the beginning of a greater conversation. My intention for this book was to provide helpful information, relevant strategies, and perspective based on my research as well as my own work with students. From that, I hope administrators, educators, parents, and students are inspired to step back, reflect, and plan and implement systems that work for their home, school, and greater communities. It's true that what works in one family, in one classroom, in one school might not in another—but I hope that we can work together to find meaningful solutions that promote social media wellness.

To that end, I wanted to conclude this book with some thoughts on planning and implementation both in the schools and at home. The abbreviated lists of questions found here can provide a starting place and an opportunity for you to design your own blueprint for success.

THINGS TO THINK ABOUT AT SCHOOL

When a school decides to adapt or bring in a one-to-one program, a great deal of planning needs to happen on the front end, ideally long before a tablet or computer is ever placed in front of a teacher in a professional development workshop. Many schools bring in classroom technology without really looking at the potential academic, social, and emotional impacts on the school community. School administrators and educators need to think about the messages they want to send to the school community about technology use and time spent online. Is your school implementing a personalized learning program in which students spend the bulk of their learning time online? Are you hoping that classroom teachers will use technology to enhance lessons as needed but that the bulk of instruction will occur offline? As you consider the questions related to school-level reflection and planning in the next section, think about the overall message that your school community is hoping to create around technology use and how your plan and implementation reflect those goals.

An important note: Whenever individuals (administrators, educators, students, or parents) have a tablet or computer in front of them for professional or educational development, the conversation automatically shifts. Regardless of age, giving someone a device with Internet access often means they become either distracted, surfing and thinking about all the possibilities, or overwhelmed with all the things they need to keep track of, and the conversation becomes more of a technology lesson than anything else. It doesn't take long to shift away from a discussion of best practices, and overall thoughts on how a system could potentially work for all involved, to a distracted discussion focused on how to use and implement the tool at hand.

REFLECTING AS A SCHOOL

Some of these questions are designed to be asked before a technology or tablet program is in place, but they can easily be adapted for reflection after a program has been in existence for several years. When I visit schools, I ask similar questions to gain a greater understanding of a school's current situation and opportunities for growth. Though these questions are aimed at administrators, they can easily be modified and are worthy of a larger faculty and staff discussion:

MISSION. What is your school's mission (in three sentences or less)?

TECHNOLOGY. What is the goal for the program? What is the goal for the first year? How do these goals relate to your school's mission?

SUCCESS. At the end of the quarter/semester/year, what objectives will have to be met in order to determine whether or not the system is successful? How will success be measured (qualitatively/quantitatively)? What are the steps for evaluation? Who will be in charge of evaluating success?

REASONING. What are the main objectives around having technology use in class? Check your three (3) main objectives from the options below (it's always good to do this as an exercise and share and compare with other faculty, staff, and administrators). **Remember:** These reasons should be mission focused when looking at the school's overall objectives:

☐ Improve student learning outcomes (i.e., increase learning)
☐ Decrease busywork for teachers (save time)
☐ Decrease busywork for students (save time)
☐ Create more opportunities for collaboration among teachers
☐ Create more opportunities for collaboration among students
☐ Promote a deeper engagement for students with the learning material
☐ Replace pen and paper as much as possible
☐ Use technology as a substitute for teacher instruction
☐ Use technology to augment classroom or in-person teaching
☐ Other

DIG DEEPER. For each of the objectives noted, how does the current or proposed technology plan achieve those objectives? Explain how each of the objectives relates to your school's overall mission.

OWNERSHIP DETAILS. If students are required to purchase a specific device, how will the school address ownership of the device and the use of games and other apps? What is the school's policy on gaming? How will you delineate and address that policy?

If students are allowed to bring their own devices into the classroom, how will the school address differences in software between operating systems? For instance, what works well on an iPad might not work as well on a Microsoft Surface Pro, or vice versa. How will you address those differences? (*Note:* This question is not applicable if all students use the same device.)

DIGITAL CITIZENSHIP. What is your school's acceptable use policy? How will issues around physical and digital technology theft be handled? How does your digital citizenship policy link to school rules and the school's overall mission? Who will enforce the policy? Will there be a student advisory council?

TEACHERS AND STAFF. What guidelines have been or will be created for staff, and what will the professional development look like at the beginning of the school year and ongoing throughout the school year? How does the acceptable use policy apply to teacher use in the classroom and outside of school with school-issued devices? Is it acceptable for teachers to check social media sites or shop online during class? What are school policies on texting and contacting students? How will employment policies be adjusted to reflect that teachers are using a school-issued device for personal and professional reasons?

STAFF ANALYSIS. How open is your staff to bringing technology into the classroom? What can you do to encourage more cooperation and collaboration among the staff? What can staff members do when they see students exhibiting addictive habits related to technology use?

STUDENTS. What guidelines and policies have been or will be created for students, and how will the school address concerns that come up during the school year as new software and apps are released? Ideally, these policies are created and implemented schoolwide, not chosen by individual teachers.

If the computers or tablets are the school's property, will you put certain limitations on what apps can be downloaded? How will you enforce that policy? Will gaming be allowed on school-issued devices? (*Remember:* Some gaming can be seen as educational. How will you delineate?)

PARENTS. How does the school educate, inform, and update parents so that they are active participants in this process? What concerns are anticipated or have been experienced, and how will those concerns be addressed?

PUBLICITY. How and where does the school publicize current or future programs? What will be the method by which students, faculty, staff, and parents are made aware of changes and become educated about current policies and programs? Who at the school will be in charge of maintaining the parent resource page and employee policies?

TECHNOLOGY SUPPORT. What will technology support be like for staff? What will technology support be like for students? Will there be a designated IT staff person (or team) in charge of all of the technical support? Will you be able to create a Genius Bar–type atmosphere where students and staff can drop in and receive assistance on an as-needed basis? One way to get students who are more technically inclined engaged in school activities is to ask them to serve as resources in a Genius Bar–type setting, where they can help troubleshoot other students' technical challenges alongside an IT professional.

THINGS TO THINK ABOUT AT HOME

Much of Chapter 4 addressed the importance of attitude, approach, and tone (*hint:* they all matter). Social media and technology use can be emotionally fraught topics, especially if you are dealing with a tween or teen who is tethered to his or her device(s) and looks to the online world as an escape from everything else. With that in mind, I encourage families to set aside a mutually agreed-upon time—and perhaps get out of the house and share a meal at a diner or restaurant or go on a walk or hike—to discuss these topics. I've found many tweens and teens are more comfortable discussing potentially uncomfortable topics while in motion, so walking or hiking side by side might be a good solution for discussing some of the issues around social media wellness.

REFLECTING ON THE HOME FRONT

After reading this book, parents and students might be wondering where to begin (ideally, some of the exercises included throughout the book have helped). Using the framework of socialization, self-regulation, and safety, I've provided some questions here to help begin the thought process and conversation. Again, these questions are simply a starting point for reference. They can be things to think about as you begin and continue your discussion around social media wellness and healthy technology use:

MISSION. What is your family's mission statement around technology use? (I realize that 99.9 percent of families probably don't have a mission statement, but here's a chance to get on the same page around technology use.) *Sample:* Our family uses technology for [A], [B], [C], and to promote [X], [Y], [Z].

TECHNOLOGY. What devices does each child have available for his or her use? What access do parents have to those devices? What social media apps are appropriate and accessible? What are the parameters for use? What are guidelines for appropriate use in terms of healthy socialization? Self-regulation? Safety?

SUCCESS. How will success be measured with respect to technology use and social media wellness? What does success look like, and what does it feel like? What are indicators of successful social media use that has appropriate parameters to encourage healthy socialization, self-regulation, and safety?

REASONING. What are the main objectives around social media and technology use in your home? Check your three (3) main objectives from the options below (it's always good to do this as an exercise and share and compare with other family members). **Remember:** These reasons should relate to your family mission statement.

- ☐ Maintain/improve communication with family
- ☐ Maintain/improve communication with friends
- ☐ Keep track of daily/weekly assignments
- ☐ Keep track of daily/weekly schedule
- ☐ Build new relationships
- ☐ Research information faster
- ☐ Keep connected with school happenings and events
- ☐ Keep connected with current events, new media, etc.
- ☐ Improve overall learning outcomes
- ☐ Promote a deeper engagement with the learning material
- ☐ Replace pen and paper as much as possible
- ☐ Other

DIG DEEPER. For each of the objectives noted, how do current or proposed behaviors achieve those objectives? Explain how each of these objectives relates to your family's mission statement.

OWNERSHIP AND ACCESS. Who owns the devices (generally, the answer should be parents, or perhaps the school in the case of school-issued devices)? What access do parents have so that they can look at the devices? Where are passwords stored? I generally recommend parents of middle school students have full access to passwords, and parents of high school students require that correct passwords be stored in an envelope in case of emergency. What permissions are needed to download new apps? What about digital tracking?

DIGITAL CITIZENSHIP. What is your family's acceptable use policy? How are age restrictions on certain apps adhered to (some apps require users to be over thirteen years old; others require users to be over eighteen)? How does your acceptable use policy link to school rules? Who will enforce the policy? What are consequences of the policy not being followed? How often will the acceptable use policy be reviewed?

POWER DOWN TIME. Are there designated times during the day or week for technology and social media users to be offline? Perhaps there is a set time every evening, or several hours per weekend. How is that down time encouraged, regulated, or enforced?

TECHNOLOGY SUPPORT. If a device is lost, stolen, or broken, who is responsible (financially and otherwise) for replacing it?

WELLNESS. What steps can parents (and students) take to encourage social wellness when it comes to social media use? How about emotional and physical wellness? What safeguards are in place in case something doesn't go as planned? What online and in-real-life resources are available to parents and students?

Recommended Reading List

Ansari, A. (2016). *Modern romance: An investigation.* * New York, NY: Penguin.

boyd, d. (2014). *It's complicated: The social lives of networked teens.* New Haven, CT: Yale University Press.

Damour, L. (2016). *Untangled: Guiding teenage girls through the seven transitions into adulthood.* New York, NY: Ballantine.

Heitner, D. (2016). *Screenwise: Helping kids survive (and thrive) in their digital world.* London, UK: Routledge.

Jensen, F. (2016). *The teenage brain: A neuroscientist's survival guide to raising adolescents and young adults.* New York, NY: Harper.

Sales, N. J. (2016). *American girls: Social media and the secret lives of teenagers.* New York, NY: Alfred Knopf.

Turkle, S. (2015). *Reclaiming conversation: The power of talk in a digital age.* New York, NY: Penguin Press.

RESOURCES

#Being13: Inside the secret world of teens. http://edition.cnn.com/specials/us/being13.

The Common Sense Census: Media use by tweens and teens. www.common sensemedia.org

Crisis Text Line. www.crisistextline.org

---

*Even though *Modern Romance* focuses on young adults, much of the premise around the change in dating is helpful for parents of teenagers and young adults to understand.

Acknowledgments

This book was a challenge—one I had no idea would require as much time and energy as it did. I am so eternally grateful for the support of so many when I was in the process of writing, rewriting, and finishing (and then refinishing) this book. Thank you for supporting me, humoring me, cajoling me, and patiently waiting for me to get to the finish line of this book's indelible journey.

First and foremost, I would like to thank the students—the ones who walk into our Green Ivy Educational Consulting offices every week, and the ones I've met and visited at schools across the United States (and abroad). Your curiosity, generosity, authenticity, and understanding of social media and how it affects your everyday lives challenged me to think longer and harder about the topics presented in this book.

Thank you to Ariel Bartlett for her patient persistence and kindness as an editor—your cheerleading of this book in and of itself is life-affirming. Thank you, too, to Arnis Burvikovs for seeing the importance of this book—even before I did. Thank you to Kaitlyn Irwin and Andrew Olson, who worked behind the scenes to help this book along. Thank you to my amazing, ever-enthusiastic, and supportive agent, Rebecca Gradinger, for all you do.

We should all be so lucky to have such dedicated champions and friends like Margaret Miller, who has read nearly every page of every draft of every book I have written and offered her own in-the-trenches, real-world commentary. Thank you as well to Susan Marquess—this book and some of my life's work may never have found such purpose without your initial guidance.

To the wonderful people who took time out of their busy schedules to discuss some of the topics in this book, I am so appreciative of your time and efforts—especially since some of you were simply friends allowing me to bounce ideas off you. Our conversations (online and in real life) served to shape and formulate ideas, sometimes long after the discussions ended. Thank you to Britton Bitterman, Drew Bitterman, Mary Callahan, Lori Cashman, Julia Cook, Andrew Davis, Kyle Doherty, Joel Flory, Kathryn Gray, Than Healy, Amy Hepburn, Ashley Hill, Michelle Icard, Alice Kleeman, Jessica Lee, Mark Anthony Neal, Katie Orenstein, Dan-el Padilla Peralta, Steven Petrow, Mike Popek, Ari Redbord, Russ Richards, Kathy Rudy, Adam Seldow, Amy Guggenheim Shenkan, Catherine Teitelbaum, Patricia Tennant, and Sue Wasiolek.

Thank you to the many generous folks who make my life better and more wonderful by being a part of it: Charlotte Richardson, Tom Davis, Lawrence Adjah, Heather Bennett, Elise Van Middelem, Amanda Jones, Kara Edgar, Nikki Gibson, Sterly Wilder and the entire Duke Alumni Association staff, and to the many parents of students who have been so supportive of my work over the years.

Special thanks to the staff at Green Ivy, who supported my writing of this book for far longer than any of us ever thought possible: Emily Dickson, Abby Mims, Lawrence Melton, Dasha Savage, Harsh Sikka, and Ryan Taylor. Thank you as well to Sarah Haas for providing a wonderful perspective on the final draft. Thank you to Kathleen Kelly Janus, Sarah Thorton, Kori Schake, and Anja Manuel for reading sections of this book and offering your insight. And to the staff at Saint Franks Coffee, thank you for always offering divine inspiration.

A big thanks to Ime Archibong for reading and commenting on a rough draft of this book. Your insight and unique perspective were and are much appreciated.

Finally, thanks to my family, including my sister, Dr. Allia Griffin, to whom this book is dedicated and who read a draft of this book while very, very pregnant and encouraged me to "just finish it already," along with her terrific husband, Kevin Griffin, and my ever-phenomenal nephew, Cameron. My parents, Amir Homayoun and Barbara Manning, have always been unfalteringly supportive, and I am so grateful for the love and support their spouses, Afsaneh and John, bring into our lives.

Endnotes

PROLOGUE

1. Instagram photo by The White House. (2016, December 23). Retrieved January 3, 2017, from www.instagram.com/p/BOXlBS5jkj4/?taken -by=whitehouse
2. Sahm, C. (2016, October 5). Virtual reality in the classroom. *U.S. News & World Report*. Retrieved January 3, 2017, from www.usnews.com/ opinion/articles/2016-10-05/can-virtual-reality-improve-education
3. Silverman, C. (2016, November 16). This analysis shows how fake election news stories outperformed real news on Facebook. *BuzzFeed*. Retrieved January 03, 2017, from www.buzzfeed.com/craigsilverman/viral-fake -election-news-outperformed-real-news-on-facebook; Domonske, C. (2016, November 23). Students have "dismaying" inability to tell fake news from real, study finds. NPR. Retrieved January 3, 2017, from http:// www.npr.org/sections/thetwo-way/2016/11/23/503129818/study-finds -students-have-dismaying-inability-to-tell-fake-news-from-real
4. Ophir, E., & Nass, C. (2009, July 20). Cognitive control in media multitaskers. *Proceedings of the National Academy of Sciences*. Retrieved January 03, 2017, from http://www.pnas.org/content/106/37/15583.full

CHAPTER 1

1. At the time, Ask.fm allowed users to create profiles and anyone could ask questions or write posts anonymously on those profiles. In August 2014, Ask.fm was purchased by Ask.com, and new policies were put in place to prevent online bullying. In July 2016, Noosphere purchased the site.
2. *Terms and policies*. (2015, February 2). Retrieved July 31, 2016, from ask.fm/about/policy/terms-of-service
3. Lenhart, A. (2015, April 9). Teens, social media & technology overview 2015. Pew Research Center. Retrieved November 6, 2016, from www .pewinternet.org/2015/04/09/teens-social-media-technology-2015/

4. Ibid.

5. *Newswire*. (2011, December 15). New mobile obsession: US teens triple data usage. Neilsen. Retrieved July 23, 2014, from www.nielsen .com/us/en/insights/news/2011/new-mobile-obsession-u-s-teens-triple -data-usage.html

6. Perez, S. (2016, April 12). Facebook Messenger and WhatsApp combined see 3 times more messages than SMS. *TechCrunch*. Retrieved November 7, 2016, from techcrunch.com/2016/04/12/facebook -messenger-and-whatsapp-combined-see-3-times-more-messages -than-sms/

7. PR Newswire. (2013, March 19). Generation Z: A look at the technology and media habits of today's teens. Retrieved March 10, 2016, from www.prnewswire.com/news-releases/generation-z-a-look-at-the -technology-and-media-habits-of-todays-teens-198958011.html

8. Rideout, V. (2015). *The Common Sense Census: Media use by teens and tweens* (pp. 14–15). Common Sense Media. Retrieved July 31, 2016, from static1.1.sqspcdn.com/static/f/1083077/26645197/1446492628567/ CSM_TeenTween_MediaCensus_FinalWebVersion_1.pdf

9. Ibid.

10. Ibid.

11. Sales, N. J. (2016). *American girls: Social media and the secret lives of teenagers* (p. 371). New York, NY: Alfred Knopf.

12. Case, A. (2010, December). *We are all cyborgs now.* TED. Retrieved November 7, 2016, from www.ted.com/talks/amber_case_we_are_all_ cyborgs_now

13. Gary, L., Thomas, N., & Lewis, L. (2010). *Teachers' use of educational technology in U.S. public schools, 2009: First look.* National Center for Education Statistics. Retrieved July 23, 2014, from nces.ed.gov/ pubs2010/2010040.pdf

14. Lenhart, A., Madden, M., Smith, A., Purcell, K., Zickuhr, K., & Rainie, L. (2011). Teens, kindness and cruelty on social network sites. Pew Research Center. Retrieved April 16, 2016, from www.pewinternet .org/2011/11/09/teens-kindness-and-cruelty-on-social-network-sites/

15. Turkle, S. (2015). *Reclaiming conversation: The power of talk in a digital age* (pp. 128–130). New York, NY: Penguin Press.

16. Rideout, V. (2015). *The Common Sense Census: Media use by teens and tweens* (p. 24). Common Sense Media. Retrieved July 31, 2016, from static1.1.sqspcdn.com/static/f/1083077/26645197/1446492628567/ CSM_TeenTween_MediaCensus_FinalWebVersion_1.pdf

17. Ibid.

18. Brizendine, L. (2006). *The female brain.* New York, NY: Morgan Road Books.

19. Meeker, M., & Wu, L. (2013, May 29). 2013 Internet trends. Kleiner Perkins Caufield & Byers. Retrieved March 20, 2016, from www.kpcb .com/blog/2013-internet-trends

20. Smith, A. (2015, April 1). U.S. smartphone use in 2015. Pew Research Center. Retrieved March 20, 2016, from www.pewinternet .org/2015/04/01/us-smartphone-use-in-2015/

21. Conversation with Andrew Davis, March 7, 2014.

22. Andrews, L. (2012, February 4). Facebook is using you. *New York Times*. Retrieved April 1, 2016, from www.nytimes.com/2012/02/05/ opinion/sunday/facebook-is-using-you.html

23. Singer, N. (2015, February 9). Uncovering security flaws in digital education products for schoolchildren. *New York Times*. Retrieved April 1, 2016, from www.nytimes.com/2015/02/09/technology/uncovering -security-flaws-in-digital-education-products-for-schoolchildren.html

24. Ibid.

CHAPTER 2

1. Dockterman, E. (2014, June 18). How "Hot or Not" created the Internet we know today. *Time*. Retrieved April 1, 2016, from time .com/2894727/hot-or-not-internet/

2. Kaplan, K. A. (2003, November 19). Facemash creator survives ad board. *Harvard Crimson*. Retrieved April 1, 2016, from www.thecrim son.com/article/2003/11/19/facemash-creator-survives-ad-board-the/

3. Sciuto, L. (2013, April 15). Instagram beauty contests can be harmful to girls. PBS. Retrieved April 1, 2016, from www.pbs.org/newshour/ extra/2013/04/instagram-beauty-contests-can-be-harmful-to-girls/

4. Bloomquist, S. (2013, May 10). Instagram pageants: New form of cyber-bullying. ABC Action News (Philadelphia). Retrieved July 21, 2014, from 6abc.com/archive/9097109/

5. Morrison, K. (2015, June 9). How many photos are uploaded to Snapchat every second? *Ad Week*. Retrieved April 1, 2016, from www .adweek.com/socialtimes/how-many-photos-are-uploaded-to-snap chat-every-second/621488

6. Solon, O. (2013, October 11). Am I pretty or ugly? Louise Orwin explores this YouTube phenomenon. *Wired*. Retrieved April 2, 2016, from www.wired.co.uk/news/archive/2013-10/11/pretty-ugly

7. Stenovec, T. (2011, June 29). Myspace history: A timeline of the social network's biggest moments. *Huffington Post*. Retrieved July 28, 2014, from www.huffingtonpost.com/2011/06/29/myspace-history-timeline_ n_887059.html#s299496title=August_2003_Myspace

8. Dockterman, E. (2014, June 18). How "Hot or Not" created the Internet we know today. *Time*. Retrieved April 1, 2016, from time .com/2894727/hot-or-not-internet/

9. Finder, A. (2006, June 11). For some, online persona undermines a résumé. *New York Times*. Retrieved April 2, 2016, from //www.nytimes .com/2006/06/11/us/11recruit.html

10. *Company info | Facebook newsroom.* (2016, June 30). Retrieved November 6, 2016, from newsroom.fb.com/company-info/

11. Newton, C. (2015, August 27). Facebook draws 1 billion users in a single day. *The Verge.* Retrieved September 5, 2015, from www.theverge.com/2015/8/27/9217607/facebook-one-billion-daily-active-users

12. Newton, C. (2014, October 1). Facebook clarifies real name policy amid LGBT protests. *The Verge.* Retrieved November 7, 2016, from www.theverge.com/2014/10/1/6881641/facebook-will-update-real-name-policy-to-accommodate-lgbt-community

13. Fidler, S. (2015, February 23). Facebook policies taken to task in report for data-privacy issues. *Wall Street Journal.* Retrieved August 7, 2016, from www.wsj.com/articles/facebook-policies-taken-to-task-in-report-for-data-privacy-issues-1424725902

14. Gaudin, S. (2013, October 17). Facebook loosens its rules on teen privacy. *Computerworld.* Retrieved July 27, 2014, from www.computerworld.com/s/article/9243270/Facebook_loosens_its_rules_on_teen_privacy

15. MacDonald, C. (2015, December 10). Teens flock to anonymous messaging app: "After school" lets students secretly post thoughts, but is it increasing bullying? *Daily Mail.* Retrieved November 7, 2016, from www.dailymail.co.uk/sciencetech/article-3353643/Teens-flock-anonymous-messaging-app-School-lets-students-secretly-post-thoughts-increasing-bullying.html

16. Tweedie, S. (2014, November 7). Mark Zuckerberg reveals why you were forced to download Facebook's separate Messenger app. *Business Insider.* Retrieved August 4, 2016, from www.businessinsider.com/why-is-facebook-messenger-a-separate-app-2014-11

17. Setalvad, A. (2015, September 4). Facebook Messenger is now the second most popular app in the United States. *The Verge.* Retrieved August 1, 2016, from www.theverge.com/2015/9/4/9264069/facebook-messenger-google-youtube-apps

18. Rusli, E. M. (2012, April 9). Facebook buys Instagram for $1 billion. *New York Times.* Retrieved April 2, 2016, from dealbook.nytimes.com/2012/04/09/facebook-buys-instagram-for-1-billion/

19. Wortham, J. (2013, February 8). A growing app lets you see it, then you don't. *New York Times.* Retrieved April 6, 2016, from www.nytimes.com/2013/02/09/technology/snapchat-a-growing-app-lets-you-see-it-then-you-dont.html

20. Kardashian, K. (2016, November 6). Kim Kardashian west (@kimkardashian) • Instagram photos and videos. Retrieved November 6, 2016, from www.instagram.com/kimkardashian

21. *Instagram press page.* (2016, February 29). Retrieved November 6, 2016, from www.instagram.com/press/

22. Shontell, A. (2014, October 29). People are now spending a mind-boggling 21 minutes per day on Instagram. *Business Insider.* Retrieved

August 7, 2016, from www.businessinsider.com/people-spend-21
-minutes-per-day-on-instagram-2014-10

23. Hutchins, B. (2014, June 11). Social media strategy for Instagram: 7 actionable tips. Business 2 Community. Retrieved July 28, 2014, from www.business2community.com/instagram/social-media-strategy-insta gram-7-actionable-tips-0903282#!boNpjD

24. Ault, S. (2015, July 23). Digital star popularity grows versus mainstream celebrities. *Variety.* Retrieved August 4, 2016, from variety.com/2015/ digital/news/youtubers-teen-survey-ksi-pewdiepie-1201544882/

25. Sales, N. J. (2016). *American girls: Social media and the secret lives of teenagers* (pp. 111–116). New York, NY: Alfred Knopf.

26. Ibid.

27. Desk, N. (2013, October 29). Teen girls who share their melancholia online reshaping what it means to be depressed. PBS. Retrieved July 28, 2014, from www.pbs.org/newshour/rundown/melancholia -trends-on-tumblr/

28. Lenhart, A. (2015, August 6). Teens, technology and friendships. Pew Research Center. Retrieved April 5, 2016, from www.pewinternet .org/2015/08/06/teens-technology-and-friendships/

29. Wauters, R. (2012, July 18). GroupMe has 4.6m users sending 550m messages per month. *The Next Web.* Retrieved October 20, 2016, from thenextweb.com/insider/2012/07/18/groupme-has-4-6m-users -sending-550m-messages-per-month-court-documents-show/

30. Lenhart, A. (2015, August 6). Teens, technology and friendships. Pew Research Center. Retrieved April 5, 2016, from www.pewinternet .org/2015/08/06/teens-technology-and-friendships/

31. Klin, C. (2015, December 8). Study: Text messages that end in a period seen as less sincere. *EurekAlert!* Retrieved April 5, 2016, from www .eurekalert.org/pub_releases/2015-12/bu-stm120815.php

32. Abbott, T. (2015, January 20). More teachers are having sex with their students. Here's how schools can stop them. *Washington Post.* Retrieved October 20, 2016, from www.washingtonpost .com/posteverything/wp/2015/01/20/more-teachers-are-having-sex -with-their-students-heres-how-schools-can-stop-them/?utm_term= .00549c04f83a

33. Zerega, B. (2016, September 14). Education app Remind passes 20 million active users and names Brian Grey CEO. *Venture Beat.* Retrieved October 20, 2016, from venturebeat.com/2016/09/14/education-app -remind-passes-20-million-active-users-and-names-brian-grey-ceo/

34. Sales, N. J. (2016). Social media and secret lives of American girls. *Time.* Retrieved August 1, 2016, from time.com/americangirls/?utm_ content=buffer12343

35. Constine, J. (2016, August 2). Instagram launches "Stories," a snapchatty feature for imperfect sharing. *TechCrunch.* Retrieved November 7, 2016, from techcrunch.com/2016/08/02/instagram-stories/

36. Madden, M., Lenhart, A., Cortesi, S., Gasser, U., Duggan, M., Smith, A., & Beaton, M. (2013, May 21). Teens, social media, and privacy. Pew Research Center. Retrieved April 6, 2016, from www.pewinternet.org/2013/05/21/teens-social-media-and-privacy/

37. Safronova, V. (2015, November 18). On fake Instagram, a chance to be real. *New York Times*. Retrieved April 6, 2016, from www.nytimes.com/2015/11/19/fashion/instagram-finstagram-fake-account.html

38. Strohmaier, H., Murphy, M., & Dematteo, D. (2014, June 4). Youth sexting: Prevalence rates, driving motivations, and the deterrent effect of legal consequences. *Sexuality Research and Social Policy, 11*(3), 245–255. doi:10.1007/s13178-014-0162-9

39. Schaffer, M. (2013, October 14). Who can view my snaps and stories. Retrieved April 6, 2016, from snapchat-blog.com/post/64036804085/who-can-view-my-snaps-and-stories

40. Mayfield, J. (2014, May 8). Snapchat settles FTC charges that promises of disappearing messages were false [Press release]. Federal Trade Commission. Retrieved April 6, 2016, from www.ftc.gov/news-events/press-releases/2014/05/snapchat-settles-ftc-charges-promises-disappearing-messages-were

41. Franceschi-Bicchierai, L. (2014, October 13). 98,000 hacked snapchat photos and videos posted online. *Mashable*. Retrieved April 1, 2016, from mashable.com/2014/10/13/the-snappening-photos-videos-posted/#waoBEpTwUkqc

42. *Snapchat support*. (2016, April 6). Retrieved August 1, 2016, from support.snapchat.com/en-US/a/guidelines

43. Kolodny, L. (2017, April 28). Yik Yak shuts down after Square paid $1 million for its engineers. Retrieved May 01, 2017, from https://techcrunch.com/2017/04/28/yik-yak-shuts-down-after-square-paid-1-million-for-its-engineers/

44. Shontell, A. (2014, June 30). Yik Yak, A 7-month-old school gossip app that's spreading like crazy, has raised $10 million. *Business Insider*. Retrieved July 27, 2014, from www.businessinsider.com/yik-yak-raises-10-million-2014-6

45. Haskell, W. (2014, April 28). A gossip app brought my high school to a halt. *New York Magazine*. Retrieved July 8, 2014, from nymag.com/thecut/2014/04/gossip-app-brought-my-high-school-to-a-halt.html

46. Ibid.

47. Graber, D. (2014, March 26). Yik Yak app makers do the right thing. *Huffington Post*. Retrieved July 8, 2014, from www.huffingtonpost.com/diana-graber/yik-yak-app-makers-do-the_b_5029679.html

48. Madden, M., Lenhart, A., Cortesi, S., Gasser, U., Duggan, M., Smith, A., & Beaton, M. (2013, May 21). Teens, social media, and privacy. Pew Research Center. Retrieved April 6, 2016, from www.pewinternet.org/2013/05/21/teens-social-media-and-privacy/

49. MacDonald, C. (2015, December 10). Teens flock to anonymous messaging app: "After School" lets students secretly post thoughts, but is it increasing bullying? *Daily Mail*. Retrieved November 7, 2016, from www.dailymail.co.uk/sciencetech/article-3353643/Teens -flock-anonymous-messaging-app-School-lets-students-secretly -post-thoughts-increasing-bullying.html

50. Balingit, M. (2015, December 8). Millions of teens are using a new app to post anonymous thoughts, and most parents have no idea. *Washington Post*. Retrieved October 20, 2016, from www.washington post.com/local/education/millions-of-teens-are-using-a-new-app-to -post-anonymous-thoughts-and-most-parents-have-no-idea/2015/ 12/08/1532a98c-9907-11e5-8917-653b65c809eb_story.html?utm_ term=.3e56246001ce

51. Vaynerchuk, G. (2015). *The rise of video marketing on social and how it affects your business*. Retrieved April 11, 2016, from www.gary vaynerchuk.com/the-rise-of-video-marketing-on-social-and-how-it -affects-your-business/

52. Martins, C. (2016, October 20). Musical.ly's teenage revolution: How the trend-setting Lip-Sync app is changing the music industry. *Billboard*. Retrieved October 20, 2016, from www.billboard.com/articles/ news/magazine-feature/7549094/musically-app-lip-sync-billboard -cover

53. Ibid.

54. Howard, H. (2016, October 20). How Maria Shabalin, a Musical.ly star, spends her Sundays. *New York Times*. Retrieved November 7, 2016, from www.nytimes.com/2016/10/23/nyregion/how-maria-shab alin-a-musically-star-spends-her-sundays.html

55. Rideout, V. (2015). *The Common Sense Census: Media use by teens and tweens* (p. 18). Common Sense Media. Retrieved July 31, 2016, from static1.1.sqspcdn.com/static/f/1083077/26645197/1446492628567/ CSM_TeenTween_MediaCensus_FinalWebVersion_1.pdf

56. *Periscope*. (2016, April 11). Retrieved August 1, 2016, from www .periscope.tv/

57. Topolsky, J. (2016, April 8). Facebook Live: Now you can never leave. *New Yorker*. Retrieved April 11, 2016, from www.newyorker.com/ business/currency/facebook-live-now-you-can-never-leave

58. Ingram, David. (2017, May 03). Facebook tries to fix violent video problem with 3,000 workers. Retrieved May 11, 2017, from https:// www.usnews.com/news/top-news/articles/2017-05-03/facebook-to -add-3-000-workers-to-monitor-live-video-other-posts

59. Pinsker, J. (2016, April 4). The hidden economics of porn. *The Atlantic*. Retrieved April 11, 2016, from www.theatlantic.com/business/ archive/2016/04/pornography-industry-economics-tarrant/476580/

60. Ibid.

61. Brown, J. D., & L'Engle, K. L. (2009, January 29). X-rated: Sexual attitudes and behaviors associated with U.S. early adolescents' exposure to
sexually explicit media. *Communication Research*. Retrieved August 1,
2016, from www.unc.edu/depts/jomc/teenmedia/pdf/xrated.pdf

62. The Obama White House. (2016, December 31). Behind the lens:
2016 year in photographs. *Medium*. Retrieved January 3, 2017, from
medium.com/the-white-house/behind-the-lens-2016-year-in-photo
graphs-9e2c8733bbb3#.2hnn6kmzl

63. WITW Staff. (2016, October 26). Woman groped in virtual reality game says experience felt horrifyingly real. *New York Times*.
Retrieved January 3, 2017, from nytlive.nytimes.com/womenanthe
world/2016/10/26/woman-groped-in-virtual-reality-game-says
-experience-felt-horrifyingly-real/

64. Google for Education. (2015, May 28). *Expeditions: Take your students to places a school bus can't*. Retrieved January 3, 2017, from
www.youtube.com/watch?v=mlYJdZeA9w4

65. O'Keefe, G. S., Clarke-Pearson, K., & Council on Communications and
Media. (2011, March). Clinical report—The impact of social media on
children, adolescents, and families. American Academy of Pediatrics.
Retrieved August 1, 2016, from pediatrics.aappublications.org/content/
pediatrics/127/4/800.full.pdf

66. Geel, M. V., Vedder, P., & Tanilon, J. (2014, May). Relationship between
peer victimization, cyberbullying, and suicide in children and adolescents: A meta-analysis. *JAMA Pediatrics*. Retrieved August 1, 2016,
from archpedi.jamanetwork.com/article.aspx?articleid=1840250

67. Suldo, S. M., McMahan, M. M., Chappel, A. M., & Loker, T. (2012,
April 25). Relationships between perceived school climate and adolescent mental health across genders. *School Mental Health*. Retrieved
August 1, 2016, from cemh.lbpsb.qc.ca/professionals/SchoolClimate
andMentalHealth.pdf

Table 2.2

1. Funny anonymous school news for confessions & compliments.
Retrieved November 7, 2016, from https://afterschoolapp.com/about/

2. Bindel, A. After School—Funny anonymous school news for confessions & compliments—App review. Common Sense Media. Retrieved
November 7, 2016, from www.commonsensemedia.org/app-reviews/after-
school-funny-anonymous-school-news-for-confessions-compliments

3. Balingit, M. (2015, December 8). Millions of teens are using a new app to
post anonymous thoughts, and most parents have no idea. *Washington
Post*. Retrieved November 8, 2016, from www.washingtonpost.com/
local/education/millions-of-teens-are-using-a-new-app-to-post-anonymous-
thoughts-and-most-parents-have-no-idea/2015/12/08/1532a98c9907-
11e5-8917-653b65c809eb_story.html

4. About Us | About ASKfm. Retrieved April 7, 2016, from http://about .ask.fm/about/

5. PR Newswire. (2015, August 27). As digital and offline lives merge, 8 out of 10 US teens post to social media without a second thought. Retrieved from www.prnewswire.com/news-releases/as-digital-and-offline-lives-merge-8-out-of-10-us-teens-post-to-social-media-without-a-second-thought-300134097.html

6. Dickey, J. (2014, June 26). Meet the brothers behind the web's most controversial social network. *Time*. Retrieved from http://time.com/ 2923146/ask-fm-interview/

7. Instagram help center. Retrieved April 7, 2016, from https://help .instagram.com/182492381886913/

8. LePage, E. (2015, September 17). A long list of Instagram statistics and facts that prove its importance. Retrieved from https://blog.hootsuite .com/instagram-statistics-for-business/

9. Terms of use. Retrieved April 7, 2016, from www.instagram.com/ about/legal/terms/

10. Bircher, M. M. (2016, September 14). Teens are hiding their real lives from nosey parents with 'fake' Instagram accounts. *Tech Insider*. Retrieved from www.techinsider.io/teens-hiding-real-lives-on-finstagram-2015-9

11. Constine, J. (2016, July 02). Instagram launches "Stories," a Snapchatty feature for imperfect sharing. *TechCrunch*. Retrieved November 8, 2016, from https://techcrunch.com/2016/08/02/instagram-stories/

12. Smith, C. (2016, April 5). 160 amazing Instagram statistics. Retrieved April 7, 2016, from http://expandedramblings.com/index.php/important-instagram-stats/3/

13. Our beliefs. Retrieved April 7, 2016, from www.kik.com/about/

14. TeenSafe.com (2015, November 30). Everything a parent needs to know about KIK. Retrieved from www.teensafe.com/blog/everything-a-parent-needs-to-know-about-kik/

15. A new way to engage. Retrieved April 7, 2016, from www.kik.com/ partners/

16. Shontell, A. (2015, March 26). What it's like to sell your startup for ~$120 million before it's even launched: Meet Twitter's new prized possession, Periscope. Business Insider. Retrieved from www.business insider.com/what-is-periscope-and-why-twitter-bought-it-2015-3

17. How do I sign up for a Periscope account? (2015, December 30). Retrieved from https://help.periscope.tv/customer/portal/articles/ 2016596-how-do-i-sign-up-for-a-periscope-account

18. Explainer: What is Periscope? A parent's guide. Retrieved April 7, 2016, from www.webwise.ie/parents/explainer-what-is-periscope/

19. Mansfield, M. (2015, August 5). What is Periscope and how do *I* use it? *Small Business Trends*. Retrieved from http://smallbiztrends .com/2015/08/what-is-periscope-how-do-i-use-it.html

20. Ashlam, S. (2015, September 23). Periscope by the numbers: Stats, demographics & fun facts. *Omnicore*. Retrieved from www.omnicore agency.com/periscope-statistics/

21. Smith, C. (2016, April 1). 70 amazing Snapchat statistics. Retrieved from http://expandedramblings.com/index.php/snapchat-statistics/

22. Singh, K. (2014, August 4). The beginner's guide to Snapchat. *Mashable*. Retrieved from http://mashable.com/2014/08/04/snap chat-for-beginners/#m8iALVu1vZqp

23. Terms of service. Retrieved April 7, 2016, from www.snapchat.com/ terms

24. 3V Advertising. Retrieved April 7, 2016, from www.snapchat.com/ads

25. 10 Snapchat statistics you need to know in 2016. (2016, January). Retrieved from http://mediakix.com/2016/01/snapchat-statistics-2016-marketers-need-to-know/

26. Hoelzel, M. (2015, June 29). UPDATE: A breakdown of the demographics for each of the different social networks. *Business Insider*. Retrieved from www.businessinsider.com/update-a-breakdown-of-the-demographics-for-each-of-the-different-social-networks-2015-6

27. Crunchbase.com. (n.d.). Spotafriend. Retrieved March 3, 2017, https:// www.crunchbase.com/organization/spotafriend#/entity

28. Spotafriend. (n.d.). Retrieved March 3, 2017, https://www.spotafriend .co/#make-friends

29. Tagz.com. (2016, December 18). Spotafriend Teen meeting app to make new friends. Retrieved March 3, 2017, from https://itunes .apple.com/us/app/spotafriend-teen-meeting-app-to-make-new-friends/ id962892510?mt=8

30. Now teenagers have their own version of Tinder. (2016, June 28). *Fast Company*. Retrieved March 3, 2017, from news.fastcompany.com/ now-teenagers-have-their-own-version-of-tinder-4012148

31. Tumblr—About. Retrieved April 7, 2016, from www.tumblr.com/about

32. Tumblr—Sign up. Retrieved April 7, 2016, from www.tumblr.com/ register

33. Novak, M. (2014, August 3). Age ranges of Tumblr's global audience: Unwrapping Tumblr. Retrieved from http://unwrapping.tumblr.com/ post/93716151897/age-demographics-tumblr

34. Carlson, N. (2011, April 13). The real history of Twitter. *Business Insider*. Retrieved from www.businessinsider.com/how-twitter-was-founded-2011-4

35. Signing up with Twitter. Retrieved April 7, 2016, from https://support .twitter.com/articles/100990

36. Bennett, S. (2014, September 29). Minimum age requirements: Twitter, Facebook, Instagram, Snapchat, WhatsApp, Secret. *Ad Week*. Retrieved from www.adweek.com/socialtimes/social-media-minimum-age/501920

37. Twitter—Statistics and facts. (2016, January). Retrieved from www .statista.com/topics/737/twitter/

38. Lenhart, A. (2015, April 8). *Teens, social media & technology overview 2015*. Pew Research Center. Retrieved from www.pewinternet .org/2015/04/09/teens-social-media-technology-2015/

39. Carr, A. (2014, July 14). Get inside Whisper's secret economy. *Fast Company*. Retrieved from www.fastcompany.com/3032951/welcome-to-the-secret-economy

40. Ang, S. (2014, January 26). The beginner's guide to Whisper. Mashable. Retrieved from http://mashable.com/2014/01/26/whisper-beginners/ #MyLZiH0Yvgq8

41. Whisper TERMS. Retrieved April 7, 2016, from https://whisper.sh/terms

42. Dickey, M. R. (2014, March 21). The war for your secrets is on, but the godfather of anonymity is skeptical about Whisper and Secret. Business Insider. Retrieved from www.businessinsider.com/secret-whisper-and-anonymous-apps-moral-responsibility-2014-3

43. *Olson, P.* (2014, January 24). 3 Reasons to be wary of secret-sharing app Whisper's claim to anonymity. *Forbes*. Retrieved from www .forbes.com/sites/parmyolson/2014/01/24/3-reasons-to-be-wary-of-secret-sharing-app-whispers-claim-to-anonymity/#1396c82579b0

44. DeAmici, C. (2015, April 29). Whisper announces it hit 10 million users the same day secret shuts down. Here's why. Recode. Retrieved from http://recode.net/2015/04/29/with-impeccable-timing-whisper-announces-it-hit-10-million-users-the-same-day-secret-shuts-down/

45. TeenSafe.com (2016, April 3). Everything a parent needs to know about Whisper. Retrieved from http://www.teensafe.com/blog/everything-a-parent-needs-to-know-about-whisper/

CHAPTER 3

1. O'Keefe, G. S., Clarke-Pearson, K., & Council on Communications and Media. (2011, March). Clinical report—The impact of social media on children, adolescents, and families. *Pediatrics*. Retrieved August 1, 2016, from pediatrics.aappublications.org/content/pediatrics/127/4/800.full.pdf

2. Ibid.

3. Lin, L. Y., Sidani, J. E., Shensa, A., Radovic, A., Miller, E., Colditz, J. B., . . . Primack, B. A. (2016, January 19). Association between social media use and depression among U.S. young adults. *Depression and Anxiety*. doi:10.1002/da.22466

4. University of Pittsburgh Schools of the Health Sciences. (2016, March 22). Social media use associated with depression among US young adults. *Science Daily*. Retrieved August 2, 2016, from www.sciencedaily.com/ releases/2016/03/160322100401.htm

5. Luthar, S. S., & Ciciolla, L. (2016, January). What it feels like to be a mother: Variations by children's developmental stages. *Developmental Psychology*, 52(1), 143–154. doi:10.4135/9781473960749

6. Garner, S. (2016, February 25). Men's Wearhouse and Snapchat celebrate "National Promposal Day." *MR*. Retrieved November 7, 2016, from www.mr-mag.com/mens-wearhouse-and-snapchat-celebrate-national-promposal-day/

7. Dweck, C. S. (2006). *Mindset: The new psychology of success* (p. 7). New York, NY: Random House.

8. Ibid, p. 49.

9. Ibid, p. 49.

10. Ibid, p. 73.

11. Lynch, A. (2015, April 20). Teens are using bottle tops to get Kylie Jenner lips on social media and it's terrifying. METRO. Retrieved August 2, 2016, from metro.co.uk/2015/04/20/people-are-using-bottle-tops-to-get-kylie-jenner-lips-on-social-media-and-its-terrifying-5158382/

12. Mychaskiw, M. (2015, October 22). Could this be the end of Kylie Jenner's big lip phase? *InStyle*. Retrieved April 23, 2016, from www.instyle.com/news/kylie-jenner-small-lips

13. Federal Trade Commission. (2015, March 20). *Complying with COPPA: Frequently asked questions*. Retrieved April 17, 2016, from www.ftc.gov/tips-advice/business-center/guidance/complying-coppa-frequently-asked-questions

14. Stevens, H. (2015, August 13). Parents expect teens to text back ASAP—even while driving. *Chicago Tribune*. Retrieved August 2, 2016, from www.chicagotribune.com/lifestyles/ct-parents-text-kids-too-much-balancing-20150813-column.html

15. Insurance Institute for Highway Safety, & State Highway Safety Offices. (2016, April 19). *Distracted driving laws*. Retrieved August 2, 2016, from www.ghsa.org/html/stateinfo/laws/cellphone_laws.html

16. U.S. Department of Transportation. (2014, April). *Traffic safety facts*. Retrieved April 17, 2016, from www.distraction.gov/downloads/pdfs/812012.pdf

17. Madden, M., & Rainie, L. (2010, June 18). Adults and cell phone distractions. Retrieved March 7, 2017, from pewinternet.org/Reports/2010/Cell-Phone-Distractions.aspx

18. Madden, M., & Lenhart, A. (2009, November 16). Teens and distracted driving. *Pew Research Center*. Retrieved April 17, 2016, from www.pewinternet.org/2009/11/16/teens-and-distracted-driving-2/

19. Federal Communications Commission. (2015, November 3). *Children's Internet Protection Act*. Retrieved August 2, 2016, from www.fcc.gov/guides/childrens-internet-protection-act

20. Ibid.

21. Federal Communications Commission. (2016, October 25). FAQs on E-rate program for schools and libraries. Retrieved March 7, 2017, from www.fcc.gov/consumers/guides/universal-service-program-schools-and-libraries-e-rate

22. *AASL executive summary: Filtering in schools.* (2012, October). American Library Association. Retrieved January 3, 2017, from www .ala.org/aasl/sites/ala.org.aasl/files/content/researchandstatistics/ slcsurvey/2012/AASL_Filtering_Exec_Summary.pdf

23. Ibid.

24. Ibid.

25. Federal Communications Commission. (2015, November 3). *Children's Internet Protection Act.* Retrieved January 3, 2017, from www.fcc.gov/ guides/childrens-internet-protection-act

26. DOMO. (2015, August 15). *Data never sleeps 3.0.* Retrieved August 3, 2016, from 1.bp.blogspot.com/-xrFZeI05Oqs/Vc3T5IHgHrI/AAAAA AAA1Vo/AQp4BN0nSQA/s0/data-never-sleeps-infographic.jpg

27. Interview with Jessica Lee, July 25, 2014.

28. Cain, S. (2012). *Quiet: The power of introverts in a world that can't stop talking* (p. 75). New York, NY: Broadway Books.

29. Ibid, p. 85.

30. Ibid, p. 63.

31. boyd, d. (2014). *It's complicated: The social lives of networked teens* (p. 23). New Haven, CT: Yale University Press.

32. Ibid, p. 9.

33. Ibid, p. 11.

34. Rideout, V. (2012). *Social media, social life: How teens view their digital lives.* Common Sense Media. Retrieved August 2, 2016, from www .commonsensemedia.org/file/socialmediasociallife-final-061812pdf-0

35. Mcphate, M. (2016, April 18). Teenager is accused of live-streaming a friend's rape on Periscope. *New York Times.* Retrieved August 2, 2016, from www.nytimes.com/2016/04/19/us/periscope-rape-case-columbus -ohio-video-livestreaming.html

36. Uhls, Y., & Greenfield, P. (2012, March). The value of fame: Preadolescent perceptions of popular media and their relationship to future aspirations. *Developmental Psychology, 48*(2), 315–326. doi:10.1037/ a0026369

37. Kardashian, K. (2016, April 5). *Kim Kardashian west (@kimkar dashian)* • *Instagram photos and videos.* Retrieved April 5, 2016, from www.instagram.com/kimkardashian

38. Stevens, R. (1983). *Erik Erikson, an introduction* (pp. 48–50). New York, NY: St. Martin's Press.

39. Best Vine Feed. (2013, September 15). *Jumping over a moving car FAIL!* Retrieved April 17, 2016, from www.youtube.com/watch?v= tpu3QDXduVQ

40. Milo, P. (2012, March 29). "CNN of the ghetto": WorldStarHipHop becoming YouTube for urban violence. CBS (Atlanta). Retrieved November 8, 2016, from atlanta.cbslocal.com/2012/03/29/worldstar hiphop-website-becoming-youtube-for-urban-violence/

41. Monae, A. (2016, September 7). 15 best quotes from "Atlanta" season premiere. *Billboard*. Retrieved November 8, 2016, from www.billboard.com/articles/news/list/7502729/atlanta-season-premiere-quotes

42. Lenhart, A., Madden, M., Smith, A., Purcell, K., Zickuhr, K., & Rainie, L. (2011, November 9). Teens, kindness and cruelty on social network sites. Pew Research Center. Retrieved April 17, 2016, from www.pewinternet.org/2011/11/09/teens-kindness-and-cruelty-on-social-network-sites/

43. Ibid.

CHAPTER 4

1. Gayomali, C. (2014, February 25). How VSCO grid plans to set itself apart from Instagram. *Fast Company*. Retrieved November 8, 2016, from www.fastcompany.com/3026722/tech-forecast/how-vsco-grid-plans-to-set-itself-apart-from-instagram

2. O'Brien, S. A. (2016, December 6). Instagram finally lets users disable comments. Retrieved March 7, 2017, from money.cnn.com/2016/12/06/technology/instagram-turn-off-comments/

3. Henion, A., McGlashen, A., & Altmann, E. (2013, January 7). Brief interruptions spawn errors. *MSU Today*. Retrieved August 4, 2016, from msutoday.msu.edu/news/2013/brief-interruptions-spawn-errors/

4. Perez, S. (2016, July 12). Moment's new app unveils a "Phone Bootcamp" to help you break your mobile addictions. *TechCrunch*. Retrieved August 4, 2016, from techcrunch.com/2016/07/12/moments-new-app-unveils-a-phone-bootcamp-to-help-you-break-your-mobile-addictions/

CHAPTER 5

1. Mueller, P. A., & Oppenheimer, D. M. (2014). The pen is mightier than the keyboard: Advantages of longhand over laptop note taking. *Psychological Science, 25*(6), 1159–1168. Retrieved August 4, 2016, from pss.sagepub.com/content/25/6/1159.full.pdf html

2. WebdesignerDepot Staff. (2009, May 11). *Advantages and disadvantages of working with multiple screens*. Retrieved August 4, 2016, from www.webdesignerdepot.com/2009/05/advantages-and-disadvantages-of-working-with-multiple-screens/

3. May, C. (2014, June 3). A learning secret: Don't take notes with a laptop. *Scientific American*. Retrieved August 7, 2016, from www.scientificamerican.com/article/a-learning-secret-don-t-take-notes-with-a-laptop/

4. Mueller, P. A., & Oppenheimer, D. M. (2014). The pen is mightier than the keyboard: Advantages of longhand over laptop note taking.

Psychological Science, 25(6), 1159–1168. Retrieved August 4, 2016, from pss.sagepub.com/content/25/6/1159.full.pdf html

5. Morrissey, J. (2016, 15 October). Your phone's on lockdown. Enjoy the show. *Scientific American.* Retrieved October 20, 2016, from www.nytimes.com/2016/10/16/technology/your-phones-on-lockdown -enjoy-the-show.html

CHAPTER 6

1. Turkle, S. (2015). *Reclaiming conversation: The power of talk in a digital age* (p. 3). New York, NY: Penguin Press.
2. *Snapchat support.* (2016, August 3). Retrieved August 3, 2016, from support.snapchat.com/en-US/about/snaps
3. Chowdhry, A. (2016, January 30). Most of your Facebook friends are not your real friends, says study. *Forbes.* Retrieved August 3, 2016, from www.forbes.com/sites/amitchowdhry/2016/01/30/most-facebook -friends-are-not-your-real-friends-says-study/#1fd9276a387d
4. Orenstein, P. (2016). *Girls & sex: Navigating the complicated new landscape* (p. 33). New York, NY: Harper.
5. Ibid, p. 35.
6. Orenstein, P. (2016, March 19). When did porn become sex ed? *New York Times.* Retrieved July 11, 2016, from www.nytimes.com/ 2016/03/20/opinion/sunday/when-did-porn-become-sex-ed.html
7. MobileMediaGuard. (n.d). *California—Laws pertaining to sexting in the state of California.* Retrieved from mobilemediaguard.com/states/ sexting_laws_california.html
8. Chamberlin, J. (2011, October). Facebook: Friend or foe. *American Psychological Association, 42*(9), 66. Retrieved August 3, 2016, from www.apa.org/monitor/2011/10/facebook.aspx
9. Turkle, S. (2015). *Reclaiming conversation: The power of talk in a digital age.* New York, NY: Penguin Press.
10. O'Connor, M. (2014, February 20). Addicted to likes: How social media feeds our neediness. *New York Magazine.* Retrieved August 4, 2016, from nymag.com/thecut/2014/02/addicted-to-likes-social-media -makes-us-needier.html; Wexler, S. Z. (2016, June 03). Why your likes don't actually mean anything. *Cosmopolitan.* Retrieved August 4, 2016, from www.cosmopolitan.com/lifestyle/a57384/why-your-likes -on-social-media-dont-mean-anything-addiction/
11. Conversation on June 20, 2016.
12. Homayoun, A. (2012). *The myth of the perfect girl: Helping our daughters find authentic success and happiness in school and life* (p. 203). New York, NY: TarcherPerigee.
13. boyd, d. (2014). *It's complicated: The social lives of networked teens* (p. 23). New Haven, CT: Yale University Press.

14. Girl Scout Research Institute. (2016, August 3). *Tips for girls. Who's that girl? Image and social media.* Retrieved August 3, 2016, from www.girlscouts.org/content/dam/girlscouts-gsusa/forms-and-documents/about-girl-scouts/research/whosthatgirl_tipsforgirls.pdf

15. Ibid.

16. Rideout, V. (2012, June 26). *Social media, social life: How teens view their digital lives* (p. 23). Common Sense Media. Retrieved July 23, 2014, from www.commonsensemedia.org/research/social-media-social-life-how-teens-view-their-digital-lives

17. Stober, D. (2012, January 25). Multitasking may harm the social and emotional development of tweenage girls, but face-to-face talks could save the day, say Stanford researchers. Retrieved July 23, 2014, from news.stanford.edu/news/2012/january/tweenage-girls-multitasking-012512.html

18. Turkle, S. (2015). *Reclaiming conversation: The power of talk in a digital age* (p. 9). New York, NY: Penguin Press.

19. Heirman, W., & Walrave, M. (2008). Assessing concerns and issues about the mediation of technology in cyberbullying. *Cyberpsychology: Journal of Psychological Research on Cyberspace.* Retrieved August 3, 2016, from www.cyberpsychology.eu/view.php?cisloclanku=2008111401

20. Chamberlin, J. (2011, October). Facebook: Friend or foe? *American Psychological Association, 42*(9), 66. Retrieved August 3, 2016, from www.apa.org/monitor/2011/10/facebook.aspx

21. Cain, S. (2012). *Quiet: The power of introverts in a world that can't stop talking* (pp. 62–63). New York, NY: Crown Publishing.

22. Summers, J. (2014, August 28). Kids and screen time: What does the research say? NPR. Retrieved August 6, 2016, from www.npr.org/sections/ed/2014/08/28/343735856/kids-and-screen-time-what-does-the-research-say

23. Rubin, B. F. (2016, December 6). Instagram to let users turn off commenting. CNET. Retrieved December 29, 2016, from www.cnet.com/news/instagram-turn-off-commenting-comments-like-heart-icon-facebook-twitter/

24. Sulek, J. P., Salonga, R., & Gomez, M. (2013, April 12). Audrie Pott suicide: Grim picture of Saratoga teen's final online cries of despair. *San Jose Mercury News.* Retrieved July 25, 2015, from www.mercurynews.com/ci_23016658/audrie-pott-case-saratoga-teens-friends-told-mom

25. Sanchez, K. (2014, January 15). 3 boys plead guilty to sexually assaulting Audrie Pott. NBC. Retrieved August 3, 2016, from www.nbcbayarea.com/news/local/3-Boys-Plead-Guilty-to-Sexually-Assaulting-Audrie-Pott-240379051.html

26. Muller, M. G. (2016, October 17). Instagram's new update may be its best one yet. *Teen Vogue.* Retrieved October 20, 2016, from www.teenvogue.com/tag/story/instagram-support-feature

27. Sullivan, N. (2012, February). *Texting that saves lives*. TED. Retrieved July 26, 2016, from www.ted.com/talks/nancy_lublin_texting_that_saves_lives

28. Gregory, A. (2015, February 2). R u there? *New Yorker*. Retrieved July 26, 2016, from www.newyorker.com/magazine/2015/02/09/r-u

CHAPTER 7

1. Gentile, D. (2009). Pathological video-game use among youth ages 8 to 18 A national study. *Psychological Science, 20*(5), 594–602. Retrieved October 18, 2016, from www.drdouglas.org/drdpdfs/Gentile_ Pathological_VG_Use_2009e.pdf

2. Adams, S. K., & Kisler, T. S. (2013, January). Sleep quality as a mediator between technology-related sleep quality, depression, and anxiety. *Cyberpsychology, Behavior, and Social Networking, 16*(1), 25–30. doi:10.1089/cyber.2012.0157

3. Adams, S. K., Daly, J. F., & Williford, D. N. (2013). Adolescent sleep and cellular phone use: Recent trends and implications for research. *Health Services Insights*. Retrieved October 14, 2016, from www.ncbi .nlm.nih.gov/pmc/articles/PMC4089837/

4. Levenson, J. C., Shensa, A., Sidani, J. E., Colditz, J. B., & Primack, B. A. (2016, January 11). The association between social media use and sleep disturbance among young adults. *Preventive Medicine*. Retrieved October 18, 2016, from www.ncbi.nlm.nih.gov/pubmed/26791323

5. Owens, J. (2014, August). Insufficient sleep in adolescents and young adults: An update on causes and consequences. *Pediatrics*. Retrieved October 18, 2016, from pediatrics.aappublications.org/content/ early/2014/08/19/peds.2014-1696

6. Adams, S. K., Daly, J. F., & Williford, D. N. (2013). Adolescent sleep and cellular phone use: Recent trends and implications for research. *Health Services Insights*. Retrieved October 14, 2016, from www.ncbi .nlm.nih.gov/pmc/articles/PMC4089837

7. Sleep Foundation. (2006). *Summary of findings: 2006 Sleep in America poll*. Retrieved October 18, 2016, from sleepfoundation.org/sites/ default/files/2006_summary_of_findings.pdf

8. Adams, S. K., Daly, J. F., & Williford, D. N. (2013). Adolescent sleep and cellular phone use: Recent trends and implications for research. *Health Services Insights*. Retrieved October 14, 2016, from www.ncbi .nlm.nih.gov/pmc/articles/PMC4089837

9. Calamaro, C. J., Mason, T. B., & Ratcliffe, S. J. (2009, May 26). Adolescents living the 24/7 lifestyle: Effects of caffeine and technology on sleep duration and daytime functioning. *Pediatrics*. Retrieved October 18, 2016, from pediatrics.aappublications.org/content/123/6/e1005

10. Ibid.

11. Williamson, A., & Feyer, A. (2000, October). Moderate sleep deprivation produces impairments in cognitive and motor performance equivalent to legally prescribed levels of alcohol intoxication. *Occupational and Environmental Medicine.* Retrieved October 18, 2016, from www.ncbi.nlm.nih.gov/pmc/articles/PMC1739867

12. Andrews, S., Ellis, D. A., Shaw, H., & Piwek, L. (2015, October 28). Beyond self-report: Tools to compare estimated and real-world smartphone use. *PLOS One.* Retrieved October 18, 2016, from journals.plos.org/plosone/article?id=10.1371/journal.pone.0139004

13. Ibid.

14. Lepp, A., Barkley, J. E., Sanders, G. J., Rebold, M., & Gates, P. (2013, June 21). The relationship between cell phone use, physical and sedentary activity, and cardiorespiratory fitness in a sample of U.S. college students. *International Journal of Behavioral Nutrition and Physical Activity.* Retrieved October 18, 2016, from www.ncbi.nlm.nih.gov/pmc/articles/PMC3693866/

15. Iannotti, R. J., Kogan, M. D., & Boyce, W. F. (2009, January 9). Patterns of adolescent physical activity, screen-based media use, and positive and negative health indicators in the U.S. and Canada. *Journal of Adolescent Health.* Retrieved October 18, 2016, from www.ncbi.nlm.nih.gov/pubmed/19380098

16. *Free coloring app for adults.* Retrieved October 18, 2016, from www.colortherapy.me/

17. DiFiori, J. P., Benjamin, H. J., Brenner, J., Gregory, A., Jayanthi, N., Landry, G. L., & Luke, A. (2014, January). Overuse injuries and burnout in youth sports: A position statement from the American Medical Society for Sports Medicine. *Clinical Journal of Sport Medicine.* Retrieved October 18, 2016, from www.ncbi.nlm.nih.gov/pubmed/24366013

18. Gentile, D. (2009). Pathological video-game use among youth ages 8 to 18: A national study. *Psychological Science, 20*(5), 594–602. Retrieved October 18, 2016, from www.drdouglas.org/drdpdfs/Gentile_Pathological_VG_Use_2009e.pdf

19. Hilgard, J., Englehardt, C. R., & Bartholow, B. D. (2013, September 9). Individual differences in motives, preferences, and pathology in video games: The gaming attitudes, motives, and experiences scales (GAMES). *Frontiers in Psychology.* Retrieved October 18, 2016, from journal.frontiersin.org/article/10.3389/fpsyg.2013.00608/full

20. Ibid.

21. *Teen online & wireless safety survey: Cyberbullying, sexting and parental controls.* (2009). Retrieved October 18, 2016, from www.cox.com/wcm/en/aboutus/datasheet/takecharge/2009-teen-survey.pdf

22. Ibid.

23. Chan, R. (2016, June 9). *Sorry teens, your Tinder party is over*. Retrieved October 18, 2016, from time.com/4362915/tinder-app-minors-teenagers/; Manrodt, A. (2014, May 7). Teens on Tinder: Why high schoolers have invaded the social dating app. *Teen Vogue*. Retrieved October 18, 2016, from www.teenvogue.com/story/teens-on-tinder

24. *Now teenagers have their own version of Tinder*. (2016, June 28). *Fast Company*. Retrieved October 18, 2016, from news.fastcompany.com/now-teenagers-have-their-own-version-of-tinder-4012148

Index

Kik Messenger, 35 (table), 46 (table)
Klin, Celia, 36–37
Kutcher, Stan, 34

Language
  of social media, 6–11, 83–85
  of social media socialization,
    138–141
  of technology in schools, 109–111
Law of diminishing returns, 123
Learning methods, online *vs.* paper
  study methods, 126
Learning styles, flexibility for
  differences, 129–130
Lee, Jessica, 67
Legal issues, of sexually explicit
  photos, 143
LGBTQ community, 29
Likes, and personal values
  development, 73–78, 144
LinkedIn, 35 (table)
Lip synching songs, 44, 48
Live-feed streams, 44, 48–50
  and bystander effect, 159–160
  of sexual assault, 74
Location trackers, 175, 176
Lonina, Marina, 73–74
Love, Yeardley, 147
Lubin, Nancy, 158–159

MakeupbyMandy24, 34
Marketing/marketers, 44, 59
Martins, Chris, 48
Math problem #3 example, 19
Media multitasking. *See* Multitasking
Messaging, private
  commentary, 34–37
Minecraft, 20–21, 36
Minimum age requirement, 1–2, 28, 43
  COPPA law, 63
Mission, questions to reflect on
  implementing strategy, 180, 183–184
Mixed messages, 62–66
Moleskine's Smart Writing Set, 130
Moment app, 94, 128 (table), 146
Monotasking, 93, 123–128, 166
Multitasking
  in class, 124

effect on connection and
  isolation, 150
and entertainment media, 6
incremental creep of, 92
and self-regulation, 18
and sleep deprivation, 166
Musical.ly, 44, 48
Music-sharing apps, 44, 48
myHomework app, 128 (table)
Myspace, 27, 31
The Myth of the Perfect Girl
  (Homayoun), 17, 18, 41, 148

Name policy, at Facebook, 28
Naming files, 120
Nass, Clifford, 150
National Highway Traffic Safety
  Administration, 64
National Sleep Foundation's 2006
  Sleep in America, 167
Negative compensatory behaviors, 148
Net Nanny app, 98 (table)
Networked public spaces, 72–73
Never good enough feeling, 57
Nike+ app, 170

Oasis point, 156
Obama, Barack, xi, xii, 50–51
O'Brien, Ron, 74
Off-campus postings, 12, 14
On-all-the-time mentality, 69–73,
  115–116, 145
One Love Foundation, 147
One-to-one tablet programs, 8, 21
  considerations, 179–180
  organizing files in digital folders,
    107–109
Online accounts for students,
  set up by parents, 38
Online comparison culture, 57,
  113–114
Online digital journal, 33
Online learning management
  systems, 110–111
Open-ended questions, as approach in
  conversations, 86–87, 90
Open time, 72
Orenstein, Peggy, 143

Organization
with digital folders and IRL
binders, 116–118, 133
of files in digital folders, 107–109
teaching daily habits, 111
OurPact app, 97 (table)
Oversharing, 57–58
Ownership details, questions to reflect
on implementing strategy, 181,
184–185

Paperless culture, 114–115
Parental control apps, 97–98 (table)
Parental pressure and mixed
messages, 63
Parents
acceptable use agreements for social
media, 96, 104
access to passwords, 176
blaming schools for problems, 21
checking children's cell phones,
143–144, 168–169
guidelines for meeting in-person, 175
implementing strategies for classroom
technology, 182, 183
influence on teens, 9–10
modeling behaviors, 62, 63–64, 153
technology-tracking devices and
safety, 176
Passwords
in acceptable use agreements, 101,
102, 104, 106
privacy vs. safety, 176
questions to reflect on implementing
strategy, 184–185
Peer pressure, and mixed messages, 63
Periscope, 46 (table), 48, 74
Personal appearance, fixed mindset
and altered expectations, 61
Personality development, 142–144.
See also Developmental process
Personal productivity, 123–128, 133
apps for, 127–129 (table)
Personal values development, 73–78
main concepts, 76
Pew Research Center, 5
"Adults and Cell Phone
Distractions" while driving, 64

on fake accounts, 39
on kindness, 77
"Teens, Technology and
Friendships," 34
Photos
sexually explicit, 143–144,
147, 156–157
student use of, 30, 40
Physical wellness, 161–177
addiction, 171–174
functional exercise, 170
safety from harm and
danger, 174–177
sleep deprivation, 164–168
stress management, 168–170
teetering imbalance, 161–164
Pinterest, 35 (table)
Plagiarism, 131–132
Planners, written, visual,
62–63, 111, 119–121
Policies. See Rules and policies on
social media
Pomodoro app, 169
Pomodoro Technique, 122, 125
Pornography, 49–50, 65, 143, 157
The Pornography Industry
(Tarrant), 50
Porterfield, Tony, 22
Pott, Audrie, 157–158
@POTUS Twitter account, xii
Power Down Day, 70, 72, 154
Power down time, questions to reflect
on implementing strategy, 185
Predators, 21, 37, 174–175
Privacy
parental access to passwords, 176
parental guidelines for meeting
in-person, 175
safety issues with classroom
technology, 20–23
and sexually explicit photos,
143–144
See also Ephemeral interactions
Private commentary, 34–37
Private profiles, 31–32
Productivity, personal, 123–128, 133
apps for, 127–129 (table)
Promposals, 59

A SAGE Publishing Company

CORWIN HAS ONE MISSION: to enhance education through intentional professional learning.

We build long-term relationships with our authors, educators, clients, and associations who partner with us to develop and continuously improve the best evidence-based practices that establish and support lifelong learning.

The Association for Middle Level Education (AMLE) is dedicated to improving the educational experiences of all students ages 10 to 15 by providing vision, knowledge, and resources to educators and leaders. AMLE is committed to helping middle grades educators reach every student, grow professionally, and create great schools.